For good neighbors
Milt and Helen

Betty and George

Christmas 1968

Roots
in the Rock

Roots
in the Rock

by

CHARLES CHILD

illustrations by the author

An Atlantic Monthly Press Book

LITTLE, BROWN AND COMPANY · BOSTON · TORONTO

ATLANTIC-LITTLE, BROWN BOOKS
ARE PUBLISHED BY
LITTLE, BROWN AND COMPANY
IN ASSOCIATION WITH
THE ATLANTIC MONTHLY PRESS

*Published simultaneously in Canada
by Little, Brown & Company (Canada) Limited*

PRINTED IN THE UNITED STATES OF AMERICA

To my wife, to my children,
to the sun, the sea,
the forest, and the rock

Give me solitude,
Give me Nature, give me again O Nature
Your primal sanities!

— WALT WHITMAN

Preface

THIS is the story of a cabin that grew and grew like a game of dominos, over twenty summers; of a man, a wife, their three children, together with sundry dogs and cats, who fell in love with a certain Point, and at first all unwitting of the nature of the task, tackled its forest trees, wrestled with rot and weight, fought against time, coped with insects and hurricane winds, got drenched with rain, blasted with sun, jagged with saws and axes, but with time survived to learn a new respect for nature, and to build a home and a life to which they have returned each summer with increasing joy.

Contents

Roots
in the Rock

1

Why Maine?

THE year was 1920 and I was young and happy. I had just landed a summer job with Professor Lionel Marks, a witty and learned teacher of engineering at Harvard. It was like this: I was to go to Maine with the family, help clear a tract of seaside land they had recently bought, run the motorboat, assist in putting up a portable house, and make myself useful and agreeable to the two Marks children, a boy and a girl. Who could ask for anything more? As they say Down East, "I was fierce to go," being at that time eighteen years of age, strong as a bull, and possessed of a small store of woodcraft acquired in various summer camps. Moreover, I was filled to the brim with a mixture of confidence and ignorance. I didn't know the difference between a turnbuckle and a bucksaw, and I didn't care. I had never been near a motorboat, couldn't read a blueprint, and was unaware of any problems connected with the care of children. But the thought of Maine, tree-chopping, exploring new land, putting up a house, boating with the kids — this could be good.

I packed my duds, including watercolors and pastels, for already I was bent on a career as an artist, then joined the Markses, and by train and boat we made that kind of journey which is still possible in this country: forward in space, backward in time, to a more primitive epoch. The Marks family had rented a house in the nearby village of East Blue Hill, as their new land had nothing on it but forest and a couple of open meadows sloping down to the sea.

In East Blue Hill after breakfast we would take the doddering old motorboat and putt-putt along the coast till we reached their domain a few miles away. The first day was pure impressionism: coming in to the shore, we could see the two meadows with a rise of land between, and the remnant of an old granite dock poking its snout into the bay. On landing we found and followed the trace of a road which ran uphill into the woods till it died in a bog. Not far away we came upon a number of splendid granite cliffs, apparently hand-quarried about a century before, which now half concealed here and there a number of rock pools, some shallow, others deep and quiet except for the occasional *bloomp* of a frog.

These mossy old quarry pools had long since gone back to a state of nature but at the same time they retained a vestige of their romantic past — a rusting ringbolt set into the rock, the trace of a twisted steel cable, now no more than a wandering pile of rust, a lonely block or two of granite that for some reason had never been taken away, wild iris, roses, and the sweet raspberries of the region which carpeted and softened the edges of the pools as did the slow creep of green and gray lichens across the cut surfaces of the rock. The woods too were romantic reminders of the struggles of my New England forebears. Dim tangled wildernesses of fir and spruce for the most part, with here and there the brilliant green of a deciduous tree, or the white of a birch — the shaggy trunks grew so close together that it made one shudder to think of trying to penetrate this unyielding mass without the help of modern tools. The old road itself was hardly more than two wagon ruts filled with black water and humming with mosquitoes. I knew that we were planning to open this trail to the sun in order some day to be able to get a car through. It seemed like an endless task.

But the meadows were lovely: two long swales covered in wild grasses over which the swallows dipped and soared all day. One of these sloped in a gentle grade down to the old granite dock, now merely a jumble of square-cut blocks jutting out some forty feet or more into the waters of Blue Hill Bay. The other ended at a rocky beach. Here, toward the top of the rise where the two meadows came together, Professor Marks intended to erect his portable house, sections of which we were bringing over daily in the boat.

Life settled into a pleasant routine. Each morning we would run the boat to the dock and then disperse to the work of cutting, clearing and building. The land itself seemed all greens and grays, and the forest covering the gray cliffs kept beckoning one into the shadowed, sinister depths. On my time off I roamed and sketched. Coastal Maine can vary its mood in a few hours — sometimes in a few minutes — from piercing color in water and sky to the very nothingness of heavy fog.

I recall standing late one afternoon by a gigantic old fir tree: I had been reading a book, and having become absorbed in it, had not noticed the passage of time till I suddenly became aware of a strange transformation in the quality of light falling upon the page. Everything was bathed in luminescence. Every needle, every twig of the tree, each crusted plate of bark was the color of a glowing rose. Up above, an intense ruby light seemed to radiate from the clouds, and the sea below me seemed now to have drawn a veil of purple gauze over its surface, while in the west, ever more intense as my eyes turned toward the setting sun, there streamed out a rose, a salmon, an orange, a poppy red, in rivers of fire. My book was red. I was red. All the world was red as a cardinal's robe. Stunned with color, I stood there with my red hand on the red tree till the glory faded and was gone.

From the Marks's cliffs on clear days I could see in the distance a line of blue mountains looming up over the sea. This was Mt. Desert Island, the site of the newly created Acadia National Park, of Bar Harbor, and of lakes, waterfalls, cliffs, forested slopes, islets, and inlets, in character rather like a miniature Norway. For days at a time these island mountains would shimmer with extraordinary clarity, then abruptly fade and disappear. They became my Bali-Hai, my dream. I should go there someday but now there was that last fifty yards of corduroy road to lay before the weekend, the children had a hut in the woods that needed a roof (that's it! a cabin in the woods, in a secret valley) — and don't forget that list of groceries to bring from the general store. Perhaps because I never did get to Mt. Desert that summer, though I visited many of the islands in Blue Hill Bay, this dream, this seed remained deep in my subconscious. More than a decade was to pass before I set foot in northern New England again, but the call of those mountains remained to echo in my mind.

Some years later, through a portrait commission, I met a superbly beautiful girl who had Seen Everything, Been Everywhere, spoke French like a native (well, almost) and strangely enough, had a love of the wilderness equal to mine. Her stepfather, an enthusiastic traveler, had taken

his family to Algonquin Park in Canada a number of times
for long canoe trips and fishing. This paragon had roan
red hair, hazel eyes, a deep soft voice. And Fredericka (that
was her name) was as sure of her woodcraft as I was.

The portrait, thank God, took a long time. As I struggled with it we used to talk of Maine, of the Canadian
wilderness, of faraway places. We became friends, friendship grew to love. The portrait was finished (I have done
better since), we found that we had a whole world in common, and in time we became engaged. Life was glowing,
my work was beginning to go well, and in 1926 we were
married.

We studied in Europe; spent a glorious year in Asia;
and then came home to settle into a small house in Bucks
County, Pennsylvania, about halfway between New York
and Philadelphia, a practical base near the cities from
which my commissions might come. I began to do fabric
designs for various New York Houses, advertisements for
Bethlehem Steel Company, illustrations for some of Stephen
Vincent Benet's poems and stories. Our house was set in a
delightful little valley with a brawling stream which swept
along the base of a hill, called in those parts Coppernose.
Tradition had it that the Indians of the valley used to have
a primitive copper mine there. But no trace remains. This
part of Bucks is old Quaker farming country, deeply rural.

Here two children were born, who we named Erica and
Rachel. Erica, the eldest, was a blonde, like her father,
Rachel a redhead like her mother. The girls grew up
through the depression years as country children, helping
with the cooking, bringing in wood, tending the garden,
shoveling snow, with time off for snowmen. There were
trees to cut, terraces to make, floors to double — jobs of

maintenance for those who like to use their hands. Busy, happy days, with the regular rhythm of school beginning to dominate our calendar.

In 1939 a summer trip began to look possible. Would it be west or north? Of course! It *must* be the coast of Maine! And now for Mt. Desert! A route was worked out. Limpopo, our great gray-green greasy station wagon, was packed, our shaggy French sheep dog, Grey Brother, climbed in, we waved goodbye to Coppernose valley and headed northward.

We ground on and on, pausing every hour or so just long enough to put food in, or let it out. "Mother, is this Maine?" "No, dear, this is Rumford, New Jersey." "Mother, I feel sick . . . Mother, where are we now? Mother, Mother, Mother . . ." Briefly I recalled how in Bali and Sumatra we had seen pigs being transshipped among the islands: they were fed opium, then thrown into the depths of the hold, like cordwood — well, no!

Three days of this brought us to Mt. Desert and the vigorous little town of Southwest Harbor. There was a Coast Guard station, a considerable fishing industry, a rash of summer cottages, and a native population of energetic people to give it a salty tangy flavor. With the help of a real estate agent, we rented a cottage on a point of rock pushing into the sea like a ship's prow. Every wind that ever blew hit that old house broadside. It stood there on its granite in splendid isolation, groaning slightly from time to time under the pressure of the blowing air, rather ugly, rather faded, but on the whole as fine and sturdy as the folk who built it. The kerosene stove seemed to be in the last stages of a serious disorder, but there was a gorgeous great fireplace and plenty of wood.

As we unpacked, fog drifted through the living room in

palpable waves, and penetrating it came the sound of the gulls and the clash and sigh of the waves as they broke over the ledges near the house. Grey Brother, having explored the place to his satisfaction, turned round three times and collapsed on a moth-eaten bear rug like a slowly deflating tire. As for the children, once fed they dropped off into trancelike slumber, and so did we.

Next morning I looked around me, considering. There was Erica, blonde and prim in her new dungarees. She was seated at an old grand piano in the living room plonking out "Good King Wenceslaus" with one finger. Fredericka was whistling in the kitchen — after all, she had just completed some radical surgery on the stove, and it was working. This whistle of Freddie's was a delight. It came out with a slight wildness, like the trill of a canary — spontaneous music that could lighten the mood of the whole family. The dog was barking at the surf. As for headlong Rachel, whose clothes when she undressed always hit the four walls of the room before they fell to the floor, she had run full tilt into a tidal pool in the rocks, and now lay there in knee-deep water howling for rescue. In short, everything was normal.

2

Old Point

IT was time to explore. A couple of days of rest had
made us eager to poke around. We said to the friendly
real estate agent: "Mr. Robinson, what we're looking for
is a nice piece of land — really *just* land: actually we would
prefer not to have anything on it. And certainly not a
fancy house, you understand. Something a bit on the
wilderness side if possible. Of course, by the shore! Shore
property is hard to come by? You mean *here,* on this island?
Well, I suppose so. Old families don't want to sell? Yes,
I can see that, but . . . but, you must have things listed.
Let's see what you have that might be available."

Two days later I said to Fredericka, "Fred, how many
places have we seen now? Twenty-one, is it? And all with
cottages. Look, I have an idea. Let's make a grid over our
map, covering this whole end of the island. Then we can
explore each section in turn, on our own. If we see anything promising we'll ask Mr. Robinson to look it up for
us. I think we'll turn up something. Okay? Let's go."

We tramped. We ducked down forgotten lumber roads;
I remember one dear little road which ended up at the
town dump. We inquired. We persisted. The region was
beautiful and beckoning. But all the best bits seemed for

one reason or another to be out of reach. We could see
that shore property was going to be very hard to find. Most
of the land around the shore was owned by people who
didn't want to sell. And who could blame them?

The girls were having a marvelous vacation. They were
enchanted. "Look at that little pond! And the lovely
farm: with cows! Someone else owns it? Wouldn't they
sell us just the barn? . . . Let's have a picnic here! I'm
hungry! Mother! Mother! How about here? What's a
Public Beach? Let's try *that* road! It has someone's name
on it? Oh, never mind — aren't we having fun!" Fun?
Well, yes, perhaps we were.

"No, no, we've been on that road. No, that's part of the
National Park area. Don't you see? It's shaded pink right
there. Say, didn't we do that one three days ago in the
fog? Hey, Fred! Whoa! Looks like this road ends in a
beaver dam, or a swamp, or something — better back up.
No, not this one. I know the land is beautiful, but we
can't afford it."

There came a day when I became insistent: "*That* land?
You mean out there to Old Point? Now, Mr. Child, you
wouldn't really want that. Just woods, about ready to blow
down any time now. I do a bit of lumbering on the side
when winter comes round and business is slow, and I can
tell you right now that forest out there isn't going to last
much longer. All old trees. Hardly any new ones coming
up. And of course, no cottage on it. Years ago there used
to be a barn somewhere but I seem to recall it was moved
over to the village to serve as a selectmen's office. The old
fellow who owns it lives in Boston and only comes down
to this part of Maine from time to time. What does he
do with it? Mebbe nothing, but I'm pretty sure he won't

part with it. All right, I'll inquire, but t'won't do much good."

"Well" (a few days later), "you remember that piece of land you were asking about? The owner happens to be down here for the week and he says he might be willing to go over to the Point with you tomorrow if this weather holds out. But he's not sure he wants to sell."

Old Point, the land in question, we had seen one day from a hilltop where there was a gap in the trees. It appeared to be a dense sword-shaped mass of forest, blue-black in color, jutting to the sea. We could see no house on it, no camp, not even a wisp of smoke . . . only a few gulls, pinpointed momentarily against the dark woods. It seemed detached from the rest of the island and, to us, invested with a romantic isolation.

We met the owner and liked him on sight. What was all this talk about his being tough? Here was a quiet old-ish man with quizzical eyes and a fine leathery face. He reminded me of a sea captain. Taking him in the car, we all drove out toward the property along a road which we might never have found. It wound obscurely and slowly downhill through a wooded area, then suddenly debouched out across a great bog, with water lying on both sides. Evidently it was this bog which almost isolated Old Point from the rest of the island. On either hand the sea shone and shimmered like mercury and seemed ready to spill over the road which at its lowest point could not have been more than two feet above water. Gradually rising, the road ended in a meadow, against which some distance farther on, one could see what appeared to be a solid wall of fir and spruce, immovable, silent. As the car drew to a halt, the dim trace of a logging road was visible — two wheel tracks wandering off into a dark green silence. "Listen, girls, that's the white-throated sparrow," said the old man, as the quiet was broken by a triple note.

As we walked along, the old road began to peter out, leaving us on a foot trail. On either hand the forest floor was a brilliant emerald green, mossy for the most part, and sown thickly with the red sparks of Cornus Reptans, northern cousin to the dogwoods. Old stumps were covered with wild cranberries just beginning to blush a delicate pink, not yet ready to eat. Here and there where a tree had fallen letting in the full sunlight, long silken grasses grew abundantly, waist high, looking exactly like threads of green glass. The little girls were delighted with this grass and soon picked enough for two woven bracelets. This forest was not gloomy. It gave one the sense of life. Often old trees would be spaced as much as twenty feet apart. Here and there a birch would drive its shaft of silver up and up through the green shade to reach the sun. We trod quietly along after our aged guide. In the heat of midday

a faint perfume of balsam enriched the air. Now and then with the winding of the path we became conscious of the sea murmuring quietly along the outer edge of the trees as they descended to the shore. We knew our time was short and the urgency added to our appreciation of the place.

"There's a spring somewhere if I can find it. We used to come out here to the Point quite regular when I was a kid to play Indians. That spring now. Never freezes over even in the dead of winter, and as far as I know has never run dry. Yep. Thar she be." He points to a large granite boulder some distance off. We hurry forward, squishing downhill toward the rock through hundreds of wild iris, the two girls leaping ahead like puppies. At the foot of the slope lay what appeared to be a small green carpet about the size of a bathroom rug. Algae. Taking a couple of sticks, we carefully pushed the mass to one side. There lay a crystal clear pool about four feet deep and five feet across. It was ice cold, brimming over into the surrounding vegetation, and laced with hundreds of gigantic mosquito wrigglers. Some kind soul had left an old tin cup on the rock. We dipped it in and took a long drink. Ah, but that water was good — even exquisite — and possessed of a palpable sweetness. It seemed to go down and down into one's insides and ring a bell somewhere. This was the Moment of Truth. Fred and I gave each other that familial look which means, "This is it," as we rose dripping and confirmed.

Years ago the old man had cut a trail of sorts around the Point and this we followed up and down, sometimes at the water's edge where great rock ledges swept to the shore, sometimes sixty feet above on magnificent monoliths of granite garnished where the sun struck in with the soft

gray of reindeer moss. Here at the very spine of the land
facing southeast to the open sea the Point reached its cul-
mination. On this bouldered dome magnificent old trees,
never very high, but muscular, girthy, ragged, were rooted
in the rock, and festooned with the gray-green moss called
Usnea, which gave them the dignity of bearded Druids.
"This is a Magic Forest," said Erica firmly. It was; a perfect illustration for a fairy tale. Little pools of water lay
here and there in the rock, bringing a note of sky color
to the soft carpet underfoot.

"You folks might not be able to see it — can't myself,
come to think of it — but right about here us kids had a
little baseball diamond: see where it stretches out nice and
flat? T'weren't much of a clearin', but it did for us. And
right here some place, off to one side — all overgrown now,
some young fool clumb up into a tree one day and got to
figgerin' he could make a 'monkey-trail' — know the kind
of thing? You pass from branch to branch and never need
to come down at all. Well sir, after we'd all got up there
and took a sight, we started cuttin' out branches, and fust
thing you know we had a clear hundred yards of trail from
tree to tree. Time went on and we kept hackin' away at
it and improvin' it and by the end of summer that monkey-
trail went clear around the Point till it come down to the
baseball diamond again on t'other side. Now these raspberries is mighty good eatin', ain't they? Same as they used
to be — not quite as big though — seems like them bushes
has shriveled up a mite since my day. Trees is older, for
one thing . . ."

As far as we were concerned, it was as if we had already
bought the place and settled on it. After all those cottages
it seemed an untouched piece of Maine. The old man had
loved it, obviously, and for years in his younger days, he

told us, he had carefully culled out the worst of the wind-falls. This is perhaps what had given it its spectacular open quality, especially on the upland slopes. "But now hardly anybody even bothers to come and pick the raspberries any more, and this here trail around the shore — well, as you can see, you kind of have to push your way through and pretty soon there just won't be any trail at all." Here a long speculative look, which met ours halfway.

Perhaps we and our children were possessed of a certain innocence that appealed to him. Or did he sense in us the inheritors of his love and care? Or did he just need hard cash? I asked, "I don't suppose you had thought of selling this land, had you?"

"Well, now, I jest thought you folks wanted to look at it. I've held onto this Point all my life, and I've told Robinson time and again not to bother me about sellin'. But bein' as you ast, I'd be willin' to consider it. Couldn't let you have part of it, though — all or nothin'." (He names a price.)

"Holy smokes! We can't afford any such sum. Impossible! We're sorry, but we had no idea you wanted anything like *that* . . . matter of fact, I don't think we could afford even half that much, and then, what with the taxes and all . . . no, sorry: we might as well go back to the car and call it a day. Now if we could have bought, say, just half of it . . ."

"Which half? T'other one or this one?"

"Why, this one, of course — with water on three sides and that spring . . ."

"Jest as I thought: now if it had been the other half, I might have considered partin' with it, but as you can see, this here is the good half. If I sell off this half, the other one won't be wuth the price of stumpage, hardly."

"Then you *might* sell this half? This is almost our last
day in Maine, and anyway, this is so beautiful, you have
taken such good care of it, and now it's beginning to go,
and I don't think you're ever going to find anyone who'd
care for it as we would. And a year's a long, long time —
who knows where we'll all be a year from now?"

"Tell you what I'll do — don't hardly know why I'm
doin' it — and I wouldn't want it to get around, but I
could let you have twenty acres — that'll just take in the
spring, mebbe a little more . . ." (He names a lesser price.)

"Oh, thank you, thank you, but couldn't you shave the
price a bit? The way it works out . . ."

Here we enter a long palaver with the old man, now a
kind of back country saint, now a land shark, as the argu-
ment sways this way and that. But by the time we had
retraced our steps to the car he had finally agreed to part
with the twenty acres for a price which was just a little
more than we could afford.

As evening fell, all in a glow we sat around the living
room of our cottage. It was September first. That very
morning at 4:45 A.M. European time, Hitler had launched
his hordes upon Poland. Here were our little girls warm
and safe sitting on the old polar bear rug in the center of
the room playing with a teddy bear. We had turned the
radio on, and there in the midst of happiness and peace
came the news of the invasion. Our thoughts turned to the
children of that unhappy land, and we shuddered. No one
knew . . . But one thing was certain: the old world appeared to be crumbling, and even our own world would
never be the same except perhaps for this magic place of
our domain. Here was something tangible, solid, beautiful,
unchanging in the midst of chaos, or so we thought.

The next day with the old man and the real estate agent

we worked out a right-of-way clause, embodied in the contract of sale, giving us a legal right of access to our own land — the right to cross the land that we had not bought. The method of payment was settled and a title search was begun. Now to sign, and the land would be ours!

Almost on our last day we filed through the forest: Charles, Fredericka, Erica, Rachel, Grey Brother, and two teddy bears. We gathered round the spring and held a solemn water-drinking ceremony in which we pledged never to betray the essence of the land, never to allow commercial enterprise to take over, always to respect its wilderness character as far as possible. Erica, an artist in matters of this kind, held the dog's paw, poured spring water on his head, and pledged for him not to chase wild animals. He

sat there, water dripping off his head and running in rivulets into the spring. Then, unable to stand the tension,
he suddenly put both feet into the water and took a good
long drink.

Then we proceeded to the minute examination of our
domain. Beginning at the bog the land mass of Old Point
rises gently to the south, where it ends in a series of sea
cliffs. In this region during the last glacial epoch the south-
ward-moving ice smoothed most of the north-facing slopes
somewhat but tended to pluck loose rock off the southern
slopes, leaving a series of great cliffs facing out to sea. This
gives the land hereabouts a notched appearance. Our Point
exemplified this glacial action. As one moved south, tumbled rocks gradually appeared, then ledges which gradually
rose until one found oneself on the spine or backbone of
the land where it fell sharply in a series of small escarp-
ments to the sea. On the long eastern slope there grew a
heavy close-knit forest, watered continually by sea fogs.
Here we found another spring in a thicket of swamp alders,
its mucky bottom land much trodden by deer.

To the west, the forest was more open, running in a
series of gentle slopes, broken here and there by masses of
rock, down to Blue Hill Bay. The beaches were not sandy
— not really beaches at all, properly speaking. Everywhere
one looked the forest ended abruptly in rocky ledges, for
the most part granite, but interspersed with the glacial
detritus and occasional volcanic dykes which distinguish
this part of the island. Here and there one could find a tiny
patch of "sand" apparently made of crushed and ground
up mussel shells — curious stuff, light and fragile. The great
lower branches of many of our older trees sank into the
ground, then rose again fifteen or twenty feet out from the
butt. There were hundreds of enormous anthills, large as

an overturned bathtub, made of a kind of light sawdust or, more properly speaking, ant-dust, a mixture or compost of minute bits of shell, crushed clay and mica, chewed and rotted wood. We traipsed up and down and round and round over rocks, under half-fallen trees, along the ledges, thinking of a suitable place to put some kind of dwelling. Romantic, inviting, but how did you get materials into this paradise? Bringing heavy timbers around by boat seemed impossible — a landing would be exceedingly rough and dangerous. Or could we more easily widen out some kind of trail over the half-mile road and path? We simply didn't know.

For the moment, then, the obvious thing to do was to find some kind of builder who might be willing to come, look the place over, and give us a tentative plan and estimate of costs. We thought of Robert Kennedy, a young architect friend from our Cambridge days. Kennedy had the reputation of being hard-boiled, objective, a close estimator. Whatever figure he gave us, provided he agreed to come, we felt would be realistic and give us the basis for further action. Putting in a long-distance call, we found Kennedy willing to come, as he was at the time working on estimates for a house on Mt. Desert. He agreed to outline a plan for a minimal house: no basement of course, no central heat — just a large fireplace, and the essential kitchen, living room and bedrooms. We mailed him a set of the survey blueprints showing the contours of the land, and now that we had committed ourselves, and now that the school year was about to begin it was time to leave Maine, just beginning to glow with the first faint hint of autumn color. We departed, filled with a mixture of trepidation and hope. And Robert Kennedy would come. He would tramp and he would estimate. The house was to

be on the spine, of course. You know, built-on-a-rock: it
might last forever.

And so we had found our land and had bought it.
Everything was there — trees, rocks, the sea, and a certain
element of mystery. Beyond the mere fact of its existence,
what did we really know of it, of its secret heart, of its
yield for good or ill? This was a first step, the merest
beginning, a challenge, a rune that could not be read.

Back at Coppernose on a certain Monday, the blueprints
came. Robert Kennedy had done his work well. The plan
was all anyone could ask in the matter of simplicity and
directness of approach. One could see the house standing
there high on its ridge: elegant, modern — and we couldn't
afford it. Not in a million years. Not on my earnings as
a painter.

And so that was that. We had a hunk of land (we and
the bank), a vanished dream house, and four pairs of
hands — just slightly more than a vacuum. We were licked.
That is to say, blueprint-licked, architect-licked. But the

momentum of a decade is not overcome in a day. After all, the land was there. It was ours. We were in love with it. And we were going to go back to it.

"Well, of course there are those two old tents up in the garage loft somewhere."

"Those? Haven't used 'em in years. Old tent poles? Rotten ropes? Never mind, let's get 'em out and take a look. It will make us feel better, and it can't do any harm."

The obvious alternative began to grow. My wife said to me one day at breakfast, all dewy-eyed and innocent: "Charlie, you remember all that marvelous axework you did around the Lionel Marks place?" (What marvelous axework?) "Have another cup of coffee. Remember those huts you built for the kids? I don't see why we couldn't do something of the kind — slightly more grown-up, of course. Build say just a small lean-to of logs — perhaps with a sod roof . . ."

"Well," I said, "with you always yakking about what a great camper you are, and loving to live in tents, I might have guessed it. Lately I've been looking through a book I got out of the library. It's all about how various National Park structures * were made. And it's full of photos and drawings of all kinds of buildings, some of them actually log cabins — quite exciting, really — but they've all been done by experts. We couldn't build anything like that — those trees aren't very straight, for one thing. I don't think you'd . . ."

"Nonsense!" said Fred. "I always knew you could build a log cabin with one hand tied behind your back, if you only set your mind to it."

* *Park and Recreation Structures*, United States Department of the Interior, National Park Service, 1938.

There it was, out in the open, and it's amazing what a
lot of literature there is on *any* subject if you only dig.
We dug. We soaked in log lore — everything from Tierra
del Fuego to Norway. What straightforward construction!
All alike, really. You fell your trees (raw material for nothing!). You peel them, notch them, stack them, cut a door
and a window or two. And presto! You're in! Simple as
that! So I drew cabins and cabins, plans of cabins, eleva-
tions of cabins, cabins on hillsides, hilltops, hollows, with
a single room, with an ell, a wing, a kitchen, a porch, a
loft — all with beautiful straight logs fitted together like
cabinetwork — that is to say, fitted with a pencil, not an
axe. Drawing is so easy.

We settled on a drawing of a cabin about twenty-four
feet long by eighteen feet wide. It had a kitchen wing at
one end, slightly offset from the living room, a big chimney
in between, with two flues, which were to serve a kitchen
stove on one side and the living room on the other. There
was to be a porch with an overhang supported by log pillars. The ceiling of this porch would make a floor for the
loft on the inside. There would be built-in bunks — everything nice and simple. Oh, and a window, of course, and
a door. The kitchen was to have no outer door, in order
to save wall space for shelves, but would have an open
doorway into the living room, which could be curtained off.

We made lists of tools and gear — endless lists. Block
and tackle, shovel, axe of course, rope, tubs, steel measuring tape, hammers, saws, spokeshave, bits and brace,
mason's trowels, hoe, sickle. Lawnmower? Don't be silly!
Cooking utensils, bedrolls and ponchos, an assortment of
fishing tackle, writing materials . . . We renovated one
of the tents to serve as a forest tool shed. The other tent
was really in pretty bad shape so at the last minute we

decided to rent a cottage for sleeping and clean-up purposes. That just about did it.

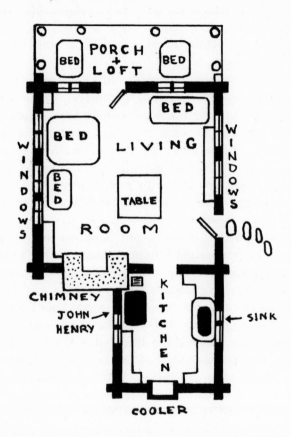

"How could we fail?" I asked myself. Of course, there were certain gaps. Whoever mentioned how much a log weighed, for instance, or that it had curves, bumps, burls? Logs were logs, as a rose is a rose. Nor was I ever able to find out what makes the log cabins, farm storehouses and churches of Norway last for six hundred years without rotting while in the equivalent climate of Maine they can suddenly turn to mush. We had come across one or two of these old cabins in our search about Mt. Desert. Neglected and forlorn, they seemed to have gone to pieces rather speedily. Ours, by gum, would be different, kept with loving care.

But there were doubts, questions. For example, could you run log-ends directly into a chimney? Could a cabin be chinked between the logs with reindeer moss? The Indians, I seemed to recall, had used this material to provide a dead air space between doubled walls of bark.

My brother Paul came over about this time to look at the plans. "On the whole it's pretty dreamy," he opined, "but of course totally unrealistic. How do you know you can lift a log twenty-four feet long? Have you ever tried? You, and who else? Who do you think you are, Houdini? I'll bet they weigh eight hundred pounds if they weigh an ounce. My advice to you, even though I know you won't take it, is to hire a good local carpenter and build a simple straightforward house — no logs! Your love affair with logs is nothing but schoolboy nonsense. You're romancing the whole thing like a Boy Scout on his first four-mile hike. Get wise! Come down to earth! You know what's going to happen? You'll get into that forest, cut down a few trees, and then find yourself sitting on a pile of logs and sawdust — probably all cut wrong, too — biting your fingernails and wondering why you didn't take my advice, and why . . ."

"For God's sake stop sitting there drinking up my likker and croaking like a superannuated bullfrog!" I yelped. "I don't want a carpenter-built house, I want a Charlie-built house, or a Charlie-and-Freddie-built house — can't afford a carpenter, anyway. The damn logs are there just waiting for me and I'll build a log cabin if it's the last act of my living life!"

"Calm down, calm down!" said Fred. "We've got to begin somewhere, and we've got to use the materials and skills God gave us. We can at least try it and see how it goes. Here, let's drink a toast to success — a little branch water on top? Okay. Here's to Our Land and the Cabin."

3

We Tackle the Forest

W E arrived in Southwest Harbor after another grueling three-day battle, the wagon covered with dog hairs, chewing gum papers, lollipop sticks, and crushed Kleenex. Our cottage, rented in advance, was not the same one as before, but it was charming, a nice homey white clapboard house. It had a woodshed fragrant with logs, and a living room absolutely dominated by a large moose head evidently stuffed with plaster of Paris, which fell all day and all night in tiny driblets from an empty eye socket. But the moose had kept one large bulging yellow orb which followed us about in friendly fashion. We grew quite fond of Peeping Tom, and took to hanging things on his antlers.

Once again we crossed the familiar boggy area which separated the Point from the rest of the world and found ourselves on the outer fringe of our domain. We knew the old road and trail combined made a half-mile walk. Tent and tools came out of the wagon and were distributed to the troops in descending order. But the going was tough. A combination of soggy ground and hidden rocks made burdens twice as heavy as they normally would be. Slips and falls were frequent under our loads. Almost at

once we came to the decision that the road had to be fixed
up and made passable for a car. This would involve tree-
cutting and corduroying, but if enough smallish trees were
cut and laid in the low spots, then covered with turf or
branches, it would bring the car and the necessary supplies much nearer our end of the Point. The hitch was,
of course, that we didn't actually own this part of the
road. We simply had a right-of-way over it, and it might
be years before anyone else bought this section and put
in a good bottom. All that work for someone else? Yet,
when the chips were down, wasn't it easier to do the fill,
slow as it was bound to be, and then *roll* in with sand,
cement, lumber, tools, tents and food?

Having spent a good half day bringing the whole wagon-
load in, we felt confident that our judgment had been
correct. Well, what's half a day? We went out to the
rocks on the shore and built a temporary fireplace and
there with a fresh sea breeze to cool us off had a grand
feast of sandwiches, cheese, fruit, hot tea. An extraordinary number of yellow jackets hummed about feasting on
the spilled juices. And we found that if we hurled sand-
wich remnants far enough out, the gulls which had been
soaring overhead would dip and snatch them from the
water. Fred and I at least were eager to tackle the forest.
And there was Erica, already sharpening her Boy Scout
knife on a rock. As for Rachel, she couldn't care less, but
was delighted at having discovered a little rain spring
seeping from the rocks and was trying vainly to construct
a pool for Grey Brother with walls of seaweed to hold the
water. How long would it take, we wondered, before we
could be living under our own roof? There didn't seem
to be any way of telling. Some of our ancestors, working
in village teams, had put log cabins up in a single day.

The waves were bright, the sun shone. My wife's hair gleamed like polished pine needles. A tuft of down from one of the gulls floated softly onto this copper thatch, a fitting resting place for a substance so miraculously beautiful.

It was time to act. But first we climbed the spine again, anxious to see the Magic Forest, site of our erstwhile dream house. If anything, it was more enchanting than ever. Here and there we saw little piles of stones left by Robert Kennedy in making his survey. Rachel, with a sense of the appropriate gesture, kicked them all down again, leaving the place as it had been before we came. It was a marvelous spot. But, a log cabin? The trees on the ledges were certainly not suitable for building. Too short. Too lumpy. Considered as raw material, utterly worthless. Yet, hauling a hundred good logs uphill? One man, a young wife, and two little girls? No go. Then and there we abandoned the site.

Hard by the shore, a hundred yards nearer the spring, was a gentle slope unencumbered by masses of rock. There were some smallish boulders to be sure, but they could be moved and the heavy ones tipped into holes. Here the trees stood tall and straight for the most part, the biggest some seventy or eighty feet to the tip, and three feet or more across the butt. The moving waves beneath us shot silver shafts into the branches. Gulls were crying up aloft somewhere and in the air there was a mingled fragrance of bay and balsam. Why wasn't this a good choice for a cabin site: near enough for water, near enough for chimney rocks, near enough to hundreds of good logs. On a little rise nearby we set up the tool tent, first staking down a canvas floor to keep off the damp and digging a drainage ditch all round. We cut a few long stakes and after mooching around a bit, for this was the moment of final decision, we said, "Okay, kids, let's put it just about here." Using the steel tape we tried to lay out a rectangle for the principal room, running white string from stake to stake. But the trees grew so close together that we couldn't run the string in straight lines. Every shift of the stakes left us with a perfect parody of a rectangle. Finally in exasperation at our amateurishness, I realized that the thing we should have done in the first place was to cut enough trees to clear a space in which one could work. Yanking up the stakes and balling the string once again, and feeling like a fool before my children, I went to the tent and got out the axe and a long saw. No more pussyfooting. This was it. Sending up a prayer for strength I began to cut the first tree. The girls dithered around asking silly questions till I sent them off to the spring to fetch water.

Chips flew, sawdust spurted. Blood pounded in my ears. This was more like it! But twenty mortal minutes had passed. "At this rate," I thought, "I'll be ten years building the cabin." Two little figures now appeared in the clearing, each holding a small tin bucket. Grateful pause. With hangdog expressions: "We just can't find the spring!"

"Well, never mind," I said. "You're just in time to see

this tree go down. 'TIMBER!'" Nothing happened. Not a thing. "T I M B E R !" I cried again, even louder, as if to fell it with a shout. But the tree remained standing, its branches so interlaced with those of its neighbors that it could not fall. "Perhaps the tree doesn't want to fall, Charlie," said Erica. I went to the tent and got out the block and tackle: two double pulleys arranged with ropes so as to increase the pulling power of a man about eight-fold. I fixed one end to a nearby tree, slowly mounted the living corpse of my enemy, ants, mosquitoes, and bark slithering down my spine, and attached the other end to a point about twelve feet high. Then — finally — everyone pulling and grunting in unison, down it came with a wonderful crash. On the whole, that rates as one of the most satisfactory moments of my life.

We found the spring again. It turned out to be about a hundred and fifty yards from the cabin. We blazed a trail to it, and filled a tin tub with water, pouring it through a cloth mosquito net to strain out the wrigglers. Now with a bit of space cleared near the cabin site the trees began to fall one by one, and were limbed close to the trunk. If a tree fell to the ground in such a way as to crush its lower limbs in the fall, the job of limbing was easy. But one tree could fall so as to lie half over another, the trunk ten feet off the ground. Then one had to chop upward, or mount the swaying log to limb the top branches with an axe that whizzed an inch or two from one's toes.

The books had said, "Peel off the bark, or you'll have insect trouble." So we set about it. For the most part this bark came off in gorgeous strips, six or eight feet at a time, revealing the astonishingly white sweet-smelling wood beneath, smooth as the tummy of an eel, dripping with sap. Strip by strip. Hundreds of strips, thousands of strips, coil-

ing like brown snakes, piling up in windrows. "Timber!"
Another tree bashing its way through tangled branches into
the clearing. Then another. And another. I was in a kind
of rage. The forest for the moment had become my enemy.
Day by day branches were hauled away, bark strips were
piled, and the logs, like fish newly caught, glistened for an
hour, then slowly dried as the sun came over the clearing.

The place had the look of a battlefield. Here were
white log-corpses lying helter-skelter, mountains of branches
not yet dragged off, writhing bark strips, stumps studding
the forest floor; here a tub of water, there a saw lying
at the ready across a sawhorse, and everywhere crushed
grasses, brambles, chips, sawdust. Down there where
Father has thrown a sweater, a doll peers up through the
wood chips, her china blue eyes plainly saying, "Why?"

Looking at this disorder, I should perhaps have felt a
certain sense of elation. But my heart sank. These logs
were immensely heavy. One could say almost immovable.
Yet they did move. By themselves. Slipping suddenly sideways over another log, rolling under the blows of an axe,
crunching down when limbs were removed. Even pulling
the bark off would sometimes start them going. Then
everyone would dodge. To make these monsters easier to
handle I began to cut them into twenty-four-foot lengths.
These were painfully rolled to one side, using a cant hook,
a tool invented by the estimable Mr. Peavey — a stout hardwood pole with a steel point. Near the pointed end there
is a swinging hook which neatly catches the log and helps
to turn it over. But a week has passed. Well, don't think,
don't calculate. We're on our way.

Clearing off most of the remaining branches and bark
strips from the open rectangular cut we were now able to
move more freely. The kids had set up a dining room

table on a stump and were feeding the teddy bears with sand-and-water soup, served in mussel shells. "Now, quick! The stakes and string. Over here? A little more to the left? There?" Damn it, are women never satisfied? Well, keep at it. "Fred, I believe that's it!" We stand back. The precise pure geometry of a rectangle imposes itself on the jangle of cut stumps; here is a hope, a promise. But it looks awfully big. And the land seems to slant a lot more than I had thought when the trees were still standing. The end of the cabin toward the shore, I could see now, would be quite some distance in the air. Mm, quite. But don't measure now: just let your eyes slide round and round, following the string, a slim white imprint on the bared forest floor.

In walking about over our domain, it did not take a scientific eye to see that this marvelous substance upon which one trod was not the common forest floor of the Appalachian regions. Here was something more nearly resembling what ecologists call a climax forest — an ancient relatively untouched and stabilized bit of the true North-land which reaches down from the region of Hudson Bay past the valley of the St. Lawrence into Maine. One looks *into* such a forest floor rather than down upon it. As Ivan Sanderson has said, it is not so much a carpet or a floor as it is an open-textured, many-colored sponge, threaded with saprophytes and mycelia among deep-lying stems and roots and rich with the fungi that grow in its filtered green sunlight. There are thousands of brilliant brick-red and orange-yellow toadstools, groups of delicately translucent Indian pipes whose ghostly shapes loom in the shadows, and mushrooms of many kinds, from the deadly amanita to delicious orange morels and edible oyster fungi growing out of tree trunks like layered balconies from a modern apartment house. Marvelous ferns and mosses spread their masses over the tangle of rotting tree trunks festooned with lichens, while farther down one comes across miniature pools of rain water held in leafy cups or rock crevasses, together with wild cranberries, twigs and needles, all as it were supporting each other in a damp, loosely felted mass into which one can sink as one might into a foam rubber mattress a foot thick. A walk here can even be treacherous as we had learned on the trail. One has to learn that gullies and pockets between the rocks and logs lie ready to trip the walker as his foot plunges suddenly into a crevasse under waving ferns and grasses. Life and death here are inextricably mixed. The work of the fungi in rotting away falling fragments is balanced by the constant formation of a rich compost of natural manure in which the seeds and spores of new growth sprout and proliferate as they send out their hopeful tendrils.

Next day, the sun shone bright on the clearing and on the white logs piled off to one side. Thousands of trees stood silently around our little clearing. But they could wait. Now it was time to think about foundations. The weight of a log cabin is immense — for a solid foundation, a few stones laid on this spongy forest duff wouldn't do. The cabin would be built to stay. Having gone to the local builders and masons, we were firmly told, "You have to go down below the frost line, or she'll sag. That's forty-eight inches, and better make it fifty. Once you get them piers in she won't sag no more 'n Gun Rock, just off your Point." Just dig a few holes — say one every eight feet. We would use beach stones in making our concrete, and we could pour it directly into the holes without making wooden forms. And for the part above ground, we would use vertical logs standing on the concrete. Everyone would have to help when the time came for getting stones. Agreed? Okay then, out with the pick and shovel, and dig, Father, dig.

The earth of our Point at the cabin site came up in unctuous shovelfuls. The skin of grass and mosses could be yanked away with a single pull: one scalped the soil with a wrench, then carefully laid aside this foot-thick green tuft, feeling that it was somehow too valuable to throw away. Underneath lay a marvelous black loam, like Swiss chocolate. Intermixed with it were roots, rotted wood, rounded pebbles, and stones up to the size of footballs, which came out with a heave of the bar. They must have been rolled and scoured for centuries, perhaps carried here from some beach a thousand miles away on the last glacier. And this digging was child's play. Or so it seemed.

The first two feet were almost like spooning cocoa powder out of a bowl. Then it got harder. And harder. By degrees the loam gave way to a mixture of mineral and vegetable substances, under which there lay a kind of compressed blue clay mixed with granite chips and the same round stones, now embedded more and more tightly as one went down. The pickaxe rang like a bell, bounced six inches in the air with every stroke. This was the Maine of the Neolithic age, its substance compressed under the weight of glacial action.

Puffing like a primitive steam engine with a leaky boiler, I banged away hour after hour, knocking out mincing little chips with strokes that would have felled an ox. Grunt. One foot more. Why was I ever born? "Hey, Freddie, just come and look at this crazy stuff! Don't you think . . . ?"

"No! The man said forty-eight inches, and you've got to do it."

Looking back on it now, I believe I could have rested the Eiffel Tower on this bed of granitelike clay and it wouldn't have sunk an inch. But, like a robot who has been programmed for a fifty-inch hole, I slogged on down with mechanical fury. Bang, Puff, Bang: two holes a day, and ten to go. To vary the torture we began to think of sand, stones, cement. Particularly stones: the more stones in the concrete mix, the less sand and cement would have to be brought in over the trail to the cabin. Thank God there was the beach not more than a hundred feet away, at the foot of that steep embankment. In the area nearby the beach had only a few ledges. For the most part it was all stones, millions of stones: stones as big as houses, as elephants, as coconuts, as small as baseballs, eggs, marbles. Baked by the sun and washed by the sea, they were sparkling clean, needing only to be brought up the eight-foot-high embankment, and then to the cabin site.

We had brought along several heavy canvas bags, used at home by local coal dealers. About the size of bushel baskets, they were strongly made, with leather corners and looped handles at top and bottom. The girls were allotted a quota: a hundred little stones to each bag for Erica, fifty for Rachel, and Father was to fill the balance of each bag with bigger stones. Then *up* I go, sweating and puffing under the hundred-pound loads, Erica and Rachel racing ahead with the dog to watch them being poured out on the ground.

And, oh yes, don't let's forget the corduroy! Half the way in, a quarter mile from the cabin, there was an open glade in the forest about thirty feet across which would make an admirable turnaround. It was a lovely, almost circular forest room, surrounded by pillared trees — a woodsy Stonehenge. This glade was our immediate goal, a perfect staging area if we could make a passable road to it.

I had had enough experience with corduroys at Professor Marks's place so that I had some deep misgivings concerning the difficulties that lay ahead here. For one thing there would have to be a lot of corduroy, and though I was full of theory, my practice had been limited. Now I was faced with the actual fact of a mucky forest track and the necessity of getting a car over it without bogging down. How many hundred little trees would it take? How did one cover them to the best advantage? There were no answers hung on the trees, no experts, only the immediate fact of mud, and the need to do something about it. Of course, drainage ditches leading out from the road would help, and the turf from the ditches could be put on top of the logs. It was a challenge which had to be met.

So, leaving all thought of the foundation holes and the stones and the logs for the time being, we began the long, slow task of trying to improve the road in order to get it opened as far as the glade, teaching ourselves as we went. Inching forward day by day, we groaned our way through the woods, widening the trail to car width and trying to put a more solid floor under it, digging, filling, cutting and madly swatting mosquitoes. Mosquito lotion is only good till you sweat it off. All the low boggy places had to

be filled with small trees laid together across the places where the wheels would go. To begin with, under the impact of a moving car the logs would jump and separate unless they were covered with soil and branches. Twenty to thirty feet a day was a good day's work. The little girls could help by laying down cut-off branches over the logs. The whole mess was then given a covering of turf and loam. There was one awful passage where we had to use stones as well as logs and turf, and cut long drainage ditches out and away to an even lower area for the necessary run-off in times of rain.

There were moments when, covered with mud and legs trembling with fatigue and on the whole feeling rather ridiculous, I wondered why I had ever begun. Fred, a bandana whipped around her red curls, face streaked with dirt, as often as not would give me a cheerful grin as she spread out a bundle of small branches. She certainly didn't look made for this kind of work. But then, I reflected, women were built to endure. Erica and Rachel, anything but efficient, were nevertheless determined to help in their own ways, and I watched them treading down sods or dropping down small stones into pockets of goo with delighted yelps. Family teamwork in spite of the ache and drag made the labor well worthwhile and gave me the feeling that the roadwork was perhaps only a by-product of something more valuable.

Of course the doggy loved roadwork — happily mucking about and getting in the way. As often as not when the heat became oppressive, he would sink gratefully down into the nearest mudhole, then spring up and shake, usually trotting over first to stand by us.

In the end the slowly lengthening corduroy did provide a kind of quaking trampoline or mattress across which a car, if it didn't go more than five miles an hour, could negotiate a trembling passage.

Measured by creeping time, we had laid a hundred miles of corduroy. By distance, a hundred yards. I suppose we were still projecting ourselves into this new world on what might be called "tenderfoot time" — the feeling that this preliminary work should somehow have gone faster. We were not yet adjusted to the realities of Old Point time.

When it rained, everything turned to muck. But we allowed ourselves to forget the road now and then. On a sunny day we would often come out of the forest onto the rocks for an hour or two to dine sumptuously on lobster or swim naked in the icy water. Occasionally we took a whole day off to ramble, explore, pick wild blackberries and blueberries, or lie in the sun, dreaming. But sooner or later it was back to the Siberian pick and shovel, the stones, the corduroy, the canvas bags, midst which the cries of our children could be heard to remind us that there were other things: "Look! Look! A sailboat! A por-

poise! A seal! A pool!" We discovered one pool so marvelous that we dubbed it Cleopatra's Bath. It was a perfect size to bathe a child in, and each high tide exactly filled it with fresh salt water. Warmed by the sun, it made an ideal tub, from which one could occasionally see a seal rise up slowly just off Gun Rock to look us over with amused, doglike eyes.

Each evening as the sun went down a majestic flight of herring gulls took place, always in one direction, toward some secret destination. Sometimes these flights lasted for an hour till it was completely dark. At night, back at the cottage under the watchful eye of Peeping Tom, the moose, we would read aloud to the children, or sit by the fire making plans and listening to the wind.

Fredericka and I sometimes felt that we had not gotten anything out of it all so far, but had only given, desperately given. God knows, there were even times when our land scared us to death. At the end of a bad day I had often been tempted to abandon the whole project.

I recall one particular storm which seemed to come out of nowhere, in the very middle of a marvelous blue-and-gold day. That morning we had all been rather lazy, content to mooch about the Point in a mildly exploratory mood. We had found at the foot of a steep cliff a delightful little inlet quite separated from the rest of the littoral by two outflung ledges. This gave it the character of a secret beach. There was a lovely sloping mass of rounded stones scrubbed and cleaned by the sea till they seemed to shine with their own light. Among the rocks at the foot of the beach there was a large tide pool and as we came up to it I was enchanted to see lying on its surface like a boat in a miniature harbor a single downy white feather. Suddenly a little wind riffled the surface of the rock pool, causing the feather to glide about as if distracted. It was a charming sight, but it brought to notice the fact that a rather dark cloud had suddenly begun to cover the sun. Now I could also begin to hear a humming in the air, a sighing in the trees at the top of the cliff. And I noticed that although we were standing in comparative calm, up there the trees had begun to bend and sway.

As we scrambled out of our little private world and over the last ledge we were struck in the face by an icy wind. More clouds were piling up rapidly and racing down the bay like bats out of the mouth of a cave. Everything became the color of pewter, shot through now with silver streaks of rain, cold rain. There seemed hardly time to collect a few tools and get them under cover before everything went black, the wind rose to a shriek, and the squall rolled down on us like an avalanche. Every storm has its own personality, and this was no exception. It had an angry, spitting, snarling wildcat quality. This was a hailstorm, slashing into the clearing as if its total animus were being released in that one spot. How could it happen that a midsummer day could turn into this howling cold and fury in a few minutes? A million hailstones bounced and clanked on the rocks and beat upon the tent with a hellish roar. Fifteen minutes passed — then suddenly it was over. The world was still there, magically glazed with white in the clearing and reminding us what it must be like in winter. Ugh! We tumbled out of the tent, feet crunching on rimey frost, and as the storm roared down Blue Hill Bay toward the outer islands, we felt a vast release. I looked at my watch. Forty minutes from hot sun to frost and back again to hot sun. And there was the dog, having appeared from some hiding place, quietly crunching hailstones with every evidence of satisfaction, as if he had ordered them especially from the Almighty for his own delectation.

In addition to such sudden onslaughts there were many more personal, more immediate experiences — cuts, blisters, the threat of broken limbs. There were roots and branches like bayonets waiting to trip and pierce the unwary camper. And always those horrible weights which had to be coped with and in the long run the more subtle assaults of fatigue and nervous tension. But these things were the threads on the dark side of the tapestry. The other side showed the beginnings of a design, hardly outlined. Yet I was conscious of the fact that the lessons we were learning were hard and real, based on necessity, and taken all in all, were giving us a kind of readiness and strength that a lesser challenge would not have provided. And there were times when my response to storms was not always just terror, but rather an intense aliveness, a roaring defiance. Something of this intensity always remained afterward, luring me back, helping me to shed fatigue as I resumed the attack.

The last hellish foundation hole was dug at last. And now began a regular rhythm of bringing cement and sand from the car, which was driven as far as the roadwork had progressed from day to day, then backed slowly out again. For this part of the work each girl had a little knapsack, Fredericka had a larger one, and I used a coal bag. In this way we brought in all our supplies each morning.

But beast-of-burden work often came to an abrupt halt with some moment of exhilaration. I remember one morning when one of the girls — perhaps it was Erica, who had an eye for such things — found a beautiful hollow stump twisted like the horn of a unicorn. Around it was growing a morning glory vine in wild profusion. Everyone stopped work while I made a sketch. Sometimes it would be the sudden unexpected clearing of the sky after a protracted

period of fog. That was enough. Now all bright and sparkling, everything seemed to invite us to some special experience. "Let's go fishing! Let's build a hut in the woods! Let's go to Graham Lake!"

Graham was formed from a stream up-country near the town of Ellsworth. Its flow had been impounded by a water company years ago, and then for some reason lowered again about ten feet from its former level, leaving a vast rim of dead forest trees around the edge. Their twisted roots, now bleached in the sun, were a perfect mine of "driftwood." Our friend Wendell Gilley, the plumber, had told us about it.

Gilley was a charming man with a strong creative flair, who just happened to be a plumber. Needless to say, he was a good one. But a driftwood-and-carving interest at the

time we first met was beginning to claim more and more
of his spare time. Setting out in a car with him, we headed
one fine day for Graham Lake. As we neared the lake we
turned the car off the main highway, following a local road
along near the shore till we came to a spot where the receding water had left a mass of twisted roots drying in the
sun.

"Not much to it, really," said Wendell. "You just visualize the kind of lamp base you want, or in my case the kind
of thing that would go well with a gull or some other bird,
then pretty soon you come across a likely piece — like that
one down there." Bending down, he partially freed a twist
of roots, then using a small Swedish saw he had brought
for the purpose he cut it loose from its neighbors. "That's
as pretty a piece of driftwood as I've seen for a long time.
Notice the way it turns, like an arm and a hand? I can
put a little shag — that's a cormorant — just about there,
or mebbe a pair of 'em, paint them true to life, and you'll
have as pretty an ornament as you could ask for. Funny
thing is, people buy 'em, too. Heck, I've been thinking
lately I might do just about as well if I gave up the plumbing business entirely and went into carving birds full time.
It's more rewardin' to the spiritual part than installin' a
kitchen sink."

But we didn't even need a trip if the mood of exhilaration came. It was enough to go mooching around the Point,
or across it, looking for birds' nests, picking an armful of
wild blue iris, or if the mood was right, deciding to treat
ourselves to an elaborate picnic in some newly discovered
spot by the shore or up on the ridge somewhere about the
confines of the Magic Forest, where the crisp gray and green
lichens made such a lovely embroidered tablecloth on the
bare slopes of rock.

But there was that little matter of the cabin. So we turned to making enough concrete to finish the holes. A rather wet mix was poured into each hole in turn, filling it about half way. Then plop, in would go the stones, bulking up the mass till each hole in turn was filled to ground level. When the concrete had set I built up each pier another six inches to make a platform for tree-trunk posts, in most instances topping the concreted stones with a rounded "pillow-stone" from the beach in the manner of the Japanese who are sophisticated in matters of this kind. The bottom end of each post, slightly hollowed out, fits over the rounded surface of the pillow-stone. In this way the whole thing sheds rainwater to perfection. The

posts nearest the beach, we found, had to be about five feet high, those at the upper end of the slope where the kitchen was to be were about eight inches high. Now at last we were able to come back to our waiting piles of logs, which in the meantime had dried so they were no longer slippery. The logs were rolled up on slanting planks laid against the braced piers, not too difficult if you use a block and tackle and a rope pre-wound round the middle of the log. As you pull, the rope unwinds, pulling the log up the inclined plane till it comes to rest on top of the piers. Mortised at the ends and spiked together, these logs formed the sills. Then more logs were laid from side to side across the floor area and notched to fit the outer logs so that all the tops would come out even. Of course, we had tense moments: logs would sometimes slip and roll back to the ground, or roll off the tops of the piers to land with a crash on the other side. A log twenty-four feet long often has a decided taper. We found that we had to shape out the under sides of the butts so the tops would lie in a horizontal plane. But after the slogging work on the holes, rough work of this kind was almost a relief. And we learned as we went along. We began to realize almost at once that logs like these were never uniform. Knots, burls, butts of branches that had not been cut close enough to the trunks, all had to be taken off if we were to have a reasonably flat floor. But the wood was fresh, the axes were sharp, and each log as it was hoisted into place was given a rough smoothing treatment. Charles with a double-bitted axe, Fredericka with a light Hudson Bay axe, the girls with Boy Scout hatchets, all went at it. The girls didn't have enough power to do much but dent the wood, but chopping and swatting there beside us gave them a fine sense of participation.

Now came spruce boards from the local lumber yard. By this time we had managed to rough out a passable road as far as the turnaround. Then along the forest trail on painful shoulders, we walked them in the rest of the way. One by one the boards were spiked down onto the log sills. At long last here was a floor, or at least a platform, a wonderful broad expanse of wood. A floor! A floor! As soon as the last board went in, we piled up and onto it and began to dance madly till it vibrated like a kettledrum. Of course there had to be a ceremony. A bottle of ginger ale was brought, opened, and solemnly poured on one corner. "I christen thee 'The Floor,'" said Erica.

("Or at least *sub*-floor," I muttered to myself.)

"Oh, don't be stuffy," said Fred, who had overheard me. "A sub-floor is a floor you can walk on, and dance on, and sleep on, and it's lovely and flat, flat, *flat* and I think you are a magnificent carpenter."

"WHOOPEE!" cried Rachel, rolling a tin tub across the platform till it disappeared overside.

But time never stopped plucking at our sleeves. Nights were turning colder now, and the days were noticeably shorter. Another family council was held: no time to finish the cabin. So let's try to build up the kitchen walls at least, put on some kind of temporary roof, and use it as a winter tool shed. By comparison with the twenty-four-footers, the kitchen logs, no more than ten feet long, were easy to handle. Notched, laid, and spiked, the log walls of the little kitchen cube began to rise foot by foot, if not like Venus from the sea, at least like a shoe box from a shelf.

Sometimes we worked in drenching fogs, which wound in among the trees. These fogs, blowing in from the southeast, would be caught by millions of needles in the branches and deposited all about us in a roaring fall. Apparently this was how the forest drank and fed itself between rains. Yellow jackets were now everywhere; sometimes the trees seemed to be alive with them. There was hardly a tree without its population of humming, whining, sipping wasps. We all got stung, Rachel especially. She seemed in some mysterious way to attract these insects, or to madden them by a physical emanation which nobody could explain.

"Rachie, if you just sit still, they won't sting you. Honest they won't."

"But they *do* sting me. They do! They do! They *do!*"

Watching our poor puffed-up baby suffering under the poisoned arrows of these outrageous insects was pure torture. But no repellent available in those days seemed to work. Sportsmen's Comforter, Lollicopop, and Penny Royal could not hide the mysterious something which radiated from long-suffering Rachel.

About this time one day at low tide, we discovered a magnificent mussel bed. Great fat purple critters they were — thousands of them in a continuous bank fifty yards long. The tide here raced by Gun Rock sideways into the bay and out again and must have been carrying an abundant supply of food past these molluscs for ages. There were sea urchins, too. We had eaten them in France and knew how good they were. You cut out a circular trap door in the top of the urchin with scissors, then spoon out the tangy orange meat. For most folks it is perfect without adding anything more. This orange substance has somewhat the texture of fish roe, a rather soft and grainy mouthful. The first taste is almost a shock: one feels that this delicacy must have been prepared by a French chef and inserted into the shell at the last moment. It is ice cold from the sea, and as it slowly spreads apart in one's mouth there is an acid tang, comparable to blackberry juice, or as some would have it, to certain Spanish wines said to have a coppery taste. Then a true shellfish flavor takes over, as it suddenly melts and is gone. At any rate, it is a most decided experience for the few seconds that it takes to consume the meat: you either like it or you don't, but no one has ever remained indifferent to it. For me it has a very faint overtone of Iodine — the whole morsel as pungent and aromatic as the taste of a pine needle.

Mussels too partake in some degree of this decided flavor. When the purple shell pops open after being steamed, one sees lying there in its nacreous bed a fine robust yellow-ochre tidbit which is as tasty as the dark meat of turkey. In Europe mussels have been consumed in vast quantities for centuries, but for some reason we have neglected them on this side of the Atlantic. Slightly chewy, but soft in the mouth, and usually accompanied not just by its own salty juices but by the blended flavors of white wine and garden herbs in which it has been steeped during the steaming process, the meat of the mussel is truly a golden treat. The usual method of preparation is as follows:

Wash and beard 2 quarts of mussels. Peel and chop 1 large onion and put it in a saucepan with 2 or 3 sprigs of parsley and a pinch of thyme. Now add the mussels and 3 or 4 tablespoons of butter or olive oil and a sprinkling of pepper, pour the wine over it and let the mixture steam over a low flame till the mussels open. Put a cover on the saucepan while steaming. Some folks, after removing the mussels, combine the remaining broth with a cup of white sauce and essence of mushrooms or mushroom broth, plus the juice of a lemon. The resulting broth or sauce is then poured over the mussels which have been opened and laid out with top shells removed. To vary the taste you can add a tablespoon of curry powder to the sauce, or substitute heavy cream for the white sauce.

Pollock and flounder liked to lurk just off this same Point and we used to cast lines out, though the fishing here was on the whole too rough and unpredictable to be much fun. At night when an occasional aurora borealis walked the northern sky, we woke the girls to see its eerie searchlights.

With summer nearly over, the purple asters were beginning to lose their petals and the goldenrod had long since faded to an insignificant brown. The fireweed, having lost its fuchsia pride, was now transforming its blossoms into cottony gauze wings which on a breezy day would suddenly fill the air with thousands of insectlike seeds, each one sustained in a mass of finely divided silver threads: a lovely sight as they drifted like feathery white moths among the trees.

We finished the three outer log walls of the kitchen, put on a temporary roof of boards and tar paper and made a rather jerry-built wall on the living room side, leaving just enough of a gap to pack the tools inside. That was it. The last few boards were nailed by hands numb with cold and fatigue. Then, blistered, burned, hardened, sad with the thought of leaving, yet in a curious way triumphant, we ate a last meal on the great board sub-floor of the cabin-to-be and bid our Point goodbye, leaving it again to its native inhabitants, the fish crows, ospreys, owls, chipmunks, and the ants, who hardly aware of our existence, were already feasting on the remnants of our final repast.

4

With Paul's Help

OFTEN that winter our Point seemed not only very
far away but unreal, perhaps something half-remem-
bered from a dream. The prosaic steady rhythms of school
and work came and went like the beat of a good engine
at the heart of a ship. I thought about my girls. How
different they were. Erica, beautiful and precise, an artist
to her fingertips, carried around with her an aura of order,
measure, and a fierce determination to grow, to be a woman.
She seemed almost to resent childhood, as somehow a waste
of valuable time. What could she get from that primitive
existence on the Point, which in retrospect seemed to present little but the hard, the necessary, the brutal facts of
a physical experience? And it was an experience that so
far had succeeded only in smashing down a part of the
forest: destroying one kind of perfection without having
created another in its place.

And Rachel, the life-lover? Living from day to day,
marvelously lazy, absolutely charming, *she* didn't want to
be a woman — not she! She loved being what she was. Yet
Rachel, breaking out of her little papoose mold from time
to time, would erupt with volcanic energy, crunching
through all opposition like a baby tank. Did she need a

doll's dress? Snip-snap-snout: any available cloth would do — handkerchiefs, window curtains — nothing was sacred. Making cookies? The kitchen would be a shambles. From sharpening pencils with the sewing scissors to hammering nails into the table legs, nothing stood in her way. There was something there, something powerful, which had not yet managed to declare itself in other than destructive terms. When Erica built a sand castle, it would be shaped pat pat pat pat with nicely calculated strokes. Rachel was all Bang Bang Bang, and Kick it if it didn't work. This fascinating difference appeared even in their language: in learning to talk, Erica had called flowers *fowfs:* precise, definite. But Rachel, not satisfied with Erica's attempt, called them in her all-out way, *wows!*

Now at home once more in Pennsylvania, the winter rolled around and slowly retreated, like the tides at Blue Hill Bay. Migrating birds were coming through our Pennsylvania valley. Especially, lines of honking geese on their way north reminded us poignantly of our little wilderness domain. The chickadees and juncos were leaving Bucks County, too, and we knew we would see them again on our land, where they remained all summer. Now like those blue mountains once so far away, the Point began to loom near and clear with the change of season. I had put on a one-man show that winter largely of canvases done on a western trip some years before. It sold well and this together with a series of illustrations I was doing for a history textbook helped to keep us in financial health.

We were ready for another summer. But no more cottages for us. During the winter we had repaired the old tents and had bought a smashing new one guaranteed to keep everything out but fear of the dark. We ordered a cast-iron stove and some stock windows, these to be delivered at the railhead in Ellsworth. The last week of school came and went. We packed, reconsidered, packed again, and at last were ready to go. But this time with a difference. Not only were we going to live in our own cabin, or at least on our own land; we now had two cars, and there was the children's nurse, Callie Burnett. Callie was, and is, a beautiful woman, built like a fortress. Raised in the little mountain town of Old Fort, North Carolina, and having lived in a log cabin — a real log cabin — all her early years, she was eager to go, able to take the other end of a two-man saw, and just as ready to split a bit of kindling or peel a log as to stuff a chicken and cook it to perfection. Callie had superb manners, melting black eyes, a brown skin, and a nature of pure gold. And she could also drive a car. This made it possible to change drivers during the trip, two driving and one resting all the way.

The "road" onto the Point had almost turned back into a primitive bog. The corduroy held, but barely, as we bumped and sloshed and burped to the turnaround. Whether we would ever get out again we didn't know, but at least we were in, mud-covered, grinning in triumph. "Callie, Callie, here's my stone castle from last year! And Callie! Look at the ants, and Callie, look, look, Callie, there's the cabin!" There it stood, a lonely gray platform in a forest clearing, the log box at one end and the spread of flooring all covered now with needles, branches, leaves, crab shells, bird-droppings. There wasn't much that one could call a home, but what there was was solid.

Down came the boards of the temporary kitchen wall, to be used in making tent platforms. Up went the tents, now all in a row under the trees along the shore. Then to garnish them with mosquito nets, lanterns, branches of fir balsam for mattresses, cardboard boxes full of dolls,

books, first-aid materials, bug lotions. Quick now, sweep
the platform, bring some water from the spring, make the
beds, and *where* is that leftover salami? "Hey, Grey Brother!
Come back here!" Well, never mind, he's hungry, too.

We could clearly see that this was to be the year of the grunt, the heave, the gasp. We had talked often the previous winter about the problem of raising logs really high, and were thinking perhaps we could manage by fastening the block and tackle high up in a tree and from that vantage point hoisting the logs to the top of the cabin walls. But now Fortune smiled upon us and with the smile another possible solution appeared. A couple of days after we had arrived and were beginning to settle to our routine, my brother Paul turned up, eager to get in on the fun. A serious fellow, Paul, and a nice perfectionist. We are identical twins, and in some respects mirror images of each other. But where I rushed in, Paul stopped to make a detailed plan. Where I would madly slash, Paul would carve. Where I would butt, Paul would nudge. A master of judo, he had learned to yield to an opponent better to bring him to defeat. But being my twin he was exactly my equal in strength, though perhaps not as experienced in the matter of woodcraft.

"See that tree? That's just what I've been looking for. It'll make great special pieces where I want some kind of decorative surface. It's got those knobs and burls I was telling you about."

Paul looked quizzical and said, "You think just because you've had some Boy Scout training you can knock this forest to pieces, cut it up and lay it out in little pieces like strips of dough? Huh. Now listen to me: you haven't any idea of what you're letting yourself in for. Out here with your bright little axe, which I may say isn't near heavy enough for these trees, and that crazy gleam in your eye, you think all you have to do is to make a few passes and the whole bloody forest is going to turn into a cabin, just like a fairy story. Haven't you any sense at all? I'll never know why I bothered to come up here. Now I have to follow around after a half-wit who thinks because he's wearing a lumberjack shirt he's Paul Bunyan's little brother."

"Oh, shut up. I'll bet you a buck right now I'll find a use for that tree before long that'll make your eyes bug out."

"Cha, I tell you, you can't get that tree down! Haven't you learned anything in the last few days? It's right in the middle of all those rocks, and you'll waste a week trying to get it out!"

"I don't know myself right now, but there's one thing I *do* know and that's the fact that I want it. C'mon, let's try."

"Well, if I hadn't agreed to let you be boss on this operation I'd say you were losing your mind. But okay — if you want to suffer . . ."

Yet all in all, we made an excellent team, our different temperaments sometimes weakening but more often strengthening our collaboration. In this respect twins have an advantage over most — they can work all day in an atmosphere of intuitive awareness, hardly needing to utter a word, a single four-armed, four-legged creature. There were other days when we totally and simply jarred on each other. But such episodes never lasted for long.

We were face to face with the serious problem of getting enough trees cut, brought to the site, peeled, notched, shaped top and bottom, and lifted exactly into place. It soon became obvious that our problem would be somewhat simplified if we worked our way uphill toward the spine so the majority of logs could be brought downhill toward the cabin. Another thing: we found that we often had to cut three trees to get one good enough to use. A Maine forest is like a city: its citizens are thin, fat, healthy, morbid, cavernous, bulging, and everything in between. The tall, straight, strong Olympic Champion trees were there all right, in about the same proportion as perfect physical specimens among a human population.

The finding and cutting turned out to be fantastically difficult for us amateurs. The basic idea was simple enough — to fell each tree in the direction of the cabin, cut off the limbs, saw the boles into sections of the proper length, put log rollers under the sections and ease them downhill. *Ease?* Some other word will have to do. Just picture this: you have managed to cut a great tree which was supposed to fall true, exactly in line with the corner of the cabin you can see a hundred yards downhill through the trees. But then, that big puff of wind came up at the worst possible moment and because the tree was balanced just so, the wind caught it and twisted it as it fell. Now the tree is lying in just the wrong direction, tightly wedged down among a group of five other trees. It seems to grin up at you, an enormous mass of tangled and smashed branches perhaps seventy feet long and to the unaccustomed eye as big as a stranded whale, lying there on a tilted hillside floor which at the moment seems to be made of nothing but gigantic granite boulders covered with slippery moss and the detritus of centuries. The tree in its fall has dis-

rupted a wasps' nest. Now with the sound of rising wind, thousands come swarming out, keening like a horde of Apaches. WHOOSH! You find yourself racing pell-mell, projecting yourself over boulders and under branches with the mad force of an avalanche. And by the way, where have you thrown that axe? That saw? And the stings are painful, more painful by far than the sting of a domestic bee. One of these fast-moving critters can sting you, jab-jab-jab-jab, four times in one second. Ironically enough, considering the identical gene structure that Paul and I must have, Paul reacted far more violently than I did. Stung in three or four places, I would yelp, glare at the rising welts, cuss my fate, and go on from there. In an hour or so they would subside to fiercely itching red areas. But Paul suffered outrageously. His wasp stings swelled up like balloons. I remember one in particular on the back of his hand: in half an hour his whole arm had swollen to an angry bloated smoothness, the hairs standing out like the sparse growth on a bald scalp. The arm was useless and had to be carried about in a sling for a day. This kind of thing happened over and over again. In those days we had not become aware of the modern antihistaminic agents, and doctors were few and far between.

To kill the wasps we used liquid paradichlorobenzene. Having located the entrance to a nest, we would wait till evening, then taking a twenty foot section of pipe and placing one end — oh, so gently — at the hole, we would pour the chemical down the length of the pipe and into the nest.

So, having killed the wasps and found the tools, an hour passes: we are in the process of limbing and cutting the tree into sections. "For God's sake, watch my foot, you clumsy ox!" The tree, with the economy of a railroad track-switch, has suddenly moved sideways just one inch, pinning Paul's foot neatly to a rock. Howls of pain. "Do something, you idiot! Get a crowbar! And hurry!" Learning the hard way — not to stand too close when things are slippery, always to cut the limb off on the far side so if the axe slips it won't chop your leg off, cursing our ignorance, we gradually learn that we must fashion long slots or troughs in the forest floor, rolling aside small boulders, laying branches in the lowest spots, throwing in sod where needed. Down these skidways we pull and roll the logs.

Sometimes a log that had balked like a donkey for forty-five minutes, even though poised on short log rollers, would begin to drift of its own accord. Perhaps an extra two or three degrees of downhill angle, a slippery roller, a bit of muck, and before you could say "Hi!" the thing would get away and zoom downhill without benefit of any agency. This usually happened on wet days when moist boughs and soggy duff under the pressure of constantly moving logs and rollers can become strangely slick. Just as the two of us had perhaps given a good heave together, thinking: That's the best heave of the day — your feet slip out from under you and you fall flat on your back. An inarticulate cry from brother Paul — you know only too well what that means: the tree is on its way — boom, bop, bounce. Mad yells from the hilltop: mad scrambles below as the girls duck for cover. In the midst of one of these runs a log can be brought up short, can bury its head deep in the ground, can leap sideways out of its proper channel, and then you're in for it. Dig, Dig, Dig, and the block and tackle, the cant hook, and the bar come out. Inch by inch it comes sucking from its bed of mud or rock and is started on its way again.

Then there was the menace of falling trees. Watching

a tree fall doesn't seem at first anything more than the dramatic and satisfying moment of the yielding-of-the-enemy. But there is a curious shadowy half-light in the forest, especially on dark or foggy days, which often made it difficult to see exactly what was happening. On the way down a tree could suddenly catch momentarily on the hidden limb of a neighbor tree, roll halfway over and complete its fall in an entirely unlooked-for direction. A "safe" distance could then turn instantly into no distance at all. Again, a tree could wait, till the last moment standing absolutely erect, then at once, without warning, down it could come: crack, swoop, hurling broken branches in every direction, and often seeming to aim itself with deadly precision at the man who felled it. There were times after such a crashing fall when whipping branches came near enough to lash the face of the unwary tenderfoot below. A tree could hold and have to be pulled down with block and tackle. But it could also fall and catch on a kind of hair trigger somewhere forty feet up, then at the slightest wandering breeze break away and come thundering down. Worst of all were the ones that fell in such a way as to come halfway down through a group of five or six dead or dying trees, all of which under the impact would suddenly let go. This happened more than once and left us white and shaken for a few minutes wondering how in the world we had managed to escape annihilation, and what to do to improve our technique. Eventually we learned to cut felling lanes into which we dropped our wanted trees. This meant cutting every tree in sight in certain areas, but it saved time in the end, and as the forest around the cabin site diminished somewhat and more open places appeared, the problem of trees catching in other trees diminished, too. But we nevertheless grew wary, respectful of the dull fury so often unleashed when a tree gave up its life. And we learned never to be without a saving latent fear, a hair-trigger readiness to jump and run into escape routes plotted out well ahead. But we never had a serious injury from falling trees.

So one by one down they came, log by smoking log, ninety-eight of them in all; some with the bark half torn off, some as smooth and bland as an apple dumpling. Lovely raw material, to be sure, and all, all for free. But that subtle curve, half seen as you glance up aloft through a tangle of branches ofttimes turned out to be a two-foot arch when you tried to lay it on its neighbor in the wall.

"Cha — the butter melts all the time. Can't we do something?"

"Why sure — just sink that old stone crock you bought the other day at the church sale into the spring and you'll have a perfect cooler."

But the crock, heavy in air, was light as a feather in water. "Look, it won't sink!" (She pushes.) *"See?* I tell you it *won't sink."* (Pushes farther.) The crock mutters "Ploop," turns over, and goes to the bottom like a tor-pedoed sub. Later, let into the side of the pool and weighted with pebbles, it learned to behave. The water in the spring had to be husbanded carefully. The inflow was so slight that one could not tell where it came from. At the top it seeped off into a boggy area, but now with a whole family using the water, this area became increasingly dry. Moreover, the level in the spring sometimes fell alarmingly. I put this problem in the back of my mind for further study.

All the newly cut logs now had to be peeled and stacked ready for building. The men generally used pinch bars and axes to pry up bark strips. The girls used Boy Scout hatchets or knives. You push the instrument under the bark, pry up a section, then the reward: with a tremendous yank a long spurting strip comes off. Sometimes almost the whole skin of a long section would yank away like a strip of birchbark, in one terrific pull. A yell of triumph would echo round the clearing. In other cases, where the sap had dried up to a certain extent, the peeling was monotonous and dull. In such cases the whole carapace had to be taken off with a spoke shave, and might take an hour or two, compared with five minutes or less for the best logs. It took us a long time to realize that logs cut early, with their sap still running, were the ones that peeled like bananas. Testing each tree before felling became a standard procedure: coming across a likely tree, we would cut a blaze on the trunk and rip down a section of bark. If it came away easily, we would shout, "Okay! Here's a banana!"

The rush of work could not continue without an occasional break. After a particularly tough tree had been felled and brought downhill, by mutual consent we would often take a thermos jug of hot tea to the bluff which overlooked the bay and lie back against the rocks to relax. A favorite spot was a certain ledge which sloped down to the south in a long incline, warmed by the sun even in coldish weather. We came to call this particular place the Hot Rocks, and here aching muscles and tired bones could be gradually baked out after an exhausting struggle. "I don't know about you, but I've had it for today. That last tree was a double dyed-in-the-wool b—stard. When it slogged down into that rock, I felt a million years old, all of a sudden. Say, look at that! Is it a whale or something? Whoever he is, I wish we could hitch him to a rope and use him to pull those damn trees downhill. They train

elephants in India — why not whales here in Maine? Trained whales for rent!"

"Tell you what: for a change of pace, let's make a swing for the kids. There's that great big tree near the cabin — you know the one — with the limb that sticks out just right to take a couple of ropes. Okay, let's go."

We made a fine swing, with a broad seat adjusted to the height of little legs and bottoms and cut the brambles and forest grass away from underneath. Now almost any day the children could be seen seated firmly on the swing, together with their teddy bears, little legs in air, Grey Brother bounding up and down after them as the swing arced across the clearing. And from time to time, Father, with a new duty to perform, could be seen responding to the imperious command: "Push harder, Charlie, harder!"

Occasionally I took a day off for sketching. On one such occasion, I heard a hearty voice as I sat drawing some rocks down near the harbor docks. A grizzled man in hip boots was standing just behind me.

"Well, it's interestin' to see the way you go at it. Used to think all artists was probably crazy. Now you sit down there nice and sober like a man mendin' a lobster pot. I can see you know what you're doin', though I can't always tell what the hell you're drivin' at till I see the finish. Then I can sometimes make somethin' out here and there.

"I had quite an education in the art business, though you wouldn't know it to look at me. Come about this way: there was this other painter appeared down to the dock one day some years ago. He was dressed fit to kill — fancy hat like a mushroom and sandals on his feet. Wanted someone to take him out on the water so's he could paint from there. Well, I had nothin' better to do at the time, so I obliged. From then on he began to hire me some regular to take him in my boat into them little inlets and such, up the bay. He'd sit there all afternoon with a bottle, slappin' mosquitoes with one hand and paintin' with the other while I fished. Now and then he'd take a swig from the bottle. By the end of the day he'd be so full he'd like to fell overboard and usually wiped so much paint off on himself that he could of framed his own pants and sold 'em for one of his pitchers. I couldn't tell the difference myself: all colors of the rainbow in a wrestlin' match till it made your head swim to tell where one began and the other left off. As far as I could see he might jest as well stayed home and threw the paint on from there. Paid good though.

"He gave me one o' them things once, in a fit of absent-mindedness, and after castin' round a bit I found an old toilet seat that had been layin' round the woodshed for years. I framed her up in that, but never did know whether I had it upside down or rightside up. After a while it made Martha so nervous that I finally took it out to the back-house and hung it on the wall — figured it might kind of felt more at home out there. And I'll tell you this: it turned out to be real handy: all you had to do was to look at it long enough and it was just as good as a dose of salts!"

5

Our Walls, Our Roof

DURING this period we built a more elaborate fireplace in the rocks to replace last year's, which had been destroyed in winter storms. We gorged on lobsters, grilled fish, blueberry pancakes and bread baked by Callie in a tin reflecting oven. Then back to the bark-peeling as before. This peeling made rather elaborate cleaning necessary, as the juices stained the hands and clung like glue as they dried. Turpentine was used to get the mess off, then soap and water and plenty of suds to get off the turpentine, which sometimes burned tender skins. A regular cleansing routine was established: once a week an all-over bath in a rubber tub, and daily scrub-ups in Cleopatra's Bath, with salt water soap. Clothes were laundered in a round tin tub till we discovered a hand-cranked contraption called by its maker in a moment of enthusiasm "The Happy Home Laundry." On the whole we managed to keep reasonably clean, by eighteenth-century standards.

The excitement mounted now. Skirmishing was over and the real battle was about to begin. The piers were in place, the sills were spiked down. The sub-floor had been nailed fast. The logs brought to the building site had been peeled and cut to the measure of our plan, so as to make a room twenty-four feet long and eighteen feet wide. But every log, as we were soon to find out, had its particular personality. The beauty of modern standardization was never more apparent than now, as we contemplated those great baulks of timber resting there in their primitive state. Lumps and bumps, of course. But all those subtle curves, like the hollows in a woman's back! Not a single log was really ready to lay athwart its neighbor. It became apparent with the setting of the very first log that every one would have to be shaped and straightened both top and bottom along its entire length. Using two similar saw horses, one under each end of a log, we flattened tops and bottoms with the axe till in effect they became beams with two parallel sides and two curved sides. Then blup, blup, blup, we rolled them into place. Many had to be taken down again and reshaped for a more perfect fit.

We didn't just lay those logs together. We spiked them down with twelve-inch galvanized spikes driven down through each log to the bottom of holes drilled halfway through at intervals of about six feet. The first log would have its butt at one end, the next at the other, to compensate for the difference in girth between top and bottom. Pulled close by the spikes, the logs at last fit tolerably well and were caulked with oakum, a kind of tarred rope fiber used by boat builders. Twisted slightly and driven into the cracks with cold chisels this material virtually waterproofs a wall, as it swells when wet. Paul took a fine series of pictures showing hands and tools working on the caulking of the logs. In fact, work was brought to a standstill from time to time while he prowled about in order to find the perfect camera angle. On the whole I enjoyed these moments but there were times when I had to grit my teeth with impatience to get on with it.

Now, a joyous day! Here was a notice from the railroad, saying that the stove and windows had come. With its large crate the stove weighed three hundred and fifty pounds, and it seemed as if it might be far too bulky to shove along the forest trail from the turnaround without more tree cutting. But it was there waiting at the railroad siding. We arranged to have it brought to the turnaround by truck along with the windows. We then inched the stove along the trail on two planks and two rollers, improving our forest roadbed as we did so, and feeling rather like Mayan slaves bringing up a block of stone for Chichen-Itza. A half day's labor got it to the clearing, where we rolled it up inclined planks onto the platform. Here we broke open the crate, and nudged the stove into our box of a kitchen. It was put in place opposite a secondhand cast-iron sink we had bought from Wendell Gilley, the plumber. As there was no chimney yet we set up a couple of sections of stove pipe to provide draft, filled the hot water tank on the side of the stove, and suddenly, oddly, felt almost effete. It was a silly-looking thing with its pipe chimney sticking up into the air, but it introduced an element of civilized life into our primitive environment which had hitherto been missing. Ah, that first roast chicken, that first blueberry pie! Purple mouths, greasy fingers! And did the king of England ever dine as well? I doubt it.

As most families who live in close association do, we had developed nicknames for each other. They varied according to the need or the mood of the moment. My children, for example, never called me Father, though I often secretly wished they would. The word has a certain dignity, and carries with it the honorable connotations of authority. But alas for status, such authority as I possessed did not stem from my position, unalterable though it was, but could be employed only in the context of our close friendship. So it came about that for the most part I was called Charlie, further pared down from time to time to the one-syllable "Cha." During moments when I was being subjected to amused family pressure, or opposition to one of my endless suggestions for the expenditure of a further quantum of family energy, they hit me as a last resort with the monniker "Bald Eagle."

When we were in a teasing mood we called Erica "Ricky." And if there were moments when she exhibited a hoity-toity quality, as older sisters often feel it their right to do, she might be addressed as "Madame Eroica von Childersleeve," a name which had to be used with a certain reserve. Rachel in her softer moments was known as "Rumple-Bumple," and when she got the sulks, as "Old Bear." "Now hear this, Old Bear: No workee, no eatee!" Paul became "Paulski," which for some reason fit like a glove.

Fredericka's full name was too overwhelming for most. She was almost always called Freddie, in time shortened to Fred, which seemed to suit a certain forthright quality which she exemplified. Along with this particular quality, Fred possesses an incredible memory for names, telephone numbers, whole conversations from years back, which come reeling out with tape-recorder accuracy. When, in her role as family memory-bank, she had characteristically performed one of these feats of legerdemain, we would often shout, " 'Total-Recall' has done it again!" As time went on we two parents were given a kind of blended or corporate name, "Chafred." "Are Chafred going out to lunch today? Hey, Chafred, how about giving those doors another coat of paint?" Other more fugitive names came and went, but over the years these were the names that clung.

As the semanticists say, "The Word is not the Thing," and though we had drawings of the cabin fireplace, and had talked "fireplace," there *was* no fireplace — only an empty space. With Paul, I toiled away at a foundation for the chimney, a hole six feet by six feet in girth and four feet deep: one hundred forty-four cubic feet of torture. But two men working together often have the effectiveness of four. Slogging away in the bottom of that hole I had visions of the folk on the other side of the island, who in my fancy were at that very moment dressed in spotless white, playing tennis, tripping lightly along the decks of palatial yachts with enormous trays of gin slings, martinis and rum sours.

Bit by bit the fireplace hole was filled with beach-stone concrete. We found too that working as a team we could quite easily roll large boulders free of the forest floor with the crowbar. After a period of drying in the sun the peculiar soil of our Point would come off almost completely with a few swipes of a stiff brush. This gathering of forest stones had a double effect. It yielded us an abundant supply of raw material which did not have to be lifted up the eight-foot bank, and it helped to clear and smooth the terrain in the vicinity of the cabin. Many of these stones were far too big to be lifted, but they could be rolled to the lip of the hole and tipped into the wet concrete mix with a fine splash. After about the sixth or seventh day the concrete reached the level of the floor. The core of the whole house was now mortised into its mother earth like those rock masses which geologists call horsts, so solid that nothing can compress them or move them further till the end of time. With this concentration on the chimney we had been carrying in eleven hundred pounds of sand and cement each morning before starting work. If you want to harden your shoulder muscles I can think of simpler ways to do it.

Since the log walls of both kitchen and living room were going to be set directly into the chimney, we now decided to do one week's work on the walls, then one week's work on the chimney, and so mounting step by alternating step, all would progress together. As the work went forward, Paul took record pictures each week. These pictures now constitute an almost complete visual story of the construction of the cabin at various stages. The day when the walls got as high as the windowsills and the fireplace sides and back had been laid up to a height of three feet or more marked a magnificent turning point. We could begin to see, in the solidity of three dimensions, how our half-house might one day be a whole house, how the crowded tents might be emptied, how we might have a table and chairs, how we might read in comfort at night, or go to sleep by the light of a fireplace fire.

On the tops of our log walls all the way round we now set up window enframements made of two-by-eight planks. An upward leap! The presence of these more sophisticated shapes suddenly gave our little enclosure the air of a banquet hall. By chance a lobsterman friend had come by the Point that very morning, and seeing our girls playing on the beach had put his boat in close to the shore and tossed them a half dozen lobsters. A ceremony! A ceremony! Or better yet, a feast, with speeches to mark the occasion. Tossing the lobsters into the Happy Home Laundry with an inch or two of sea water, we set up a banquet table in the middle of the platform. It was made of planks set on short legs about fifteen inches high, as we had no chairs and would have to sit on the floor. This gave it an oddly Oriental look. We had the lobsters with cole slaw, apple pie à la Callie, cool beer from the spring for the grownups and ginger ale for the kids. In our hair we wore twisted wreaths of forest grass spiked with goldenrod, and for the moment we were beautiful and shining.

The window units themselves fitted inside the enframements sideways, two to a frame, so as to open horizontally. They would create a long continuous bank of light on either side. The spaces between the frames would be filled with short logs. For the time being ignoring the chimney, we worked on our living room walls, filling up the spaces and bringing the level of the fitted logs up as far as the tops of the window frames. In the process of building, enough trees had been cut in the vicinity of the cabin so that the ocean could be seen through a fringe of trees on the southern and western sides. This newly framed view of trees and water from inside our almost-room, far from giving us the sense of being blocked off, created a series of lovely long vignettes. Strangely, the panorama was not destroyed; it was enhanced.

Only two courses of logs now remained to be set above the window frames before the walls would be finished up to the springing of the roof. A roof! What a delightful thought. But now we had to get back to the fireplace. To top the aperture we used the gigantic old knurled log I had salvaged from the first days. This kind of construction was used by the pioneers in our part of Pennsylvania, who sometimes ran a baulk of oak ten feet long across the great fireplace opening from one stone side to another. The inner face of this log we lined with a heavy sheet of zinc, stuffing asbestos insulation down between metal and wood. The log itself was covered with knurls and knobs and fine muscular bulges, and had the sheen and lustre of old pewter. Here was triumphant vindication of my interest in "fancy" logs!

Now I began to taper the chimney back in a series of little steps or shelves incorporating the ends of the logs from kitchen and living room walls as I went. This tapering in theory should have made the work go faster as the cross section of the chimney was gradually reduced. But my calculations had not taken into account the fact that passing stones up higher and higher took more and more time. Rough staging had to be erected round the working face every three feet or so. Then the stones were handed up from stage to stage. As the stages got higher we began to pass up smaller and smaller stones to save work, producing the effect of a quite sophisticated gradation of surface from rough to fine, though this had never entered our minds.

From time to time winds would come scouring in, whirl around the room, and leave a few calling cards. The windows, set loosely in their frames, would rattle like snare drums. And showers fell in our almost-room: rain coursing down *in*side the windows! "Get out the mops and sop it up, but *who* left that book on the table? Haven't your mother and I told you time and again . . ." And there was that roofless kitchen with its silly stovepipe sticking up to nowhere: we rigged ponchos over the stove corner, which served after a fashion. Finally the stove pipe was set into its proper place when the chimney got high enough. But still, a good long rainy day would set everybody's teeth on edge. John Henry, the stove, would go out sometimes, unable to keep up the unequal struggle against blowing rain and drafts swirling and whirling about in all directions.

"I don't have to stand *this*," I growled one morning when the weather was particularly hideous. I jumped into the nearest car and drove to town where I bought two large brown tarpaulins. We stretched them taut over the kitchen and one corner of the living room from wall-top to wall-top. "Why didn't we think of this before?" Here in effect were two abbreviated tents with wooden walls and glass windows. Paul at once moved his sleeping bag inside under the living room tarpaulin. By night one could hang lanterns under this corner and feel almost as if the room had a ceiling. If one went to the other side of the clearing and into the woods to look back at the half-cabin dimly seen through the dark, one could see a row of soft square lights in the forest, a rough sketch of things to be.

Out on our Point, cut off for days at a time by work and distance, it was not difficult to forget the war and the gradual building of tension. Nevertheless Fred and I were apprehensive, and sometimes compared ourselves to the ants now garnering the last seeds before the onset of winter. But the work went on, with a sense of poignancy hanging in the air like woodsmoke, hazing over our delight. Working now at my chimney top, I could look down to see Callie and Fred, heads wrapped in red and blue bandanas, whipping the two-man saw through a log with a swish, swish, swish. The girls were down on the beach supposedly picking up little stones for the bags, but actually trying once more to dam up the tiny rain spring which was seeping out of a crevasse in the rocks so the dog could have a pool of drinking water. A bit of concrete would help there. Immediately below, Paul was putting the hoe through a mass of sand and cement, and here was I, looking like a neglected bronze statue covered with bird droppings, splashed as I was with nuggets and ribbons of wet cement mix.

From time to time one or two of the local children would appear on the Point to see how things were going, and they often stayed to help with the work: peeling logs, picking up beach stones, running along with the girls to get needed materials. And if we stopped for lunch there would be peanut butter sandwiches, ginger ale, or a piece of candy. We were delighted to welcome them and to realize that our girls were by degrees beginning to make friends in the village. We had heard much talk concerning the suspicious or unfriendly Down Easter, but we never felt this quality among our neighbors whom we were meeting casually at the post office or the local stores. Quite the contrary. They were gay and friendly, full of wit and a vast curiosity concerning life on Old Point. There was a quality however which impressed itself upon us with increasing force as time went on. Maine folk, even the children, are often masters of a certain lank, four-square comment which can bring a conversation to an abrupt halt as if it had run into a brick wall. I recall one such conversation which took place just as I emerged from the cabin one day dressed for a rather elegant lunch. Here I encountered a young friend of the girls who looked me up and down for a long ten seconds with the inscrutable air of a Sachem reading distant smoke signals. Thinking to ease the situation a trifle I remarked, "Well, how do I look?" Whereupon the tot replied, "You wouldn't look half bad if you'd only zipped up your fly!" End of conversation.

Sometimes a day would unfold with an ominous tension. For no reason we would bite and snap, or go broody. "Oh, shut up!" someone would yelp when no one had spoken. From a tent one might hear: "Damn this typewriter anyway! Why is it sticking just *today* when I have an important letter to write?" From the kitchen a plaintive wail: "Mr. Child, would you mind coming down here a minute — I just can't make John Henry behave." From my perch,

I might shout: "Do this! Do that! Why can't you leave me alone? Can't you see this concrete is drying up on me right in the bucket?"

Sometimes we would come across one of the children tight-lipped from a quarrel, or at rare intervals, blubbering quietly in a corner. All families have these moments. But the proffered balm of a friendly "What's the matter, darling?" was not always effective. "Nothing, nothing," the child would mutter, turning away, for the moment beyond help. We had to learn that children's sorrows are often mysterious, veiled from us and our fathoming probes, for there are times when they fear our understanding, too. The rough intrusion of an elder can be a bruising thing, though it is hard to admit that it does not always solve the problem it seeks to analyze. You can advance harshly into this domain beating your drum in victory only to find that the field is strewn with the corpses of hope and wonder. Children in these instances often remind me of "natives," and parents remind me of anthropologists. Just as with the anthropologist and the native, a touch of compassion may open more doors than a thousand theories.

There were times when tension built up in the air itself. The forest would produce strange sounds. Insects would suddenly disappear. What, no mosquitoes, no wasps? Of course! A storm's coming! That's it. "Find the kids! See to those tent pegs." Now to cover the wet cement with a poncho and lash it fast. A hollow wail from the treetops. A sudden flight of gulls. The sky turns to slate. If one had time to rush out to the fringe of trees one could see a dark mass approaching, its cumulonimbus fingers reaching out ahead to rake the light from the sky. Such sharp squalls and line storms often came without warning. Or perhaps I should say that the warning often went unheeded. Under the trees, hard at work, it was easy to be too preoccupied to notice anything till the first enormous ice cold splashes of rain came hurtling down. With a roar the squall would break. Trees would twist and groan and lash at each other. Salt spray would batter the tents, shuddering in their ropes. Inside the tents, or cowering under the billowing tarpaulins, we would sit it out. John Henry would hiss and sputter; smoke and sparks would lash the room as with a whip. Grey Brother, under the floor, head to tail, would wait with stoic calm.

Then suddenly everything becomes bright. Whew! We look around. The trees are sparkling in the sun, millions of drops clinging to everything. A sudden lurch from the kitchen — Oops! The tarpaulin has just discharged a quart of water on Rachel's head. Woe! That stealthy reach for the cookies high on a shelf has been her undoing. "Ho, ho, Old Bear! Clean up your mess!" Now out with the mops, off with the poncho-lashings round the chimney, adjust the tent lines and pegs, try to coax John Henry back to life.

Of course there were hours, even days, when we both felt nearly overwhelmed by discouragement. We could not change our method of building to a more modern type of construction for that would have involved an impossible additional expense. And we could never abandon the project: we were too proud. The only way out was simply to keep on, keep on, never to give in.

Lunching on the rocks and looking out to sea one day we had said to each other, "Why not a boat?" Well, why not? Among our friends in the nearby village were people who could give us good advice in the matter. "There's that Clifton Rich, he's a dern solid man with a boat," said a local man. So we went looking for Mr. Rich. His

house was one of those modest gray-as-bark dwellings that one sees in this part of Maine, their front yards often filled with lobster buoys being painted or repaired and like as not alive with a pride of tow-haired children. Rich was a grizzled man, not unlike his house: a bit gray and worn at the edges, but solid and substantial. I had the feeling that he himself might have been turned out by a fine ship-wright, and that if one could have opened his hatches one would have found everything down below in fine shape, probably varnished with Hongkong Spar. On the day of our visit he was just putting the finishing touches to a fine skiff, slowly and lovingly sandpapering her gunwales in preparation for a coat of paint. There is a lingering quality to good craftsmanship. The important considera-tion is never time, always quality. Delighted with the look of the work and the fine lines of the little craft, we asked him if he would consider making us one just like it. This he readily agreed to do.

Under his hand in the course of some weeks there emerged a good solid boat, the twin of the one we had seen. Now we were able to extend our range into another dimension and another element. Callie turned out to be an ardent fisherman and one of the typical sights of the Point from that time on was the skiff floating quietly some distance off Gun Rock, Callie hunched at one end, Freddie at the other, immobile as two stone figures, till suddenly with a lurch, up came a line hand over hand, with its wriggling prize — or maybe just a piece of seaweed. I fashioned a glass-bottomed box with handles at the sides with which the girls and I could peer down at the amazing submarine life just off the Point. Rowing about, we could envisage our little world as a whole, a domain of forest, rocks, cliffs, ledges, inlets, floating on water. At times

when the mackerel were running one had only to toss handfuls of oatmeal, "chum," overside and the fish by scores would rise to a bare hook. Split and grilled over an open fire, there is nothing more delicious.

There was another occasion, while working merrily at our house-building, when we were brought up short by an experience akin to that of Crusoe as he came upon the imprint of Friday's foot. Everyone was pounding oakum into the walls that day, chirping like a flock of sparrows. Suddenly out of nowhere there stood a man in the clearing. He was rather elegantly garbed in tomato-red Concarno trousers and a soft blue sailor's shirt. He looked us all over with a piercing eye, an astounded expression on his face. This face and form had a finish, a refinement, a certain force. Our work came to a standstill. Like Living Statues in a circus we all froze to immobility. I was breathing hard, stark naked except for a pair of shorts, covered from head to foot with sawdust and sweat. A nice moment. For a second I thought he might be going to say, "Mr. Livingstone, I presume?"

We both said simultaneously, "Er, how d'you do?" He said, "My name is Walter Lippmann, and I have a camp here back where your road begins." (Invasion!) "I've come walking down this trail along the shore before, but I never knew . . ."

"I am Charles Child," said I, "and my family and I (gesturing toward the ragged crew) have a camp here, as you can see, and I never knew . . ."

We smiled. "Well, I hope you don't mind . . ."

"Not at all, not at all." (Slight grinding of teeth.)

This was the beginning of something — perhaps one could call it an invasion, as my first impulse had it. But seen in perspective, I would call it rather a gentle knocking at the door. The world was beginning to enter our domain, and in the person of Walter Lippmann this entry was a most happy augury of an expanding life and the beginning of twenty years of friendship.

But what is a home without a roof? We had cut and dried some long slim trees to serve as rafters, and these we now edged one by one over the tops of the walls. A ridgepole had been set, running from end to end, and now the rafters were slid up into place pair by pair, holding it secure. Horizontal rafters had been run across over the porch, needing only a platform to provide at one and the same time a ceiling for the porch and a floor for the loft. At last the whole skeletal form of the cabin was apparent, glistening in the sun, ready for the skin of boards that would close it in. Paul was sitting up there on the ridgepole slicing off knots and bumps with a razor-sharp axe, the final stage before boarding up. Suddenly there was a gasp. His light Hudson Bay axe, slicing across a knot, had gone through a soft spot and had buried itself in his shin bone. Disaster!

For a moment immobilized with horror I stood there looking at the blood dripping to the floor. I felt as if it were my own blood, and perhaps it was. For a moment in which time seemed to be suspended, my breath stopped, and my heart seemed to stop with it. We had coasted along week by week managing to avoid all but the most ordinary accidents — minor cuts, a few bruises, now and then a nasty scrape from a mass of barnacles. I suppose we had grown careless. But here it was. The Big One: the kind of thing I had avoided even thinking about. It was a thing sudden and final, like the springing of a trap. The axe clattered to the floor, spattering it with blood. Paul's face had gone white. Instinctively he grabbed for the cut to try to keep it closed, his free arm clinging to the ridgepole with a desperate grip. There was a deathlike silence, in which the figure on the roof, motionless as a statue, seemed cemented to the ridge, the only motion a red stain which slowly spread out from between its fingers and trickled down the wounded leg. Then suddenly my breath came back with a rush. Grabbing a ladder and snatching a bandana from Fredericka's head, I made it to the top as fast as trembling legs would take me, and began to apply a rough tourniquet. "Damn it, damn it, damn it," Paul kept muttering to himself while I twisted the knot. Now to get him down.

"Over here, Paulski. Easy now. Here's the top step of the ladder." The blood was now beginning to run off the right foot onto the rungs of the ladder. "Easy boy, easy. One step at a time. Fred, for God's sake get the car engine going; we've got to get him to a doctor. Now girls don't

look so scared, Paul's going to be all right. Okay, now put
your arms over my shoulders. I'm going to carry you to
the wagon. Step by step. That's it."

Somehow we got him to the wagon, made him comfortable on a blanket and we were off. Then came a desperate
search for a doctor, no mean feat in those days when there
was only one doctor to every eight thousand people on
our side of the island. The cut was serious, but I am glad
to say that the doctor was quite efficient. The wound was
dressed and stitched together and we brought him back to
camp. Although exceedingly painful, the cut in time
mended without complication. But our chief helper was
unable to do any heavy work from that time on.

A day or two of blind casting about followed. We were
trying to find someone who could take Paul's place, as it
was now absolutely necessary to have a man on hand who
could lift heavy stones and mix cement if I was to continue working at the top of the chimney. Information
from a local mason eventually provided the answer. We
found a strong young man of the vicinity named Seth who
seemed delighted to come and help with the work. I
rigged an arrangement with a pulley and ropes so that
Seth could put stones or wet cement in one of the coal
bags at the ground level, and haul them up to me on the
working face of the chimney, now some fifteen feet above
ground. This arrangement worked quite well, and the
chimney was topped off in excellent style a week later.

Boards for the roof were brought in and we began the
final phase, sheathing the roof day by day with sweet-
smelling wood. Indomitable Paul came back on the job
after a fashion, managing to be amazingly useful in hand-
ing up boards, caulking logs, raking and cleaning up
around the cabin, and now more constantly than ever tak-

ing snapshots and carefully staged record pictures of the work in progress. The last board in place, we covered the roof with tar paper. *Now* let it rain! The air in the room had become still and, best of all, with the roof in place John Henry had begun to function properly. The porch looked like a porch. Of course the roof did bulge here and there: no one had the heart to cut off any more knots, and the rafters, like all the other logs, were not perfectly straight. "Never mind," said Freddie, "it's a beautiful roof." And so it was. Bundles of cedar shingles were opened: This was fun! All day long, tap, tap, tap, tap, like a woodpeckers' convention. The kids were up there also, with the result that the lines of shingles came out a bit wavy. But it was their roof too, and the slight irregularity simply carried out the general rough handmade character

of our dream house. All in all it was a rewarding thing to
see that ultimate surface, like a rough golden frosting on
a cake, spread slowly to the very top.

When the last shingle had been laid, bedrolls were
brought in from the tents, and lanterns hung round about.
No more mosquito nets! And why not a fire? Just a little
one? Well, the chimney was not quite dry, but who could
say "No"? So a small fire was lit. We sat there after dinner at our plank table feeling, in Erica's words, like "de-
cayed Romans." It was a banquet feast: who dares ask for
peacocks' tongues and stuffed ortolans after two helpings
of Callie's fish chowder? The fire dies down. Out go the
lanterns one by one, leaving only the last embers to cast a
copper glow against the ceiling. I listen to the soft breathing of my children. Warmth. Love. Contentment . . .
Sleep.

6

Wartime Intervals

OUR thoughts turned often that winter of 1941-1942 to the land and the cabin, now boarded up and sleeping away the season like a drowsing bear. How far away it seemed. Yet more desirable than ever: a point of stability in a world of storm and war. No one knew what the future held. I was illustrating another history book, doing a fresco mural for the living room of a house, working on decorative screens. The children were back at school, and on the surface life went on very much as before.

As the spring turned toward summer, Fredericka gave birth to a boy, whose roan red hair matched her own. We named him Jonathan. The girls were enchanted. Here was a real living doll to play with. He was a happy infant, healthy and strong. But alas, there was to be no Maine that summer. I had accepted a job in Washington to work at the National Planning Association. Not many people seemed to want to buy pictures — at least not my pictures — during that confused and hectic time, and the prospect of a steady salary, and work with interesting people from government, farming, labor and education, was pleasing and challenging. Summer, fall, winter, passed like whirlwinds. I was writing, arranging conferences, editing, meeting scores of people. Washington throbbed with the tension of wartime, and vibrated with the shock of new ideas. Occasional weekends with my family provided a quiet counterpoise. It was good to see Jonathan with his absurd crop of copper curls sitting sturdily between his two sisters, to take long walks with the dog, to sit by the fire with Fred and call up images of our magic land.

"What do you suppose it really looks like now? Hey, I remember, we forgot to pull the crock out of the spring. Probably frozen and cracked. Wonder what the old place looks like with snow on the porch? Do you suppose all that forest grass has grown right back and up to the walls of the cabin? Will we be able to get to it next summer? Cha, how much time off will you have? Only *two weeks?* Oh, no! What can we do in two weeks? But perhaps we could make it there after all? Would it be worth it?" Yes, now more than ever.

Here's a letter from Seth I received about this time:

DERE MR. CHILD: I bin working down to yor place quite some the last few days now the whether is let up and yor rode is to muddy to walk and had to wear rubber boots to get in. Come inside to eat lunch and counted seventeen red squirls but appears no harm done and porch has snow on it about 2 foot deep. Two trees down in the cleering and got them cut up and found a ded bird in the spring where you drink yor watter so. put lime in ther to sweeten. I will close now as I have nothing mor to say.

Y'RS TRULY,
SETH

Sitting at my Washington desk I got a long distance call from Boston. It was the old man. "Mr. Child, I don't exactly like to tell you this, or press you too hard, but due to the war and all, prices for pulpwood Down East are going up sky high. I find I can sell all the trees between Lippmann's place and yours for stumpage, and get a

dandy price for 'em. But I thought I'd just better call
you first. Maybe you'd like to buy the land yourself? I
knew you was so fond of it I thought you might like to
take the whole thing off my hands. I can give you about
a week to think it over."

Frantically I got on the phone to Fred. "You know we
can't possibly afford any such sum," she said. "The nursery,
Jonathan, everything. It would be madness . . . but why
don't you call Walter Lippmann and see if by any chance
he might be interested in going in on it with you. We
might just work something out."

Calling Mr. Lippmann, I outlined the situation to him.
"Charles, this is dreadful news," he replied, "but I'm pack-
ing this minute for a European trip, and I'll be gone by
tomorrow morning. See if you can't hold him off for six
weeks until I get back. Then we'll work something out."

A week passed. Two. Telephone calls back and forth.
The old man seemed for the moment to be reconsidering.
In the midst of my work the thing was there like an itching
sore. Then a call. The trees had been sold for stumpage
and a gang of Canadians was that very moment beginning
to cut. Damn the old man! Damn the war! Damn my
salary!

I kept my eyes on our fortnight of vacation as summer
came on, as one who sees the light at the far end of a
tunnel. We packed the cars, making the painful decision
to leave Jonathan at home with Callie. Two and a half
days this time. The roads were getting better. At last,
the village and the road through the woods. Hold your
breath, here we go, across the bog, over the meadow and
to the corduroy.

Everything had changed, Now a vast openness, a desola-
tion, cut across the Point from shore to shore. It lay before

us, a moon-landscape of stumps, branches and dead trees. We could see the gang of French Canadian woodsmen busy down at one end, like mongrel dogs finishing off a corpse. Our right-of-way was still visible, curling and twisting through the slash like a cast-off snakeskin. In fact, the men had been using it to get the wood out. They had kept it up of course, even improved it here and there. But nothing would ever be the same. Now it had a wide and desolate look like the terrain over which it wandered. On the far side of the cut there was a harsh abrupt unnatural line of forest — our forest — standing naked to the sun. Already many of the older trees, tall as masts in the center of the woods, had begun to fall. Shallow-rooted, top-heavy, they had been bowled over by the force of winds roaring through the cut. And those cursed men were like army ants chewing up everything in their path. No selective cutting here: this was total destruction. We could hardly blame the dark feral little Canadians who were doing the cutting. They apparently knew no better. They were living in the past century, logging off the land without regard to the future. The hand of war had reached the very doors of our paradise and had beaten them to pieces with one vicious swipe. Rachel burst into tears. "There's no more forest any more! It's all gone! Did they take away the cabin, too?"

"Of course not, silly," said Erica, glancing apprehensively at Fred for reassurance. "It's still there, I know it is." I looked at Fred, too.

Her whole body had tensed like a coiled spring. I felt that she might claw me to ribbons if I moved a muscle. Two sharp lines had sprung from the base of her nose and down across an absolutely white face to the corners of her mouth, which was drawn into a tight red line. Those hazel eyes, usually so soft and twinkling, were now full black and staring, with the white showing all round their rims.

"Damn those men!" she hissed like a snake, hands clenching and unclenching. "I could kill them. Don't they see what they're doing?"

The forest closed over us. The quarter mile was passed in silence. What was there to say? Yes, the cabin was still there, logs and roof graying now almost to the color of granite. A giant tree had fallen across the roof but had apparently done no harm. These trees, forced over in winter storms, often come down slowly, in their fall upending a vast pancake of roots and soil, which acts as a partial counterbalance. This tree had descended till it just touched the roof. Now in its dying condition, shedding thousands of needles, it had deposited a long windrow of brown across the graying shingles. Coming directly up to the cabin we could see that somebody, irresistibly attracted by our wooden window shutters, had shot several blasts of shotgun shells through them. Inside, glass lay all over the floor. And here was something new: wild flies by the million had discovered the delights of a roof, beds, boxes, rolled-up tents, and had made themselves a happy winter home. A buzzing and droning filled the air, which put me suddenly in mind of the felted Mongol tents of Siberia which we had seen similarly crawling with masses of black flies. As the shutters came off, letting in the light, the last fifty thousand stragglers came pouring out of every crack and cranny and whizzed off into the forest. Whew!

Work! Work! The fallen tree was fortunately so balanced that we were able to haul it back nearly upright, using the block and tackle. It was then felled and cut up for firewood. We set ourselves to making shelves and to building tables and beds. We dragged the old bark strips over the cliff, and began the business of rooting out stumps in the vicinity of the cabin.

This uprooting and grubbing of stumps was to go on for years. Luckily, with the forest soils lying no more than a few feet deep over the clay and granite underburden, none of these trees had tap roots. Each tree manufactured its own pedestal as it grew, a great spreading system of lateral arms, knotted and interlaced underground with those of the next trees till the whole became on a grand scale a kind of felted web. After chopping and sawing through the top layer of this system, we could hook one block to the top of the stump, then fasten the other end

to a neighboring tree and more often than not manage to tear it out of the earth. But this was never easy — these roots were like spring steel, and we found that a regular pattern of growth prevailed. Seedlings would almost always sprout in the shadow of a boulder, or down among piles of rocks dumped by glacial action. What this meant to us, rooting out a tree sixty or a hundred years later, was that we had not only to cut roots, but cut them away from their excruciatingly tight holds on this subterranean mass. These embedded rocks added hundreds and hundreds of pounds to the weight of each root system, as inch by stifling inch we struggled to pull them from their matrices. Sometimes it seemed as if we had to employ every tool on the place — axes, saws, crowbars, sledge-hammers — before they could be loosened from a century-old grip. And that summer the crash of falling trees from the cut, like jungle tom-toms, beat upon our nerves all day.

Sometimes I was almost afraid to take a day off. There

is a momentum in struggle which supports those who do not admit defeat too soon. But the flow of nervous and physical energy which comes in the midst of an exciting project can be diverted or even cease altogether if one allows oneself to get out of the rhythm. Even at best, along with the strength and pride of construction, fatigue was a constant clinging parasite. Nasty cramps, which we finally learned were the result of salt depletion, could double one up with pain in the middle of the night. Aching joints, tired feet, and the inevitable cuts and bruises accompanying hard physical labor were always with us like heavy knapsacks. It could happen too that some trifling thing like the bursting of a blister or a little cut, could for the moment bring the whole project to a grinding halt. Great stress and tiredness have their natural limits, beyond which the addition of two ounces of fatigue will trigger the mind to go on strike.

But perhaps in the long run it was the children themselves who kept us going. Their utter faith in our strength became our strength. Their enthusiasm supported our flagging wills. And even their occasional defections from duty acted as a spur to renewed effort. Now, looking back on this long struggle with the wisdom of hindsight (someone once said, "Hindsight is the only 20-20 vision"), I will have to admit that parental egotism — the necessity for continuing to present the image of infallibility — was also a powerful, if secret, ally. And I must add one more ingredient: laughter. The crust of self-pity is often broken by a peal of laughter.

At the end of a fierce and protracted day of building, when we were all so tired, so aching, and so hungry that we just barely had the strength to wash the dirt off, Fred in the course of preparing a chicken stew for supper failed to notice that the cover of the pressure cooker had not been properly tightened. With a frightful BOOM! the cover flew off, throwing chicken parts and gravy all over the kitchen walls and ceiling. As we rushed into the kitchen and saw carrots, onions, gravy, and chicken legs running down the walls and dropping from the ceiling like manna from heaven, we all burst into insane peals of laughter. Don't ask me why, but this absurd episode had magically changed the atmosphere, and as we sat round the table eating cold cornflakes and milk, we found ourselves completely restored to enthusiasm and sanity.

And there were compensations. The girls, I noticed, were really getting to be excellent carpenters if one didn't expect too much. Our furniture was pretty crude, but it worked. And rowing the boat around the Point on a still night in which each stroke of the oars produced a phosphorescent wake — "sea fire" the locals called it — or listening to the echo of a loon's call over the water, yielded moments of quiet magic. We all missed Jonnie, back home with Callie, and our familiar, Paul, who had gone off to Washington and was doing something mysterious in the Office of Strategic Services. But all in all, though life that fortnight was a battle against time, a test of nerves, we were strangely happy.

The enormous dislocations of the war had perhaps given us a new sense of proportion. To be able to eat, to sleep, to work in comparative peace, was more than enough. We found time to drive to the top of Mt. Cadillac in the center of Acadia Park. Here a whole new world of possibilities was opened to us. Hundreds of miles of trails wandered all over this mountain area, from which one had astounding views of islands in the sea, of tremendous cliffs, immense blue distances where the white spire of a church

or a smudge of smoke might be the only reminders of man-
kind. This was a side of island life we had never had time
to see before. And the very shortness of our vacation made
each moment more intense. The simplest experience had
a kind of concentrated flavor.

Walking along our boulder-strewn shore, for instance, it
was difficult to believe that one beach could hold so many
kinds of stones. But one had only to recall that this
region had been filled with the violent conflict of volcanic
eruption and glacial action. Continuous upheaval and
sudden changes had left it rich with a fantastic array of
forms and colors, washed up from the depths of infinity to
this little shore of time. Measured by the surf, this shore
was standing still, but with a slight change of focus in the
mind one could see that everything was being torn down,
built up, crystallized, shattered, moved from place to place,
in a never ending process of transformation.

Collections of stones began to accumulate all over the
cabins. Each of us had his favorites. Erica, for example,
loved white stones, or the smooth egg-shaped stones that
felt so nice in the hand. Rachel collected "lucky" stones,
whirled and striped like marbles ready for some celestial
game. Fred and I were particularly fascinated by the
range of textures and colors. Here was a world of abstract
patterns seemingly infinite in its variety, yet somehow con-
sistent within itself — not like the patterns of the flowing
clouds, nor like the design of the forest floor, nor the ever-
changing undersea life. Each of these in its way was infinite, yet each had its own particularity, its own perfection. The little universe of the beach — rather dun-colored
if one did not bother to look closely — yielded its beauty
only when one disciplined one's self to move slowly, and
bend low.

Our brief vacation over, I returned to the frenzy and
bewilderment of wartime Washington, where I moved to
the Department of State, which was in the process of
creating a Division of Cultural Affairs. I suggested to Fred
that she join me and begin to look for a house in Washington. After a frantic search we found a charming small
white clapboard house in the Georgetown section. It had
apparently once been a modest farm, for it had the remnants of a barn across a courtyard garden in the rear
which could be fitted up without too much trouble for a
part-time studio. For my children it was revolution, adventure. For Fred and me it was peace, normalization.
Now at the end of a crowded day, it was only a half hour's
walk to rest, refreshment, the laughter of children, the
possibility of entertaining friends and colleagues. Jonnie
called the State Department, perhaps prophetically, "The
Statement-Park-It," a name in use in the family to this
day. But then, he described my typed notes as "that stuff
you do on your tripewriter."

Another summer came and it became possible to think
of getting away for a couple of weeks. Gas rationing made
a long trip in two cars out of the question. So we reluc-
tantly decided to leave the children at Coppernose with
Callie, the ever-faithful. We took two Canadian bikes
onto the train and were off. Knapsacks on our backs, wire
baskets on front of the bikes filled with groceries, we
pedaled out of Ellsworth, Maine, like two high school kids
on a lark.

The Canadians were gone at last, leaving long windrows
of burned slash behind. Thousands of stumps poked up
through ferns and fireweed. Here and there tiny evergreens
and a fuzz of baby hardwood trees were beginning to show.
And as we passed Walter Lippmann's woods we could hear

the white-throated sparrow and the hermit thrush singing as if to say that war was only an evil dream, and this was the true reality.

The beautiful orange-striped bumblebees of the region hummed in the wild flowers now coming up all over the open spaces of the Point. Our two weeks were strangely like a honeymoon. We lazed about, swam, made friends

with our neighbors of the village. Wendell Gilley, the plumber, for example, had now carried his bird carving to an amazing perfection. Setting his birds on bits of Graham Lake driftwood was easy. But what worried him was that he was having trouble with his colors. In his shop from time to time we used to talk over the problem. "Wendell, that little bird there, he's a plover, isn't he?"

"Yep, that's a plover but he don't look natural. I like to carve them, but with this plover here, trouble is how to make the paint go on so's it looks real. I don't know too much about paint. If you was to ask me about pipe-dope now, I could give you all there is to know. But as far as this painting goes, all I know is it has too much shine. A bird often has a kind of sheen — like a wood duck, for instance — and mebbe I tried too hard to get it. Now I've come around to thinkin' that the best way is to color them without shine at all. But I'm stuck. Now if you was to paint a bird like that, would you use varnish in your paint, or what?"

"Well, you know, there's a whole range of paints — egg tempera for instance, or flat oil paints, or gouache — that's a kind of watercolor that goes on flat: why don't you try all of them and see if one of them seems just right for the effect you are trying to get . . . ?"

About this time I began a series of fabric designs, using ferns, shells, moth wings, stones, tree rings, as motifs. Bobby Rich, son of the old boatbuilder, and a maker of boats in his own right, had become a friend. He was interested in what I was doing and suggested that we might go "island-hopping" to look for more raw material for the designs. He loved exploring in the vicinity of Mt. Desert, and took us along on several trips of this kind. The region is rich in lonely forest-covered islands, many of which were occupied a century or more ago and are now deserted. One in particular had a name that rang in the ear: Orono. For us this island was the quintessence of wild coastal Maine. In the first place the whole island exhibited the glacial syndrome to perfection, slanting upward gradually from its northern end to a series of sea cliffs on the south. Here a tiny meadow seemed as if it might lose its struggle with the forest which surrounded it on three sides. At the foot of this meadow a beautiful spring burst forth almost at the shore. The whole island could not have been more than forty or fifty acres in extent, yet this spring had water untainted by salt, coming up clear and cold from some underground source. Years ago Orono had supported a considerable quarry. Its fine gray granite is said to have contributed to buildings in New York City, going off by schooner direct from a dock at the base of the cliffs. But now the island was as it has always been, silent and alone. Near the spring and the cliffs we came upon a great midden of clam shells hinting at ages of Indian encampments. Where the lichened cliffs dropped off to deep water no trace of house or shed remained, only a rusting ringbolt here and there, or a squared block of stone left behind because of some invisible imperfection.

Back at our own Point we were conscious on cold days of the wind skirling up through the cracks in the sub-floor. We decided that we had time to double it with matched tongue-and-groove boards of fir. A truckload of these boards was dropped off at the turnaround and carried in to the cabin site. Laying a finish floor is a very pleasant occupation. Each board in turn is yanked up tight to its neighbor and fastened with nails driven in at an angle. As you progress, the true floor seems to unroll slowly from one side of the room to the other like a carpet, the silvery surface of new wood decorated with a fine abstract pattern of brown knots and rhythmic lines of grain.

Sitting on this half-finished wooden carpet one day with a few sandwiches and a bottle of wine, we looked up to see a pair of vivid blue eyes peering at us through the door. They were set in a magnificent Viking head, blond and commanding. This head was followed shortly by an equally commanding body, as a man — and there was a lot of him — stepped in over the threshold. He introduced himself: Hayford Peirce, from Bangor. He had a summer place not too far away, about a mile and a half back along the eastern shore. He accepted a paper cup of wine

and we fell to talking of the geology of the region. Hayford
Peirce had been collecting rock specimens for years and
had a house full of them, and more back in Bangor. Excellent wine, by the way. He happened to have some Chambertin '29 in his cellar, and would we like to share it with
him tomorrow? We would. Conversation flowed till the
bottle was empty. Peirce came of an old lumbering family
of the region and seemed to have an endless store of information concerning trees, rocks, fish, forest management,
and the like. He was indignant at the method of cutting
which had been used by the Canadians. "Nobody in
Maine cuts like that any more. Absolutely senseless. Takes
years under those conditions for a forest to come back. If
you've been properly taught, selective cutting is easy and
far from doing damage to a forest area it is actually good
for it, maintaining a balance of mature trees and young
trees forever. But this pulpwood thing, with the spur of
war prices, simply mines a forest tract to exhaustion with
the result that the land erodes, dessicates under the sun,
and takes a generation or more before it can begin to heal
its wounds."

Peirce had a beautiful young wife and, as it turned
out, two boys who were eager to see the cabin. A few
days later upon completion of the floor, they all came to
the Point and we cooked lunch together. The Peirce boys
promptly took to the boat to go fishing, while we four
grownups strolled along the shore leaping from rock to
rock and exploring the miniature world of tidal pools.

Hayford Peirce's woodland lore and geological enthusi-
asms proved to be minor facets of an extremely complex
personality. He was primarily a Byzantine scholar, at the
moment in the midst of writing a book in collaboration
with Royall Tyler on certain aspects of Byzantine culture.

His mind, never still for an instant, darted from Byzantine artifacts to painting, to rocks, to French literature, to the stock market, to explosives. We saw the Peirces several times during that fortnight: we ate together, drank most of their Chambertin, examined our own rocks with a new interest, talked endlessly, and happily became aware of the budding of friendship. And, having finished the floor, we didn't do another thing to the cabin. We were in the mood simply to sit back, as a lazy swimmer sits back at the water's edge, and let Maine roll over us. This had been on the whole a wonderfully quiet time, an interval in which there came a renewal of faith.

Back in Washington the Department of State had given me a new responsibility and a new title, Adviser in the Arts and Humanities. Weekend painting was almost out of the question, though from time to time I did go into my small studio and try to pick up some design I had been at work on two or three weeks before or in a desultory fashion try my hand at something new. This little room at the far end of a garden court was quiet, isolated, and above all, a place where no telephone rang, no staff meetings ever occurred, no files were misplaced, no secretary asked banal questions. It served to remind me that I had another life to which I could return with the return of peace. I could take up a little beach stone I had brought back, and holding it in my hand see all the rocky shore and hear the sound of waves. It was a concrete reminder in the midst of this four-square office world with its grinding machinelike tempo, that the other world was still there in all its vivid reality.

Jonathan was now four years old, bright and rollicking. The girls, twelve and fourteen, were firmly enmeshed in the public school system of Washington and beginning to experience the throes of adolescence. "Mother, you know I can't study with Jonnie in the room all the time. Mother, do you *have* to wear that old green shirt when we go over to the Jones's? Mother, couldn't I have just a half glass of wine at dinner tonight? Charlie, when are you going to leave that nasty old State Department? Mother, are we going to take Jonnie to Maine this summer?"

At the close of the school year the rest of the family went off to Bucks County to prepare for Maine. I joined them there when vacation time came round and we packed with joyous anticipation. Then, with a whoop and a holler we were off once more. The vast parkway systems leading north from New York were being extended farther each year. On the second day of hard driving we turned eastward around Penobscot Bay past Camden, Belfast, Searsport and Bucksport, to Ellsworth and the Mountains of Acadia.

At the point where a little bridge separates the mainland from the island we always cut loose with a wild Comanche yell, and fierce gesticulations of triumph from car to car. Now down to Southwest Harbor, stopping only long enough to pick up groceries and greet old friends. "Hi, Challes. Hi, missus! You back for the season? I bet Mr. Trundy'll be glad to hear it. He's been stockin' up on nails and axe handles jest waiting till you get back. And don't forget to drop by the house on your way in. My wife bought a washin' machine over the winter and she might help you out with your laundry. That your boy there? Red hair too I see. Any more on the way? No? Well, t'ain't much of a trick, is it!"

Now the last agonizing miles to the little road which led across the bog. This crossing-of-the-bog always seemed to be the cut-off point, or moment of the waving of a wand. It marked the very second when one left the dusty world behind and stepped into another dimension. The road itself for a hundred yards or so was almost water-borne. One could often see a heron or two peering intently downward at his own reflection. Then came a line of scraggly trees signaling the beginning of the meadow-land. Just here, up the slope, one could catch a glimpse of a little graveyard in a grove of firs off to the left, its stones covered with rich orange lichens. Now the meadow itself, the Lippmanns' woods, and then our road, the last half mile.

As we drove among the stumps of the cut we saw that thousands of blueberry bushes were coming up. An osprey had made his nest in the top of a dead tree and was circling directly overhead uttering shrill piercing cries. The wall of our forest leaned crazily in all directions, some trees shouldering back, others slanting outward into the cut. Then came a grinding, squishing halt at the turn-around. Like a double bomb the two cars burst open, belching people and animals. This time there was a cat, Wisteria, who, catlike, took one quick look around and sat down to wash. We covered the last quarter mile of trail too excited to carry much on the first rush. Now to lift up the stone by the front door and find the key for the old copper padlock, swing it wide and let in the sunlight. Take off the shutters, slide the windows open. Now it's coming alive again, and we are *all* here! Woosh, zoom, out go the flies. "Where did you put that broom? Rachie, take Jonnie and show him the spring, and bring some water. Callie, you get a fire started for some tea. Fred and Erica and I will bring in the heavy stuff." Now groceries to the shelves, blankets on beds, oil in the lamps, scrub the table, and "*Thank* you, Jonnie, for the pretty dandelion."

What a sense of quiet joy had come over us at our return. There was always a primitive, superstitious gut-feeling that perhaps the land would not be there at all. I could never quite rid myself of this foolish notion, so that at the actual moment of return, the solidity of it was all the more overwhelming, all the more delicious. Go on, stamp your foot on it! And the first impression was always the same — perfume! Odors are the thing to bring back reality! Clear salty air, damp forest grass, wild roses. And what is that? Oh, yes, raspberry blossoms. Sniff sniff: fir balsam, spruce gum — and that tangy one? Sweet fern? It was always a kind of long drawn out chord, of which the lowest note was earth and mushrooms, and the highest was cold salt air, the whole thing taken together bringing a terrific wallop of life, energy, even a touch of menace.

And our cabin! It always seemed somehow smaller than I remembered it, but it had a kind of beefy reality, and a perfume of its own — a clean woody resinous smell which now brought flooding back clear-cut memories of chips gathered in baskets for kindling, of an axe bright in a shaft of sun, and distantly the voices of my children, the cry of gulls, and forever the sound of waves, lapping the rocks of Old Point, lapping the reefs of memory, roaring in the ears, in the air, in the mind.

A voice from the water: "Hi there! I was wundrin' when you folks was goin' to get back. Comin' down the bay we get used to lookin' for your lamp lights to guide us off Gun Rock. Want some crabs? Got a whole bucketful right here. I'll just ease the bo't over to that ledge and toss 'em out to you. I see you got a new redhead in the family. Hi there, Sonny! What's your name? Jonathan?

Good solid name — see you eat plenty of lobsters now — here! Here's a two-pounder. Eat it all by yourself and get good and rugged like your pa." He chugs off.

An hour passes. We all sit down for a cup of tea. "But Jonathan! Jonathan! Drat the boy. Where is he?" Where indeed, in all this forest, among all those rocks? "Now that I think of it, we haven't seen him since that lobsterman came by. Drop everything! Spread out! You through the forest, you along the beach, you on the path to the cliffs, and make it fast!"

Strangely enough, here was something none of us had thought of. I suppose we had rather taken it for granted that Jonnie would stay close by. In one horrid moment Old Point had become quite menacing. He could have gone off in any of a hundred directions. I had visions of a little body wedged into some crevasse in the rocks, of a head rising briefly to the surface as he struggled to keep himself afloat. How about that flock of gulls over there? But no, it was only a bit of flotsam. The woods? The rock ledges? The cliff? "Go find Jonnie. There's a good dog." The furry face looks up, dark eyes sparkling with the sheer joy of life, pink tongue drooling on one of my shoes. A lot he cared!

Fifteen minutes, no Jonnie. Twenty minutes. Thirty. From time to time as we circled and searched Fred and I exchanged fearful glances. We stumbled and ran about shouting, feeling foolish and at the same time very much frightened. Suddenly, there he was, down on the beach near the base of the cliffs, gaily toddling along, stuffing crab shells and seaweed into his pockets and talking to himself in the loud arrogant tones which distinguish the male of the species. From that time on a regular Jonnie-watch was established.

One of our principal occupations that year was the construction of a woodshed. Our cabin was there, mellowing
nicely. The northwest-facing side of the roof was even
beginning to collect gray-green lichens like the trees nearby.
We arranged tarpaulin curtains for the porch which in time
of winds and rain could be rolled down and lashed fast
to the floor. But the real need for the moment was a place
where wood could be stored and kept dry. "We have plenty
of room," I said to myself, "so let's make it really big —
not just for wood but a place to store tubs, to put the boats
in winter, to hang the tools, even a bit of a carpenter shop
for something to do in foul weather. And it should look
strong, ample, and rugged, like the cabin."

To begin with we decided to leave it open on the southeast side, facing the summer sun, with an overhanging roof
set on four log pillars made of burled tree trunks placed
about six feet apart. There was to be a long loft above,
to hold extras of all sorts, for we were now accumulating
coils of rope, bits of screening, extra window glass, boxes
of nails, and the like. The northwest face would be made
of logs in the regular manner and have a central door for
easy access from the trail which we hoped would someday
be a road. This was the basic design as worked out in a
series of sketches. "It looks like a woodsy cloister," said
Erica. "Why not cut a door through from the end kitchen
wall," said practical Fred, "and simply hitch the two structures together the way so many Maine farm buildings are
laid out. Then on rainy days we can go back and forth
without getting wet."

"Splendid! We'll have so much extra room that we'll
never miss the space cut out of the kitchen wall."

The hillside at this point, when we undertook the actual
building, made it necessary to put in a little stairway of

three steps leading up into the shed. As the work progressed we added two windows on the northwest face, one for extra light, for on rainy days we expected to have tarpaulin curtains let down over the pillars to keep the shed dry, and another window near the kitchen which was made with a deep embrasure. This "window" had screening instead of glass, and would be filled with shelves so as to make it a cooler or storage place for perishables. Almost at once this curious box began to fill up with odds and ends of food. Into it went butter, milk, cheeses, perhaps a couple of bottles of wine or the remainder of a roast. There they stayed cucumber cool till we needed them. The roofs of shed and cabin were tied together with new rafters and shingles, and we built a loft along one side under the rafters, leaving a continuous open space for easy access.

This new space thus combined the virtues of wood storage, a little carpenter shop (with a bench immediately under the window), a loft, a "cooler," and occasionally a sulking place when youthful tensions became unbearable. Jonathan learned to whittle here, and here the mysteries of the saw, the hammer, and the plane were revealed to him. On rainy days we made model boats, oiled our boots, sharpened our tools, built shelves — always more shelves — and endlessly scraped, painted and sandpapered. Now we made a living room table and a desk and began to refine the design of our primitive beds which had been made in the early days of two logs with boards across their tops, redoing them one by one in a style which, while not exactly Louis XV, did boast legs and casters so they could be rolled out from the walls for dusting and tucking in blankets.

There were times when Erica and Rachel in this growing-up period could hardly stand each other. Together they used one of the tents as a dressing room and storage place. Thinking to make it easier for them to share this joint space if each girl's territory was clearly indicated, one of us one day suggested that he would draw a chalk line down through the middle of the tent floor so each girl could see where her responsibility began and ended. But we gave up the idea almost at once: what if in a crass spirit of independence, each girl, better to defy the other, exaggerated her own characteristics? Erica's half could become painfully neat and orderly. Reacting to this impossible standard, Rachel would then perhaps let her side degenerate and become more like a caveman's hideout or a bear's bed.

Something of this sort occurred from time to time. One day, in a fury over some incident which I have forgotten, the girls decided the only thing to do was to erect a curtain down the middle of the tent in order to define their respective territories once and for all. I helped them sling a sheet over a rope which went from pole to pole. The sheet was then pinned securely. Retreating to a discreet distance I placed myself behind a bush and watched the following drama unfold. Almost at once the girls became aware that in order to get the good out of the situation they had to stay in the tent. But of course this was frightfully boring. Consequently, after a few minutes of cogitation, Rachel, whose self-control had begun to slip, surreptitiously began to pile up several orange crates to make a kind of watch tower from which she could peer over the wall and see what Erica was doing. As she got to the top and looked down, what was her horror to see Erica's flaxen curls immediately below, as the latter applied one eye to a hole she had just made the better to observe Rachel. Peals of laughter! Rachel, realizing that Erica had obviously worked out a more efficient system, now got to work with a pair of nail scissors and made half a dozen holes. Erica, not to be outdone, began pushing a sharp pencil through the barrier in a neat line of at least a dozen holes, at eye level, giggling meanwhile. Now ensued a game of peekaboo, each little girl jumping from hole to hole in an effort to outwit the other. Finally the inevitable happened: they met somewhere in the middle, blue eye staring at blue eye just one inch apart. That brought the house down, and ended the Maginot Line, which was promptly unfastened, yanked down, and forgotten. But the clothesline itself remained, now draped from day to day with socks, clothes, and little bouquets of grasses and flowers fastened there with clothespins till they faded.

Outside the kitchen we laid down a little paved courtyard of flat stones about eight feet on each side, just where the back of the chimney jutted out, and here we set up a mirror and a log table against the kitchen wall, with towel racks overhead. This was our outdoor bathroom and washing place. When someone wanted hot water he let out a whistle, whereupon whoever was inside came to the stove, above which was fixed a rubber tube with a funnel in the end. This tube led through a hole in the log wall to the outside table. Water poured through the tube into a basin.

Seth came around the corner of the cabin where I was sitting toward the end of one day's work, making a pastel sketch of a sunset.

"Well now, that's beautiful! I see you're keepin' about one stroke ahead of the sun. If your hand ever slipped it would be dark before you could find your chalk! Speakin' o' which, what are you goin' to do if she goes down before you put all the colors in? Paint in the dark?"

"Seth, trying to fix the thing in your mind leaves you with plenty to go on. Besides, I'm trained for it. You can't put in everything you see anyway: too fussy. In general, memory helps by making the design simpler. Take this sketch for instance: it's more or less like a shorthand report to myself on what I've been looking at."

"I see what you're a-comin' at. But you still have to catch it before you can cook it! Reminds me, them colors you got there looks jest like lobster meat dipped in melted butter — pretty near good enough to eat. Now that dog o' yours. D'you spose he sees that sunset just like you do?"

"Don't think so, Seth: they say dogs are color-blind."

"Color-blind, eh? Well, I guess he makes up for it with that nose of his. Always sniffin' around and don't seem to mind what kind of sh—t he gets into. I know some of the boys down to the fish dock would like a nose like that when they have to fix up a load of rotten fish for lobster bait. Well, I got to be gettin' along or the missus'll be wonderin' if I fell off a limb and bust my backsides."

There were times when I was rather conscious of being entirely surrounded by women. True, I made most of the noise, and considered that in some ways I was the center of the drive and direction in our joint enterprise. But they knew what they wanted just as clearly as I did. "Man looks at the compass but woman keeps her hand on the tiller," I said to myself on more than one occasion, and how could I go against the combined will of a whole family on days when they were determined that the work could wait?

"Cha, it's a gorgeous day: let's drop everything and go out to Opeechie Island."

"Hey, Fred, you know I wanted to work on that back bank today."

"Yes! Yes! Opeechie!" say the kids. "You've done enough work this week — too much, in fact. We're all tired of Good Works."

"Don't scowl so," says Fred. "You'll only crack your sunburn. And anyway, while you were out there on that bank this morning getting dirtied up before breakfast, the girls and I were making sandwiches and getting out the clam forks and a pot and skillet and now everything's all ready. You don't want to disappoint the kids . . ."

The clamming at Opeechie was always good. We built a cooking fire, dug a mess of clams and steamed them in the pot together with a bit of white wine and a few herbs. We knew what was coming: clam hash! Here's a typical recipe which can be varied in innumerable ways:

CLAM HASH

Melt about 6 tablespoons of butter in a skillet and fry a minced onion until it is transparent, adding about 2 cups of boiled potatoes chopped up fine along with 2 or 3 cups of chopped clams. This mix should cook for about 15 minutes, the ingredients being turned over from time to time so as to obtain bits of brown crust. At this point some folks add an

egg for each hungry person, or just the beaten yolks. If you
wish to enrich the mix further you can add cream, and
sprinkle it with grated cheese. We use Romano if we can get
it. Bits of ham, chopped green peppers, cracker crumbs, or
mushrooms can be added *ad libitum*. Stir the new ingredients
in, cover the skillet and cook until the eggs bind the whole
thing together into a kind of pie.

This is a hearty meal, the perfect answer to appetites
whetted by salt air and a dip in ice-cold water. And the
dog loved clams. Nosing about among the discarded shells
he would vainly try to bite out the hardened ends of muscle
that remained attached to the shell.

Another gorgeous clam recipe which has general utility
is a particular favorite of ours. Everybody loves it. We
call it Clams Fredericka.

CLAMS FREDERICKA

Steam a peck of clams in one-half inch of water till they
open. Take them from their shells, rinse, and chop coarsely.
Chop one large fresh green onion. If it has a good top stem,
chop that in too. Dice 5 slices of bacon, add 3 kernels of
garlic, squeezed into pulp. Now put 3 tablespoons of olive
oil in a skillet, put in the onion, bacon, and garlic, and let
it simmer till onion is soft but not brown. Add the clams,
⅓ cup of cracker meal and 2 tablespoons of butter. Add 1½
cups of clam juice to the mix.

Chop up 2 tablespoons parsley, 1 tablespoon tarragon, and
1 tablespoon thyme and add to the mix. Add 4 tablespoons
of brandy, cook for about 15 minutes, stirring occasionally.
It can be served warm as a spread on crackers or the way we
do it often, as a dip, using clam shells to spoon it up with.
Needless to say, mussels can be substituted for clams in either
of these recipes.

Paul returned from the wars at about this time. He had
been working on Mountbatten's staff in India and Burma,
had been given a medal, a pat on the back, and now was

free for the time being to take a real vacation. He came on for a visit, lean and mahogany brown, thus helping to bring the male and female elements back into balance.

Lean and brown. Brown and lean. I had never seen Paul look so thin. Though it wasn't unattractive: there was a subtle air of command about him somewhere which made itself felt. His face was a deep dense brown, against which I noticed almost with a sense of shock there stood out a few gray hairs at the temples. His eyes were an intense blue against the tan. And now there was a clipped, rather square British type mustache jutting from his upper lip. On the whole, I concluded, we didn't look very much alike any more. For the moment at least he had become a rather strange echo of the brother I used to know so well. He was older, crisper, somehow more concentrated, more romantic. I wondered how I must look to him — soft and white, perhaps? With a touch of the bureaucrat's pot belly, a widening bald spot?

"Who around this place is tough enough to fix up the rest of the road so we can get cars all the way to the cabin? Besides, I want to get a photo record of road work before the damn thing gets too good! Man! Can you imagine grabbing groceries right out of the car, taking just three steps, and Plonk! There they are on the kitchen table!" Like an open wound this thought had been irritating us all season too, needing only Paul's words to produce concerted action. So back to the muck, the sods and the corduroy logs we went, sustained by the vision of driving a car right up to the front door.

A specially beautiful day might come — "sparklers" we called them — when we felt that we just had to get away. On such days the whole land and sea seemed made of

ethereal diamond dust, filling the lungs with its secret ingredient which produced extra energy and gaiety. "Let's go out to Baker Island!" The procedure for going out to Baker was to go first to Captain Bill's dock to hire a boat. One could find Captain Bill there at his desk almost any day: beet red, with a body like those little Chinese figures called laughing Buddhas. A vast amplitude, a smile, a canny blue eye. "Why, if it ain't Challes! How be you? Fleshed up a mite, too, ain't you? Well, I ain't done so bad myself! Want to hire a boat to go out to Baker? Well, I guess we can fix you up. Don't see much of you folks down to the Point these days. Keep yourselves pretty busy, eh? And I see you got one more redhead in the family. Rugged boy — like his dad! Heh, heh . . . well now, just for Old Time's sake. . . ." (He reaches down to the floor behind the desk where a pair of old rubber boots is lying in one corner, picks one up, fishes around inside, and brings out a bottle. We drink, solemnly.)

"Captain Bill, why do you keep that likker in a rubber boot?" I asked, overcome by curiosity.

"Tell you what, Challes," he replied. "I'm not what you'd call a drinkin' man myself, understand, and the wife don't like to see me doin' it. Specially as the Doc ses I shouldn't touch the stuff at all: gettin' a bit too hefty, as they say." He pats his ample tummy with a large brown hand. "So if you was a mind to, you could call this a measure of self-discipline. Like another drop? Makes it a bit harder to get at, and all neat and shipshape between times. Besides, these damn desk drawers stick somethin' awful down here on this wet dock, and I jest like to know I can put my hand on it if the need arises." One eye closes in a solemn wink.

Baker Island, a half-hour's run from Captain Bill's dock, is a rounded dome of granite and forest about a mile across. At the top of this dome stands an old lighthouse, now abandoned. On the side looking back toward Mt. Desert a group of six or eight weatherbeaten deserted houses straggle in a rough double line up the hill through the one bit of open meadowland on the island. On the seaward side the forest is dense, ending abruptly where a series of magnificent pink granite ledges sweep to the water, and a sea wall of giant boulders has been thrown up by storms sweeping in from the open sea. As the long combers come crashing onto the ledges, spouts of foam leap high and often produce momentary rainbows of exquisite beauty. Here one faces nothing but the open sea. Clumps of wild pink and white roses, lovers of salt spray, grow between the rocks. Wreckage from ages of storm lies high on the sea wall and behind it, and thousands of sea birds dart and whirl nearby in the spindrift. A glorious, abandoned, wild place, perfect for picnics, and for the discovery of magically shaped things. Paul was in his element here, wandering about, with two cameras now — a big one and a small one — getting pictures of the rocks, the driftwood, the family gathered for a picnic. As the day passes, the sun leans over the far shoulder of the island, casting long streaks of light across the granite. Suddenly it is cold. "Mother! Mother! Do we have to go? Just ten more minutes? Just five?" But the shadows are climbing rapidly up the rocks — we must collect our things and be off. "Cha, can I take this piece of driftwood, this stone?"

"Yes, if you can carry it." We turn for a final look. The white shaft of the lighthouse glows in the setting sun like a narwhal's tusk. The ledges have turned from pink to lilac gray in the shadows. Goodbye, old Baker, for another year.

The road, always the road. But not quite in the grim mood of yesterday. We had a method that had proved satisfactory, and we pushed our highway forward each day, and made time between pushes for various kinds of fun. "I bet we cut three billion of these blank-blank little trees today. And *now* look at that damned corduroy: seems like hardly a couple of rods for a whole day's work, and I can see the water coming up between the logs right now. We're going to have to ditch and drain this one before we go any farther. The Burma Road was never like this."

Work on the shed continued. All of our tools now lived here, each hung on its special hook. The carpenter's bench became a focal point for male activity. Mops and buckets and tubs found their proper niches. The firewood, cut and stacked, scented the air. At the hillside end of the shed we hung a clothesline at a point where the forest met the clearing. We had found an old ship's bell and I mounted

it here, just under the eaves. When passing boats saluted
us, as they often did with a waving of hands or a friendly
toot, we would reach for the bell and give an answering
reply.

The problem of the spring still bothered me. We could
cover it to keep out mosquito wrigglers and the formation
of algae, yet this would not solve the basic question of an
adequate supply. But the summer was drawing to a close
and would soon be over; we would have to find an answer
another year. Seth had become a rather steady helper, and
he volunteered to put up the winter shutters after we had
left, stack and grease the tools, and cover the chimney with
a box to keep out the rain. This would simplify the business of departure. But there was one thing he wanted to
do more than anything else: "You know what would be
dandy to have down there on that point of rocks — a flagpole! That's what I've been a-comin' at — a flagpole! I
can see her now — right *there!* And you could set up a
circular bench right around the base where you could set
when you was doin' that letter-writin' you dote on so."

"Well, no, Seth, not this year, anyway." Picking a last
bunch of flowers and breaking off a branch of leaves hung
with the crimson flags of autumn, we sloshed out from the
turnaround, now rimed with frost, and left our Point for
another year.

7

Many Hands

IN 1947 I left the Department of State, though not without regret, turned my back on Washington for good, and returned with my family to Bucks County. Paul had decided to remain in Government service, and had exchanged his uniform for a diplomat's hat. During his years in the Far East he had worked for a time in Ceylon, and had met there in one of the other O.S.S. establishments a delightful girl named Julia. Now they announced their engagement. Julia was a tall willowy creature with dark curly hair and blue, blue eyes, as jolly and gay as Paul was serious. She possessed more than a touch of the unexpected: she was a tough relentless worker at whatever she undertook, immensely systematic, determined to carry through anything she began. At the moment she was becoming very much involved in mastering the art of French cooking, and would spend her free hours each day at the stove, notebook in hand, enthusiastically reeling out miles of cookies, pots full of Boeuf Bourgignon and Tripe à la mode de Caen.

It became clear that for the first time in some years we would have the chance to plan a real summer, instead of two weeks devoted to the hope of doing the impossible.

I felt back in my old form as a painter. Having been at last spewed out from the belly of Leviathan, as it were, I was human and whole. But there was a certain sadness in the family: during that last winter Callie had left us to take care of her aged mother. We felt the loss keenly. Callie had been so much a part of our life and our efforts that now, with the prospect of a rewarding summer taken at a somewhat easier pace, we would miss her doubly. She had added an element of strength and stability which no one else could replace. And to compound our sadness, Grey Brother, our old shaggy friend, had died. But now, after some search, we found another sheep dog to replace him. This one we named Figaro. He was no more than teddy bear size when we got him, but before the end of the winter he was all gawky legs and great paws, and stood a full two feet high, a leaping, slavering bundle of love.

"Shaggy dog and shaggy people," I thought, looking at Figaro, whose curly hair somehow seemed to match our own. Erica had flaxen curls with a hint of strawberry, curls that shone in the sun and lay in tight little ringlets all about her curiously mysterious face with its bee-stung lips, which sometimes seemed to me, although apparently so innocent, to be as remote as those in a Balinese mask.

Rachel's hair was extraordinary. The color, though brilliantly red-orange, as soft as if a shadow had been drawn over it. Her curls had long lazy loops — "Botticelli curls," we used to call them. They framed a face full of life and wit, and softened her rather dramatic features: classic Greek sculpture come to vivid life, with deep blue eyes which always seemed to have enormous pupils.

Jonnie's hair was roan red — in places almost bronze. There was one amusing area in back, a patch of hair that was decidedly blonde. We called this his Erica Patch. Fred

and I both have curly hair. Hers grew in amazing swoops and swirls which never could be dealt with in conventional fashion, though to my mind perfectly complementing a face whose wide cheekbones, small rounded chin and subtle mouth forever seemed to change with her changes of mood. Alas for my hair: it was retreating year by year at a steady rate. "Hey, Cha, why don't you make yourself a Figaro-wig?" said Rachel on one occasion. "His hair is sort of biscuit-and-gray, like yours. It's not too late, and I'll bet no one would know the difference!"

"Not on your life, Old Bear — it would only make me into a one-man Shaggy Dog Story."

A curious side effect of traipsing back and forth from winter home to summer home had made itself felt. We often never knew just where things were: some tool, searched for all over the house in Pennsylvania, we would suddenly remember had been left at the Point. Or, at the Point, we would miss some essential cooking pot or medicine, inadvertently left at home. Now we took to making lists of things in each place: "Tools left at the Point, 1946."

"Things to bring, 1947." "Must do during summer '47," and so on. These little lists were a help, and now we began to consult them for the upcoming summer, and having made our final dispositions we packed once more and were off.

Back at the Point, we were saddened to hear of the sudden death of Hayford Peirce. Polly, his wife, had decided nevertheless to bring the boys down to the coast for the summer. This promised good fun for Jonathan, and gave

us a chance to see something of Polly, and to some extent to be able to help her through the difficult period of adjustment. This summer we promised ourselves there was going to be more than enough time to look around, to expand, to caress every tree if we were so minded, and if we were in the mood, to fill a whole month or two with lazy days. But lazy days are not my forte. For one thing, I did want to finish pushing that road through to the cabin. And I kept thinking about the spring.

The transition from war to peace and from public life to private life had not been easy to make. But there were days now when without difficulty I could take my sketching materials and wander off alone for a few hours to draw rocks, waves, terns, or merely muse and let the current of life flow through me at its own pace. Perhaps I might even build a studio up here sometime, I thought. It wouldn't have to be very big — just a box with a window. The idea was intriguing, and once having been discovered, it remained to twinkle there in a far corner of my mind like a little star.

George Richardson came galloping along one day about this time in a splendid new tractor. "Hey, Challes," he roared. "Look at her! Ain't she a beauty?"

"Great, but how about the gardens, George?" I asked. "I know you do a lot of garden work, but seems to me that she might not go slow enough, the way I saw you just now barreling along my road."

"Why, Challes," said George in the voice of a wounded child, "she goes fast all right, but does she ever go real slow! Listen, when I get aboard of her and put my hand on the tiller and set her in low-low, I can jest sit there and watch the snails rush by! Don't need no help neither. Now you take Margaret there; she's a good woman, a real good woman, and she has a nice little gardin. But she needs help and don't know it. I could do for her, but she won't have none of it. She don't know no more about gardenin' than a hog at a cocktail party. She jest put on them white gloves right up to the elbow and joined up to one o' them gardenin' societies so's she could go messin' around in a pile of hen shit! Now if you was to have a gardin up there on the hill I could fix her up for you in the spring with no trouble at all!"

"Maybe I will sometime, George," I said. "It's not a bad idea, now that the cabin's all finished. I'll think about it." Here was another idea, destined to grow in the mind as time went on.

Now Paul and Julia, newly married, came to spend part of their vacation period with us. Julia set out almost at once to master the subtleties of John Henry, a little tired now and not at his best after having spent a number of years rusting quietly through each winter in the cabin. Paul on his part was in excellent form, rarin' to go, perfectly willing to tackle a bit of roadwork, and always between times ready to photograph everything with the undying enthusiasm of an almost-pro.

Leaving Julia and Freddie and the girls to window-curtain sewing, the inevitable wrestling match with John Henry, and the mysteries of Bouillabaisse à la mode de Blue Hill Bay, Paul and I would slog out to the road, our slowly weakening adversary. There was one place in particular where it made a sharp turn, a low boggy bit which never seemed to fill up no matter how much material we put into it. I suppose there may have been a small spring which surfaced here. Every time we had a guest we would walk out to this spot before bidding a final farewell, almost certain to have to give the departing car a terrific shove. In fact, it came to be known among ourselves as "Lippmann Corner," in mute admiration for our friends who with perfect tact had never failed to smile and wave a fond goodbye as their car, spattered with the mud of our latest effort, slogged through the morass. Eventually we by-passed this insoluble problem by relocating a section of the road.

But oh how we ate! Fred was a marvelous cook — endlessly inventive. As somebody said, "Freddie can cook in three languages!" These days, coming back from the muck and grime of roadwork we could see Fred and the girls and Julia crowding round the stove, which gave forth a perfume — perhaps of strawberry shortcake, of bread, or of some delicious soup. The girls were learning from their mother, and learning fast, and by now were most competent in their own right. Erica was becoming a minor master in the art of subtle flavoring. Many a dish which I thought only Fred could have made turned out to be the product of her skill. Rachel, true to form, had a somewhat outrageous sense of experiment in bold new combinations of raw materials. She darted at the stove: "NO! Let me cook today. I have a good idea: ham with peanut butter and milk! Oh, it's been done before? Well, never mind, I just invented it anyway!" A touch of lemon peel in the chicken broth, then whirl in a beaten egg? Why not? "And who says we can't use our seaweed? The Japanese do!" And now Julia was teaching them to cook dishes straight from the Cordon Bleu. What matter if from time to time the bouillabaisse had too much saffron, the petits fours came out slightly soggy: it all tasted delicious to appetites sharpened by cold air and heavy physical labor. And to this one must add the joy of eating food prepared with loving care by members of one's own family.

Now, with time on our hands and the essential work

going forward, it was easy to relieve days of tension and
fatigue with trips out to the islands or to some spot on a
mountainside where one could picnic or wander about the
cliffs and open slopes. And there were a surprising number
of Washington friends who began to find their way to Mt.
Desert and the cabin. In those days one could take a train
direct from Washington to Ellsworth. I recall a British
Major General, proper Sandhurst mustache, monocle and
all, down on his knees in a pair of my overalls helping me
get out a stump. "Wizard, old boy, absolutely *wizard!*" he
roared as the stump finally came out of the ground, throwing rocks and loose dirt all over him. Having some of our
slightly more exquisite friends for a few hours was fun,
but overnight accommodations were extremely simple, except for the hardy few. The kids then had to be kicked
back to the tents to make room for grown-up guests, and
although by now they were learning a good measure of
self-discipline, it was still no fun. Actually we were sometimes beginning to wonder if we were not just a little
crowded!

By the summer of 1948, Erica was sixteen, Rachel fourteen. As Paul remarked, they looked like two healthy an-
gels. Now Paul's endless pictures began to feature the
youngsters more and more. That is, when he could catch
them. For in fact their world had noticeably widened. The
social life on the other side of the island was beginning to
attract their attention. Tennis, sailing, dances, all began
to be a part of the picture. And boys. Above all, boys.
Girls at this age, as any parent knows, begin to send out
mysterious vibrations which like the emanations of female
moths seem to attract the opposite sex for miles around.
Fuzzy young men began to appear. Erica was increasingly
drawn into this social stream, while Rachel, for the record

pooh-poohing the whole thing, was nevertheless beginning to neglect some of her hoydenish ways in favor of experimenting in secret with hairdos and lipstick. Emerging from a session of this kind, she often presented the appearance of a person who had been given by some over-generous God a mouth-and-a-half instead of a mouth. "Rachel! You've been using my lipstick!"

"I have *not,* Eroica von Childersleeve!"

"Mother! Make her keep out of my things."

"Well, if you must know, it was Mother's lipstick, damn you!"

"Anyway, you look simply *awful* . . ."

We were obviously at the beginning of a new era. Jonathan too was growing fast, and had left the world of toy-boats-with-paper-sails. He was carving himself a "Four-Masked Skooker," a weird contraption with real cloth "sails" and rigging of string. A spider would have been lost in that rigging. And the boat wouldn't go forward — not even backward — but did beautifully sideways till

drawn by a long cord. Then it slithered through the waves in splendid fashion.

And there was Fredericka, in a sense the heart of all our endeavors. She didn't look any older. But she had more competence, more depth, and was a person who could charm anyone from a Chinese coolie to an ambassador in full regalia — and had. I recalled how often I had seen this sophisticated creature perched up aloft, her gorgeous legs wrapped around the very ridgepole of the cabin for better balance, passing up stones to me one by one (complaining bitterly every minute) or in the kitchen with Callie concocting some superbly aromatic dish. It was she more often than not who had smoothed over ruffled feelings, patched up cuts, and told the best stories. An alert, objective critic of painting, she had often brought me up short by an incisive comment. "Well," she might say, after a careful scrutiny of a hard day's work: "your colors aren't too bad, and the forms have considerable existence, but what I don't really understand is why it all adds up to nothing." Or again: "You know, Cha, I sometimes get the impression that you're just copying some artist — and I think his name is Charles Child! Why don't you try again?" In such matters, Fred never tried to soothe my pride with flattery, never allowed me to let my standards down. If the work seemed hasty, she unerringly pointed it out. On the other hand, if I was too tired at the end of a day to know whether a painting was good or not, she often persuaded me that it had excellence, or managed to make me see that I had done enough. "I love that. Don't touch it. This one has the Old Charlie Magic!"

But as one's kids grow up, one realizes that one is being pushed into middle age — and one resists. Perhaps the process is more psychological than physical to begin with.

I must say, as far as mere aging was concerned, I didn't feel that little shortness of breath or dimming of the eyes that is supposed to tell you that you should take things easier. And looking at Fred, I could see nothing in those smiling Irish eyes or that thick thatch of red curls that looked like decrepitude to me. She gave one the impression of health and strength deeply imbedded, which expressed itself more often than not with a lurking humor, but nowadays, I felt, more clearly, more forcefully, and Fred could bring me up short — sometimes with painful impact when I disagreed with her, as husbands often do, in a mood of lordly disdain. "Cha! Stop bulldozing! Listen to me for a second! Don't treat me like your idiot child. I'm your wife, remember?"

Then, in another mood: "Dern it: just tried to kill a mosquito but I didn't hit him hard enough. Now he's just lying down on his back here on my knee, kicking his legs in the air and crying for mama. I feel awful!"

Or again, in a more incisive mood, commenting on a couple of our acquaintances: "Of course they have no family, but in a way their stomachs are their family: something to yearn over and take care of."

We began about this time to talk more and more frequently about the need of all three children for privacy. Now, considering Jonathan's burgeoning skills and interests, and the girls' legitimate need for more sophisticated activities, it even occurred to us to dream of a possible addition to the cabin, which could take care of guests more adequately and segregate the generations in times of rainy confinement. Conversations on these matters began to take on increasing importance. The idea of an addition, especially, seemed to point the way to an agreeable solution for many of our problems, most of which seemed to relate to the need for additional living space. "Charlie, if we do build, and I don't say we should — neither of us is getting any younger, I suppose — we should do it on an ample scale. You remember: 'Make no small plans.' Who said that, anyway? Now suppose we wanted a nice big living room — let's get a piece of paper and actually sketch something out, shall we? The kids are all away for the morning fishing off the dock across the harbor so we won't be interrupted."

"Good idea, Fred. Where'll we begin?"

"Why not think of a new kitchen to begin with? Here, here's a nice piece of paper — you know, eight-by-eight for a family kitchen is pretty small. Old John Henry is beginning to go. *You* don't have to cook with him. Those cracks you filled with stove cement the other day have opened up again — I forgot to tell you — and that grate! It will hardly turn, and when it does, about half the time it lets the whole mess of fire down into the ash pit."

"Well, we don't want to build a kitchen big enough for music and dancing (but wouldn't *that* be nice!) or have strings of bedrooms like a motel. But now that we're getting bigger as a family there's no reason why we shouldn't add on something that will give everybody a feeling of relief."

It was true. "And, Fred, with all due respect to Brother Gilley, that sink is pretty primitive. I admit it wasn't his fault: that's all we could afford at the time. And it made good sense. But not any more. Then we need a really good place to dry wet clothes. We could certainly use that . . . okay, let's try something: Mmmmmmm."

"NO! *Bigger* than that! We've got to have a place where we can put a decent bathroom sometime. And now that we're on it, a separate bedroom for the girls might be a good idea."

"What about Jonnie?"

"Yes, Jonnie: I've been thinking — we almost never use the porch anymore during the daytime — the air here on the Point is just too cold for comfort unless you get in the sun. We could close it in and make a room for him, too, when the time comes."

"Good idea! Cha, you just sketch the thing out so we won't forget it. Let's put these papers away and sleep on the idea for a while. No need to say anything to them for now. They'd only ask silly questions like: "When are you going to do it?" Well, the place was full of family and friends most of the time and we loved it. But there was the need for more space. We would think about that — and think — and think . . .

Now from the advancing work area on the road we could see the cabin. Nearly there! Paul and I were like two old horses at the end of a day's work who have just caught sight of the barn. One more day! One more photograph! Now everyone pitched in. Branches snapped, sods flew, logs rolled, dirt was thrown in and stamped down, as the fourteen-legged family juggernaut pushed forward toward the cabin door. "Goddamn it, why aren't girls any stronger? Look at that! Dirt all over, and only a spoonful on the right place!"

"Look here, you may be the grand Kleagle of this Klan but as far as I'm concerned, you're talking to my wife. If you don't like the way she works, I'd just as soon see her walk off the job. Damn dirty job, anyway."

"Oh, shut up, you men! Let's get back to work."

"I'm sorry. I know we're all tired, but look — there's the cabin!"

And then the glorious moment arrived. Having broken
through the last fringe of trees and into the clearing, we
threw a few hasty shovelsful of dirt into the last potholes,
and raced back to the nearest car. Everyone piled in. Furiously honking, shouting, barking, we jammed into the
clearing and skidded to a stop six inches from the cabin
door. Glory road! Now supplies, groceries, anything — even
family and guests — could arrive on wheels, and with a bit
of backing and filling, the guests might even manage to
leave again. Seven years had passed, and the improbable
road was finally finished. Or, if not "finished," at least
it had an existence and had become an augury of a new
approach to life on the Point.

To celebrate the wonder of the event, Julia made a marvelous Something, which she averred was called in Paris
a Gâteau Fourré à la Crème d'Orange. It turned out to
be, as it grew and grew under our wondering eyes, a kind
of enormous sponge cake, split in two to form a top and
a bottom. It had an orange-butter filling between the
layers, if I remember correctly, and a butter-cream icing
outside. This icing was then covered with a glaze of apri-
cots. And this, believe it or not, in turn was sprinkled
with a cupful of pulverized almonds. Almost too good to
be true, and certainly too good to last, it disappeared like
one of our own Old Point sunsets, leaving only a warm
pink glow behind.

Shortly after the completion of the "road," we were walking along the beach one day. Figaro, running up and down
and mooching about after the immemorial manner of dogs,
suddenly froze in his tracks and began to bark excitedly.
"What is it, boy? What is it? Do you see anything, Fred?
What's that crazy pup making all that noise for?"

Figaro was now alternately barking and growling, and

had taken up a position some distance down the beach, facing the water. Then we saw it: a Something — a large rather shapeless yellow-white lump about three feet long, by the water's edge. The lump stirred, reared up suddenly at one end, and we found ourselves staring into the large black frightened eyes of a baby seal. Coming closer, we could see that he had an ugly cut about ten inches long just back of one flipper. Perhaps he had gotten too close to a lobsterman's boat and had been scored by a propeller blade. This youngster had a most appealing face: two enormous quite intelligent eyes, black as pools of ink, with no discernible pupils, yet curiously soft and sweet. He had a rather doglike muzzle and a huge white mustache. He was now regarding us with a look at once tender and scared, with a soft appeal that seemed to say, "Don't hit me; I'm really very nice."

The two animals now regarding each other not more than six feet apart presented a most amusing contrast. Figaro, the extrovert, all curly fur and ponderous bony legs, was leaping and quivering in a perfect ecstacy of excitement, a sort of free-form pinwheel, with barks and growls added. The introvert seal, curved like a wave, seemed to melt halfway into the beach, a glacier-smoothed object, immobile and silent. He was clearly a creature of another element, yet doglike too in a far-off way. For a moment I could imagine their being good friends, but the thought burst like a bubble. Pulling the barking doggy back by the scruff of the neck, we took him back to the cabin and shut him in, his mournful yelps distantly audible. Fred had now fixed a large bath sponge to a stick, dipped it into a pan of milk till it was full, and made her way back to the beach. Approaching the seal with motherly solicitude, she presented the dripping sponge to the little

stranger, who now bared its silly teeth and uttered a feeble
hiss. "Plop" went the sponge as Fred pushed it into the
baby's face. He wouldn't drink but lay there, reared up
at one end like the prow of a boat, nose and mustache
now covered with milk, looking more woebegone than ever.

All that day he remained on the beach. We visited him
from time to time until evening fell, but he never moved,
never uttered a sound, merely looked at us with those
ever-tender eyes. As night fell we could see his dark shape
still dimly silhouetted against the water. The next morning he had gone, the waves of high tides having apparently
cradled him off into his natural element.

Now about this time another matter began to assume
increasing importance in our minds. This was the question of an adequate supply of drinking water. Water had
been no problem when we had to be patient over so much
else. Now I began to muse: "You know how slowly the
water comes in? Only last week when we had those people
over here for a picnic, remember? I thought it might really
go empty. Then what with baths, cement-mixing, clothes-
washing, it takes absolute hours to refill. But here's an
idea: suppose we enlarge this spring hole to three or four
times its size — why we didn't think of this before I'll never
know — then it can fill all night when no one is using it,
and every day we'll have at least twice as much as we ever
did before, and maybe more! While we're doing this, we
can scrape it out to the bottom, maybe even enlarge the
place where it comes in to increase the flow."

"Hey, Jon, and you girls too! C'mon, we're all going
to dig out the spring! Let's go!"

First having supplied ourselves with all the water the
place would hold — tubs and buckets and pails and stove

tank full to the brim — we bailed out the remaining water. At the very foot of the empty pool we could see a tiny surge of white sand where the water emerged from a fissure in the rock. But there was no way short of blasting to enlarge the orifice. Okay, that was that.

Now we went to work to enlarge the basin of the spring itself. Laying out an area about five feet wide and ten feet long, we began tossing mountains of muck out on every side. Heavy work, this. The muck sucked at the shovels like an octopus. This soaking wet stuff lay a good deal deeper than the usual two feet, but at about four feet below the surface we struck a granite ledge, apparently a continuation of the large boulder which lay at one end of the spring. This ledge had a curved slanting surface like a roller-coaster and was smooth as a polished floor. Now we shaped side walls and end walls out of two-by-eight pine planks, from ground level down to this floor, carefully scribed and fitted to the curves in the rock. We covered over the top of these walls with a wooden floor into which we let a trap door for access to the water. Over this box-like arrangement we built a little roof supported by pillars in order to keep off falling twigs and needles. It looked curiously like a miniature Greek temple, half lost among the trees and surrounded by iris and swamp alder.

This scheme, by which the spring renewed its supply of water during the night, worked very well indeed. But one day not long thereafter the girls came to me and said, "You know, Cha, there's something we've been thinking about: down at the spring we feel kind of guilty. We've covered the whole thing up, and how do we know whose drinking water we might be taking away? Deer, for instance. And of course, the birds. Couldn't we make just a tiny little pool from the overflow so they will have something to drink?" Of course! So we all traipsed down to the spring and there we fashioned an outlet of pipe a few inches underground which carried the water down to a natural hollow some distance away. Here we constructed a little pool bordered by large stones and planted all about with ferns. In a day or two it filled with water from the overflow, and was henceforth christened "The Moose-drink." Of course the mosquitoes found it at once, but so did the birds, and later the deer. Going down to inspect the level of the spring we would often see purple finches, pine siskins, warblers, and robins and in the spring, deer tracks.

8

The Idea of the Wing

THE following summer we took a short trip to Europe with the family, but unable to stay away from our land completely, we spent the last two weeks before school began at Old Point. That two weeks had fateful consequences. It was just that suddenly everyone seemed so *large*. Enormous. There is nothing larger in the entire world than a large adolescent. The shelves would hardly hold their clothes any more. Baths were becoming a problem. And more: new boy friends were coming daily — sometimes it seemed to us almost hourly — along our "highway" to visit the girls, or up through the woodwork, as someone put it. For young visitors fresh from the more sophisticated life of Northeast Harbor, Bar Harbor and Seal, this place of ours held all the romance of a gypsy encampment. It had everything! The girls were blossoming like those enormous wild roses down by the shore, and the sound of the jeep and the jalopy were heard in the land, together with stamping feet, raucous laughter, guitar plonks, and feeble jokes. We love kids, but there are times and places when you can have just too much.

That idea of the wing: by degrees it was becoming the only thing by which we preserved our sanity. We talked

of a wing, we worked on it, clung to it, let it rumble loudly about in our minds. The case was now no longer arguable. There must be a wing, or else.

But what kind of wing? What shape? What size? What materials would this extension be made of? As any person who has ever set out to build something will have observed, conversation is one thing, active planning is another, and the doing of it still another. We knew by now some of our own limitations, some of the special characteristics of the local raw materials. One thing we had plenty of was space, and the kind of nerve possessed by those who go gaily into the Grand Canyon of the Colorado in a canoe. Besides, for sheer fun, building sand castles is nothing beside planning a new addition to a house. For the moment not a thing limits you but the size of the paper. In making plans for anything we had worked out an approach which seemed ideally suited to our particular natures: for the moment forgetting all other considerations we would try to visualize exactly what we wanted. Then, but only then, allowing costs, time factors, raw material resources, and other mundane considerations to creep in, we would modify the original idea. But first the rocket flight, first the Grand View from the mountain top!

Dozens of sheets of paper became hundreds as we got into our stride. No logs this time — well, a few, to tie the new wing into the rest in an equable transition, say up to the windows on the side nearest the old cabin. And bigger windows! Yes, of course, bigger windows; the view to the sea on the southwest side was superb now that the forest had been thinned out. And that delicious new kitchen, everything planned so that food would positively *flow* from bins to stove to table.

And now that the local electric company had offered to run a line onto the point: this must be considered. (But a half mile of poles? Well, this is no time to worry about such details; let's just get the big picture.) Electric lights would reduce fire danger. We could even put in a small rotary pump at the spring, pump water to some kind of storage tank on the hill, and thus have running water for both kitchen and toilet. Hurrah! Of course, a grand central fireplace. "And why not a smaller fireplace on the back side of the central chimney to warm the bathroom," said Fred. "Yes, of course, silly, now that we're considering the possibility of running water, we can have a real bathroom, with a shower and a toilet."

"But listen, Fred — that ice-cold spring water? Oof!"

"Cha, who said anything about ice-cold water? We have a road, don't we? The gas company can bring in bottled gas — in fact I was talking to them about it just the other day. Most of the locals have it: now just say this slowly to yourself a few times and see how it sounds: 'HOT-water-

when-you-want-it' — *and* a gas stove! Think of it! We can
get rid of John Henry forever, and turn the old kitchen
into a guest room. All we have to do is to plan the new
kitchen big enough to take the heater, a new stove, lots of
shelves, and a nice little fireplace thing in the side of the
chimney facing the kitchen — not an actual fireplace, really
— just a little hole-in-the-wall at table height where we can
broil things."

"Oh no!"

"Oh yes! You know how we all love those charcoal-
broiled steaks."

"Well," said I, "I think it's pretty crazy. Gosh! I sound
like Paul, don't I? Just give me a moment to adjust. Sometimes you women leap ahead three times faster than a man.
I can see that if you have to grill steaks in the fireplace
instead of the stove, it would be better than to have the
grease all over the kitchen . . . . Then of course we want
a big table to seat plenty of guests: we both agree on that,
don't we? Now what else?"

"Well, for one thing," said Fred, "we ought to have more
beds, or comfortable lounging seats, all round the room."

"Yes, that's a good idea. And what about bookcases? We
must have bookcases. Our books and the kids' books are
stacked all over the place now, even out in the shed. But
I still have the feeling that perhaps we're being just a little
crazy. Or am I getting old?"

"No, just stuffy," says Fred. "The idea *is* a bit visionary
but practical, too. If we're going to do it at all, I think
we ought to make it work. What I mean is this — not plan
it half way, but really try to visualize the needs of the next
ten years, and then see how near we can come to it."

"Yes," I put in, "I don't want to go to all the work of
building another cabin, or a wing or whatever, and then

find it simply the twin of the first. You know, I think you've actually been quite a way ahead of me on this. Or maybe it's your practical woman-sense at work. I have to think of the actual physical labor involved, though — that's mostly my ticket — for instance, those stones, those endless stones. That's a nightmare. I've been thinking — we might just figure out something — some new approach with stones. We could send up the garden tractor from Coppernose and use it for hauling. Mmmm . . . yes . . . might work. And get Seth again for the cement work. And see if Paul and Julia could get here for a bit: they'd love to help. That makes four more hands. Of course there would have to be a lot more foundation piers. But we could have a local contractor do them for us in the spring so they'd be ready when we come . . . and that enormous fireplace foundation, too. I know, when you do things this way they seem so expensive — that's the worst part. But after all, it's only money. This is *real*."

More thoughts, more plans. The look of the new wing began to shape itself in our minds more clearly. How high, for instance? How wide? And how handsome! "That's the thing to keep your mind on!" As the plan matured we began to measure and remeasure the wing in our minds in terms of actual lengths and widths. Conversation would go like this: "Let's see now, the way it works out this big room would be about thirty-six by twenty-four, including the kitchen and bathroom. Okay? And the bathroom, if it was put behind the big fireplace, wouldn't show. And the kitchen could be half open to the main living room, with a kind of food counter in between. Does that strike you as practical, Fred?"

"I like the idea," said Fred. "Who wants to be shut away from guests in a kitchen? Especially in an informal camp? If we did put in that counter thing, we could perfectly well have a curtain to shut the kitchen off when we start eating."

"Now there ought to be a doorway back toward the shed," I continued, "and a nice big front door — really impressive — I love big doorways — and perhaps we could include two or three French doors on the side facing the view — you know what I mean? Mostly glass — you buy this kind of thing already made up. They could open onto a nice long porch, or some kind of walkway without a roof, where we could all sit and have lunch or drinks."

"Grand!" said Fred.

"Then there's another thing: if we build this whole wing at right angles to the old cabin, it would make a kind of outdoor courtyard of the clearing and it would help keep the northeast winds off. And come to think of it, Fred," I added, "now the materials can be brought right in by truck and dumped where all we have to do is stretch out a hand and pick them off the pile. Nothing to it, really, when you come right down to it. And thinking of the actual carpentry, we could use post-and-beam construction like barn builders, with curtain walls between the posts. It's quicker that way. The posts will carry the

weight right down to the piers, and the walls, with almost
no weight to carry, can stand all the windows we want."

But wasn't the old place really good enough as it was?
I went out one morning as the sun rose. A film of mist
was drifting gently toward the cabin. It came up from the
water and swung about among the branches of the trees.
There was a fine golden light increasing now by degrees
as the sun climbed higher. A lobsterman out there a half-
mile off shore had begun to idle the motor of his boat to
haul a trap. With the sudden decrease in noise one could
plainly hear him singing to himself. Marvelous how sounds
carry over water. Wisps of steam began to rise from the
cabin roof as the rays of the sun came through a gap in
the trees, warming the night-damped surface. With its
front porch, the living room, the kitchen, and the woodshed, the whole mass of building was perhaps sixty feet in
length and really handsome, I thought, as it glowed in the
morning light. But only twenty-four feet of this was living
space, properly so called. A double bed on the porch had
been one answer to the problem of space but the girls had
ultimately rebelled. So then it was two separate beds.
Then came Jonathan's bed: that made three. Then those
dark but necessary tarpaulin curtains against wind and
rain: what a nuisance! Then we had added shelves, and
suddenly it wasn't a porch anymore. It had become a noisy
dormitory. And Jon had turned the loft above the porch
into something he called his "office." Among the stacked
bags and trunks, the extra rolls of mosquito netting, old
tent gear, window glass, kites and extra coils of rope, he
had cleared himself a space, hung up a lantern, whacked
together a jerry-built table and box chair, both leaning
madly to one side. With its attendant noise and confusion
— the boy was forever running up and down the ladder,

dropping things overside, asking boy-questions — there was no more space or quiet up there, either.

The sun rose higher. Soon the whole family would be awake and clamoring for breakfast. Sure enough, there was a figure now, stealing out and down to the rocks on a call of nature. This necessary function, too, had its limitations, its restraints, and sometimes, as in rainy weather, it was just damned disagreeable. And as for guests . . . Then there were the tents. Old and baggy now, yet still serviceable after a fashion, they had become "spare rooms" for young guests. But here a certain question of prestige entered in: who wanted any more to sleep in a smelly old tent if the rest of us were in the cabin?

There were sounds of stirring, and of someone splitting wood for our friendly enemy, John Henry. Smoke began to pour from the chimney. Now a voice: *"Who* washed the dishes last night? Well, why didn't they clean the spaghetti sauce out of the skillet? Now it's stuck on like glue; the water isn't heated up yet; I can't get it off, and Oh Hell anyway!" CRASH! That would be Rachel, on the breakfast detail. But let's be fair: Rachel had a point. I thought of Callie back in Old Fort with her mother. Was she cleaning a skillet this morning, too? And perhaps thinking of us, a thousand miles away?

Yes, all in all the decision to build a wing did look practical. To both of us it was a good deal more than a wishful dream. If we were to go on living here in anything like a civilized state, it had become a necessity. A flicker darted from the shadows, landed on an ant hill, and began snapping up ants.

Later on, sitting at breakfast, I happened to glance up at the ceiling, following a spider who was climbing her invisible thread. There on one of the ceiling boards was a

little handprint, made when one of our girls had handed
up that particular board with muddy fingers years ago.
The print was clearly visible, outlining a delicate little
palm and four fingers. Probably Rachel's. It was not the
hand that had so recently crashed the skillet into the sink
in exasperation, but childish, square-fingered, immature.
I looked at Rachel's hand now as it held her fork. It was
large, quite competent, almost mature. And so, by the
grace of God, was Rachel. This was in a sense the measure
of our growth, but also the evocation of our need.

As plans for the wing developed, we finally told the children. Wild enthusiasm! Now we were for it. When? Maybe next year if everything went well. A room for each
girl, a room for Jonnie, a real kitchen, a real bathroom
with a shower, plenty of space to store things. But we
needed help. Everyone would have a job to do and most
of next summer would be filled with labor. Sure, sure.
You bet. If guests came they would be put to work. Okay?
Okay. But plans had to be drafted, an order of priorities
set up, a schedule for delivery of raw materials worked
out, and a contract signed with the local contractor to
make the foundation piers in accordance with the plan.
"Boy, oh boy, a room *that* big? And a room for us? Two
rooms? Oh boy! You mean I won't have to sleep with *her*
any more? Whoopee!"

"Yes, but of course you'll have to keep your rooms extra
neat. There'll be a closet in each room for one thing; and
maybe a desk, or at least a table of some kind. But the
rooms for you girls will have to wait till we get the big
one finished — might be another year after that, depending
on how fast we can go."

"And porches? And? And? And? . . ."

In going over the plans that fall, we decided to use a

modular system of proportions. This is a sound approach, used for more than a thousand years by the Japanese, and now common in this country. (Perhaps the Greeks used it, too, at least so Jay Hambidge had thought.) The Japanese based everything in their traditional architecture on units of measurement derived from their straw floor mats, long since standardized in size. Their rooms are thus always measured in "mats" — so many mats long, so many mats high or wide. As it began to take more definite shape in our minds, we decided that the new wing was to have its principal measurements based on a module of three feet, or on multiples of three feet. Thus, for example, the final floor area was to be twenty-seven feet wide, by thirty-six feet long, the walls nine feet high with the apex at fifteen feet, and so forth. If the theory was correct, this three, six, nine, twelve, fifteen system would make the room subtly pleasing to the eye and of harmonic mathematical proportions in all its parts. Nothing was to be left to chance. But nothing! We dubbed this dream chamber Great Hall, and now in the astral world of our imaginations it proudly hung like a floating island all that long winter.

The fireplace in Great Hall had to be big; in fact, the whole chimney complex had to be big enough for the principal fireplace to heat the hall, big enough to have another fireplace at the back of the chimney, facing the bathroom, big enough to have a side fireplace or grill for the kitchen. How big was that? "Well," I said to myself, "if you follow your module you're bound to be okay." After a good many preliminary studies, I decided on a chimney complex that would be nine feet wide and nine feet deep. This would allow for two fireplaces back to back at the base. It was to be fifteen feet high at the peak of the ceiling and would top out at least three feet above the roof for adequate draft. And it would be stepped back so it came out at the top still nine feet wide, but only three feet deep. This monument to pride was to be located more or less in the middle of the new wing, but it appeared that throwing its heat across the short way, it would perhaps not succeed in warming up the whole room. So, I modified the design in such a way as to turn the front face of the fireplace diagonally toward the far end of the room. The stepbacks were then twisted or swiveled slightly so the top of the chimney would come out parallel with the long axis of the roof.

In thinking of the probability of having more guests and larger gatherings of young, we decided to add a smaller "convenience" room beside the bathroom. This would have a toilet and a small sink. A place for large storage shelves was provided at one end of Great Hall and a ramp was drawn in, leading down to the woodshed level from its higher level. A long porch would someday run along the ocean side of the room and access to it would be provided by a triple French door about twelve feet wide, principally of glass. They would be exposed to westerly gales from time to time, but I felt that the enormous amount of light and air they would let in would more than compensate for an occasional episode when we might have to resort to mops. However, I finally modified the design, reducing the glass area somewhat by extra strong enframements all round the doors, each of which would have three glass panels: top, middle, and bottom supported by sturdy mullions. There would be two rooms off the far end for the girls but that would have to wait till the following year. However, access doors could be built as an integral part of the room. I decided that I would make all the doors myself except those leading to the porch, using a hollow core construction inside and simple textured designs on front and back made of wood strips. I wanted those doors to be rugged, big and somewhat overscaled to go with the look of the room.

The basic skeleton of the room we would build with six-by-six beams like a barn. They would carry all the weight. Walls and windows would simply fill in the nine-foot spaces between the beams. Logs to tie the look of the new wing into the whole cabin complex would be used up to the base of the windows, and wide fir boards above. The rafters were to be of logs but instead of spacing them the conventional four feet apart, on the suggestion of an architect friend I decided to pair the logs, putting these doubled rafters nine feet apart and then run two-by-eight planks from doubled rafter to doubled rafter. These ceiling boards would be toenailed together so they would not warp or sag individually.

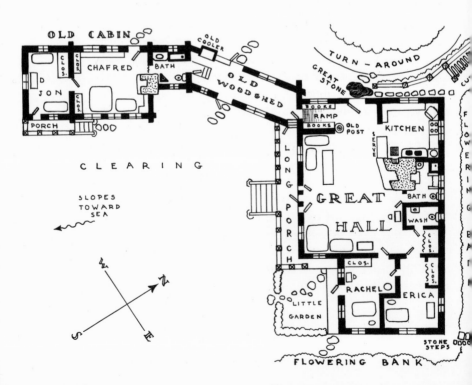

The kitchen was to be separated from the living room by a low wall or counter with an open space at one end for passage in and out. Shelves under the counter would provide spaces for linen and silver and there would be windows, windows everywhere — all around the room: large windows, made specially, six feet wide, three feet high, set solidly in their own frames. The vertical posts carrying the weight of the roof to the foundations would be fashioned of peeled tree trunks about a foot thick, set so that about four inches would show inside and out. Along the ramp leading to the woodshed we would build book shelves and game shelves which we hoped would keep people from stumbling down into the ramp as well as provide a convenient place to put things. Down the long side of the room facing the sea we would make built-in bunks or seats. The bathroom would have a shower, a toilet, a sink and a built-in seat facing the little fireplace, with shelf sides for soap, brushes, towels and first-aid materials. Here the happy bather on cold days when a fire had been lit could sit on the seat and toast his toes on the raised hearth while drying off, or even read a book curled up on the seat in a warm bathrobe.

We made a cardboard model of the kitchen in order to settle problems of traffic flow and storage to the best advantage. The girls got in the act, and fashioned miniature ice box, stove, and work-tops, and we all played with this little kitchen made of cardboard, arguing and discussing about each detail until we felt that a family consensus had been reached. We knew that the kitchen would be one of the most important rooms in the new wing. This model, crude as it was, made the whole thing so actual that we could almost believe it was already in existence. A carefully worked out plan of concrete piers and chimney

foundation was made and sent to the contractor for preliminary construction before our arrival, and lists of needed
materials were roughly calculated. Now there was no backing out. Either we had to build this dream wing or sit
and stare at those concrete piers forever.

To help get stones up from the beach, we sent our garden
tractor up to Maine. The idea was to build a ramp on
which a little wagon or box-on-wheels could run, and using
block and tackle hitched to a tree, and the tractor for
power, pull loads of stones up the incline to the level of the
cabin. The thought of those endless bags of stones of former years was just too much. Besides, the time element
was all important: we had to get enough of the new wing
built and covered by summer's end so that rain and snow
would not destroy it.

All that winter plans were drawn, discarded, modified,
drawn again, and at least firmed and crystallized in final
form with the help of a book titled *Your Dream Home —
How to Build It for Less Than $3,500.* * It had excellent
tips on all sorts of materials, and on framing, foundations,
floors, fireplaces, doors, etcetera. It was a full winter —
seven portraits, all of Washington sitters — which neces-
sitated an unusual amount of travel, as well as a rush of
fabric design orders, kept me hopping. As spring rolled
around Fred and I both felt more than ready for Maine.
"Well, what I say is," said Paulski in a telephone conversation from Washington just before we took off, "if you're
going to commit a folly, it might as well be a Big one. And
brother, this one is BIG!"

* Hubbard Cobb. W. H. Wise Co., 1950.

9

The Battle of Great Hall

"OH, my God, how enormous it looks! Will we ever . . . ?"

"Wow! Cha, we'll never finish that great mess. It looks bigger than Grand Central Station! Do you expect us to create a building on top of all *that*? We're not supermen, you know."

We had arrived at the Point, and were staring at the serried ranks of concrete piers, their gray-white rows strangely like a graveyard — the graveyard of our foolish winter hopes. I felt suddenly cold. Here it was — the battleground. Those piers, potent and menacing and above all, so solid, brought home to me the extent of my ignorance, the shortness of time. "You're no pioneer," I thought, "just a modern damn fool trying to play a game that's too complicated for you. But you asked for it. It's here. So let's get to work."

There were trees to fell for rafters and posts and walls. But we had counted the exact number and knew the exact lengths, which made it easier to see that this year there would be an end to felling and peeling. There was that crazy but hopeful tractor-pulley-wagon-ramp thing to work out. The kids were already calling it "Charlie's Folly."

There was lumber to be delivered; there were tools to sharpen, the cabin to set to rights, tents to pitch, groceries to buy, and no time to waste.

And now the mad concentration begins. Long straight trees for the rafters, shorter thicker ones for posts and walls — these come first, for they had to be peeled and dried. A truckload of lumber comes and is unloaded: six-

by-six beams, and what Maine builders call "boardin'
boards" for sub-floors and scaffolding. And of course, it
would happen, by far the best stones for the fireplaces we
found lying at the foot of a steep cliffy bank about forty
feet high.

We had hardly gotten well into our stride when who
should turn up but Paul and Julia, full of fire and ready

to help. For the moment Julia and the girls set about stripping the newly cut logs so they would have time to dry while Paul and I, with Jonnie as helper, worked out the problem of creating an apparatus for bringing stones up from the beach. Together we started to rig a double track of heavy planks from the stone beach to the top of the cliff. The idea was simple: all we had to do, or so it seemed, was to set the planks just the right distance apart to take the wheels of the sulky from the tractor. That having been done we would make a heavy box to set on top of the wheels and rig it with hooks and ropes so that the block and tackle placed forty feet up in a tree at the cliff top could be used to pull the box up the ramp when the other end of the rope was hitched to the tractor.

Two days went by while we smoothed a rough track along the top of the cliff for the tractor to run on. Then the box on wheels: half a day. Now the planks: three days. The ramp went up the face of the cliff at a sixty degree angle, and was tough to put together.

Now everything seemed ready. The only thing to do was to fill the box with eight or nine hundred pounds of stones, start the tractor, and see what happened.

"Okay? All set? Let 'er GO!" Blast it! The stones roll out at the very first yank. Well, of course: we should have built the box with its lower side twice as high. Once again half a day's work, as we realize that the planks too will have to be strengthened with heavier braces. Well, here we go again! Set? GO! The box trundles about fifteen feet up the tracks, then — WHAM! It comes off. A half ton of stone hurtles down the cliff, not quite braining brother Paul who has prudently withdrawn behind a boulder in the best tradition of the wise Government servant. Jonathan, at the cliff top with the tractor, is a fascinated spectator. We will have to make sides to the tracks to hold the wheels — that's another half day or more. And of course, a stop now and then for photographs. I had long since ceased to begrudge this enthusiasm of Paul's, as we now had a visual record which marvelously enriched our winter lives. His work was excellent, and by now of fully professional caliber.

Two hours pass: the sides are just about finished. "How about changing jobs? The mosquitoes down here are awful. There, too? Oh well, the hell with it . . . now, for God's sake, Cha, when we get going, take it *easy!* And Jon, don't start your tractor with such a jerk. What do you think you're running, an express elevator? Plonk. Plonk. "Whew! Must say, that looks better! How about if we put some more two-by-fours under the track?"

Another hour passes while we strengthen the bracing again. Everything has to be twice as heavy as we had foreseen. "Now, lower your ropes. Not there, you idiot! Another two feet! Okay. All right now, Paul and I will give her a half-load till we see how she works. But don't start that fire engine of yours till I give the signal. That'll mean she's loaded up and we're both out from under. Two whistles? Okay. Here goes! And get that crazy dog out of the way! Hey girls, call Figaro! He wants to race the tractor. Everything set up there? You okay, Jon?" Paul whistles twice. I run for cover, as does Paul. Jon eases in the clutch of the tractor, the pulley begins to turn. She starts! She moves! Up she goes! As the tractor trundles along the top of the cliff the box-on-wheels rumbles slowly but quite steadily up the ramp like a freight elevator, comes over the top onto a straightaway and is brought to a halt for unloading. Whew! It works. Cheers from all hands. The girls come running. Now in our

minds transformed, it is no longer a mere Folly, but a triumph of ridiculous science: Robinson Crusoe, plus gasoline!

The next trip will be a full load. Steadily the little vehicle rumbles up the incline, over the top, and is unloaded. Congratulations from the spectators. Yelps of masculine vanity from the men. Another full day has passed, but the stone problem has been licked at last. In this way over the next few days we laid down an enormous pile of stones at the top of the cliff ready to be hauled directly to the building site by the tractor and an accompanying dump cart.

But word now comes from Washington: only five short days and Paul has to go, at once. Something has come up and he must leave that very day. Hellish news, this: we had thought to make the greatest use of his strength and varied talents. And Julia, Fred, and the girls would have been able to solve the housekeeping end of things without too much burden falling on anybody. Now everything was changed — we'd all have to work that much harder. Very little housework would be done, I could see that. And meals would have to be at a minimum. Everyone would have to pitch in and help with the carpentry most of the time if the end of the summer was to see any sort of result. Once again my heart sank.

"Let's drop everything and lay the first six-by-six beams along the piers." Up to now, every move had been of a preliminary nature. We all want Paul to have the satisfaction of being able to say that he had helped in the actual construction. So, rather sadly, we get out the saw and nails in order to mortise two beams together over one corner. The cuts are made and the nails hammered home. Now a square is applied. The beams lie straight and true.

Feeling that a ceremony is in order, Jonnie brought a

branch of fir balsalm to lay over the two corner beams, in the name of hope. Then all being gathered at the corner, I uttered the words, "We christen thee Great Hall," whereupon, exactly at the completion of this phrase and before I could elaborate the pronouncement, Figaro, our shaggy dog, as if to get into the spirit of the occasion, delicately lifted one leg and granted the beams the favor of a small donation. Since, with this act, the ceremonies had obviously been brought to a fitting close, we hung around morosely while Paul and Julia packed their things and then, bidding them goodbye, we returned to work.

The rhythm of building was very much like that which we had established for the old cabin — three or four days of wood construction, then three or four of stonework on the central chimney in order to keep the whole complex going up together. The centers of the piers were nine feet apart. The beams were cut nineteen feet long, six inches of each end being lapped together over every other pier. All the outside piers had bolts set into the center of their top surfaces with threads uppermost so the beams which formed the sills, with holes bored every nine feet, could be bolted fast by screwing nuts down on the threads. Having fitted and bolted the outside pieces, we proceeded to lay those on the inside — which would support the floor — the grid of beams forming a series of interlocking squares. The beams ending at the central chimney were cemented directly into the stonework. Now the sub-floor was laid over the beams: the kids all helped, tapping the tongue-and-groove boards into place and nailing them fast, sawing and hammering with a will. It was almost like spreading a layer of butter on a gigantic piece of bread. Now the finished sub-floor was covered with rough building paper to keep it clean and dry.

Next came the upright tree-trunk posts, every nine feet, then more six-by-six beams spiked on top. Now we had a kind of giant cage, indicating the outside walls of Great Hall. It was time to work once more on the chimney. We made a ramp from ground level up to the sub-floor and brought our wagon loads of stone from the clifftop directly to the base of the chimney. Seth, though no substitute for Paul, was back on the job, mixing cement, sand and lime and the girls had now switched jobs and were busy peeling logs for the lower part of the walls, while Jonathan raced around after me, helping where he could.

About this time a number of the village boys, friends of Jon's, began coming to the Point. They hung around, asking questions and making suggestions till suddenly it occurred to us that we might be able to use their help. Would they like a job? They would. We worked out a pay scale according to ages and put them to work bringing in water, loading and unloading stones, clearing away log peelings, carrying buckets of concrete. We had five of these lively helpers, ranging in age from eight to fifteen. The eight-year-olds, two of them, got fifteen cents an hour, and worked mostly on command — "Hey, Bobby, bring me some nails. Oops! Dropped my hammer — Frankie! Bring me up that hammer, there's a good kid." The top pay was ninety cents an hour and for this we expected, and got, fairly skilled labor. As time went on, the boys showed up regularly each morning with their lunches and put in more or less of a day, some shorter, some longer. Being paid by the hour, they could quit whenever they got tired. But in fact, even with all the confusion and the uneven hours, this motley crew proved to be a great help, and added a tremendous element of noise and enthusiasm to the project.

And here came electricity! The twentieth century was

catching up with us. We had made a deal with the Bangor Hydro Electric Company by which, in the expectation of other families moving onto the Point in time, they would run a line out to our place for a sum that we could afford. Day by day, the crew came nearer, setting up poles and stringing wires in a direct line across the cut and through our forest to a final pole just one fifty-foot span away from the cabin. Ugly sight, with its junction box. But it held in its embrace all the glory of light, heat, music, refrigeration, running water, and communication.

The log walls between the posts went up quite fast. Pre-cut to length, they were simply spiked into place and caulked with oakum. But the place seemed to be taking on some of the aspects of a boys' camp, or zoo. Clattering, shouting, banging, dragging, the work went forward day by day, the family crew and the village crew vying with each other in a friendly but frenzied race against time. Sometimes there would be sulks, as kids who had tossed luncheon papers and Coca-Cola bottles carelessly about were asked to clean up.

"By gorry, Mrs. Child, them old sandwiches ain't mine! I et everything all up clean down to the bottom of the box!"

"Hey!" (A roar from the great panjandrum.) "Everyone stop! Who in hell threw that lighted cigarette butt down here? I don't give a damn *who* did it, but no one does a lick of work till one of you apes comes down and puts it out." Sheepish grins. Finally, the culprit comes down off his ladder and steps on the butt. "Okay, let's go!"

"Watch out, there, with that board! You want to brain somebody?"

"Oops! Sorry!" (A piece of wood has just landed on someone's back.)

"Hey, Charlie! We're running out of lime!"

"Hey, Charlie! What size nails did you say for this?"

"Hey, Charlie! Isn't it time to eat?"

"Hey, Charlie! Give us a hand with this rock!"

"Hey, Charlie!"

"Hey!"

One day, thinking to get away from the work for a brief half hour, we were rowing about at lunch time and found a magnificent old log floating in the water on the other side of the Point. It had apparently once been part of a mast or the piling for a dock. The ends were rounded off by grinding on the rocks. We drove a spike into it, hitched a towline to the spike, and brought it around to the nearest part of the beach where we rolled it up to dry. I sawed five feet off one end and brought it into Great Hall to use as a post at the end of one of the bookcases which bordered the ramp. It had an ancient crusted look. Deeply pitted here and there, mellowed by time, the color of rust and sand, it still had the look of an artifact shaped by someone's toil, old and strong.

On the back side of the chimney, the little bathroom fireplace was quickly finished with an opening about two feet high, two feet wide, and two feet deep. On the kitchen side, for the grille, a square opening for a wall fireplace eighteen inches from corner to corner was contrived at table height. And on the front, the principal fireplace whose opening was to be five feet wide and four feet high with a raised hearth, had already been partially built. Now we began the construction of a scaffolding provided with ramps for getting up more stones. As the chimney rose, we graduated the size of the stones smaller and smaller, as we had in Old Cabin, as we had come to call it, so the problem of getting them up the ramps would be simplified.

Even so it was hard work, made somewhat easier by the open spaces enclosed by the five flues which were being brought up together on the inside: one for the kitchen grille, one for the bathroom fireplace, two for the principal fireplace and one extra flue on the side opposite the kitchen for a space-heater if we ever decided to use one.

Next, the window frames were set and the spaces between were walled up. The chimney had finally risen to fifteen feet and it was time for the rafters. We set ridgepoles made of stout logs out from the chimney to the two ends of the room, held up there with six-by-six beams. Then we pulled the rafters up into place, using a rope flung over the ridgepoles. The paired rafters had their butts canti-levered out three feet beyond the outer walls and were then spiked into place. Next the two-by-eight ceiling boards were laid on the rafters and toenailed together, and the walls at the two ends were finished up to the peak: hollow walls with a grid of two-by-fours inside. Rolls of tar paper for the roof came next, then shingles. Such a hammering and yammering — there were ten of us all told — like a mad flock of woodpeckers we tapped and banged. There was a constant climbing up and down ladders with supplies and sometimes a sudden stop as a particularly beautiful boat went by. At noon we lolled about on the sweet-smelling surface of the roof eating our lunches. It was a merry time. It had been a dry summer and we had not been plagued by rains, so the roof was completed in good time. Finally the chimney was topped off at eighteen feet, and twelve sets of initials were duly incised in the wet concrete at the top, ten for the crews, two for Paul and Julia.

"What about a party?" said Rachel.

"Party? Here? Just look at the damn place: plaster all

over the floor, kitchen only a box, and those spotted windows — ugh! We've hardly had time to get the roof on and
now you want a party!"

"Aw, come on, Cha, don't be stuffy. You sound like the
State Department. Let's have a celebration for the whole
work gang. What if it is messy? Nobody'll care!"

"Okay. But let's try and get the floor cleaned up, at
least."

"Whoopee! A party! Let's go!"

We set about sweeping up the plaster and rock chips,
and rolled up the building paper underneath, revealing
the lovely clean surface of the sub-floor. While Fred began
to prepare a feast the girls took to washing the windows.
Surprising what a difference it made.

"Party's tomorrow noon, so let's do what we can before
then."

Going back up the hill, I cut forty or fifty branches of
fir balsam and put them around the walls for decorations.
We tried out the fireplace. It worked! We would have a
fire for the party. Though we didn't need it in the least,
it would look beautiful anyway. Camp chairs and orange
crates were set out for seats, and a table of sorts was
hastily thrown together from scrap lumber, and covered
with a blue and white checkered cloth. Lovely odors from
Old Cabin. Fred was inventing again. "What you makin',
Ma?" cried Rachel.

"Oh, just my idea of a Cooking Folly," said Fred.

The following morning we went to the village and got
some ice cream and some fish for chowder while Erica
picked a great bunch of wildflowers: asters, goldenrod, fireweed, and the glowing red-berried branches of the rowan
tree. Jon made place cards, and folded napkins into wig-
wams, with a gull's feather in the top of each.

With the coming of our gang of young workers the place looked absurdly festive and gay, and was filled with the sound of laughter and whoops of delight as newspaper cornucopia hats were donned. Blue jeans, khaki, colored shirts made a necklace of color round the table. "Hey, Billy! Go wash yer hands. The party can wait," said an older brother. Steaming bowls of chowder, slabs of bread and butter, hunks of cheese — everybody was wolfing down the food, and for the moment a kind of strange silence prevailed. Now came dessert: ice cream and the confection Fred had invented for the occasion. We called it Blueberry Folly. Here's the recipe, which has become a staple of Old Point feasts.

BLUEBERRY FOLLY
Bake a tart shell, using your favorite recipe for pie crust. Now take one ten-ounce jar of currant jelly and one ten-ounce jar of crabapple jelly, and having chopped up a fistful of fresh mint, put the mint into the jelly mix and melt over a low flame, stirring to dissolve the lumps. "In the meantime, back at the range," as Fred put it, fill the tart shell with fresh blueberries. When the jelly mix is melted, pour it over the blueberries. Not having quite enough blueberries, Fred added raspberries, blackberries and peach slices. Glaze immediately to retain the color. Serve cold.

Rachel's instinct had been right. The feast was a glorious occasion, the first of many, marking the beginning of a new dimension in the life at Old Point. "Well, I've et pretty good now and then," said one of the kids with a slightly glazed expression, wiping a bit of jelly from the corner of his mouth, "but t'want never like this! Here doggy, doggy, doggy — mebbe you can finish this blueberry stuff — I'm full to bustin'."

Now that Great Hall was weathertight, we could turn to the construction of kitchen and bathroom walls, shelves, shower stall, bunks and bookcases. The smaller fry drifted away by degrees as the work became more complicated with the need for careful measuring and fitting. A plumber's crew came and installed pipes, sinks and toilets, and a septic tank. I noted that Wendell Gilley was no longer a familiar figure in the team. "Wendell? Well, he's took to carvin' them birds full time," one of the men said. "Sort of retired, you might say. Nice work, too, with the driftwood and all, and now his hands is all colors of the rainbow from paintin' the birds — not like mine!" He held up two enormous hands covered with black grease.

On the hilltop back of the cabin, we began to set up a water tank in one of the clearings in the forest which had resulted from our logging operations. Pipes were laid on top of the ground from the spring to the tank and from the tank to Great Hall. A small rotary electric pump was installed hard by the spring house and the electricians wired it for power with a control switch in the woodshed. As the inner walls of Great Hall were completed, the wiring went in both there and in Old Cabin and in the woodshed. Finally, the great day arrived when, inspection completed, the juice was turned on and the whole place sprang into light.

What glory! To anyone who has lived with kerosene for ten summers, such a moment brings a transformation more complete, more compelling almost than the building of a new wing. In one second, it brings you forward into a new century. In one second, it relieves you of the immediate fear of fire. The ineffable odor of kerosene dies away. The trimming of wicks and the washing of lamp chimneys is over. And the thought of running water, hot water, instant water, instead of buckets and buckets and buckets painfully tugging at shoulder muscles — and inside toilets instead of the slippery rocks — and dishwashing made so much easier — all these things were now possible.

But speaking of water, where was the water? The tank was a knocked-down affair made of two-inch-thick redwood planks, tongued and grooved together to make its walls and floors. The completed tank could hold ten thousand gallons of water. The planks were brought together and held tightly in place by circular metal tie-rods, running around the outside and tightened with turnbuckles to make everything watertight. We had built for us a rugged supporting tower about ten feet high of heavy cross-braced beams set on concrete footers, and assembled the tank on top.

We threw the switch. The water came hopping and plopping into the tank and almost at once began to leak away through those "watertight" cracks. We had been told not to try to putty up the cracks as the wood would swell and close them as it got wet. But as the water was leaking away, the wood didn't get very wet. And, as it didn't get wet, it didn't swell. And, as it didn't swell, the water leaked away. And the summer sun beat down, beat down, and the water level at the spring got lower and lower.

"To hell with expert advice," I said to myself. I got ten pounds of putty and went to work. At once the water rose in the tank. In about three days, we had enough water to essay a test. A gas hot water heater had been installed in the kitchen and had been sitting in its corner, waiting. But now we dared fill it and light it. Suddenly everything worked. Toilets flushed. Oh, joy! Piping hot water came splashing and singing out of the faucets: no more excuses for dirty hands and faces. Now for a shower. "Ho ho! Tum-ti-tum! Yippee-i-ay!" No shower curtains yet — water all over the bathroom. But who cares?

The shower water came down into a zinc-lined box with

a hole for the waste pipe. Filling the bottom of this box with about three inches of wet cement, Erica and I laid down a design of smooth beach stones averaging about one inch across — a black fish, a green fish and a yellow fish, all against a white ground of quartz pebbles. Constant use has polished this little mosaic till the stones glow like agates.

Came the day, with the kitchen and Great Hall substantially completed, when we were able to move everything over to the new location — everything except John Henry, that is, John Henry, our old enemy, now in the last stages of decrepitude. He had served us well in his fashion, but the time had clearly come to give him a decent burial. "Goodbye, John Henry," I muttered, taking up a ten pound sledge. Bam! Wham! Bop! Crack! Klunk! John

Henry was gone. Roars of glee from the kids! A mass of rusty iron shards was all that remained, signaling the end of his long career. Filling the boat three or four times in succession, I rowed this rusty cargo out into the bay and

gave it to the sea to dispose of in its own fashion. The old kitchen now stood empty — a few crumbs, a few dead flies, and silence. What a beautiful moment! This year we would have no time to do more than clean it, ready for turning it into a little guest room at some future date. In Great Hall there were still a thousand things to do, and outside a really immense job of cleaning up.

On rainy days the whole family turned to making lamps. We created wall sconces of quarter-inch galvanized mesh curved into the form of half barrels cut down through the middle; the sides were fastened to the wall, the fronts bulged out. These were covered with Coast and Geodetic Survey maps of the region, tops and bottoms being left open. The blue and white tones of these maps were lovely against our wooden walls. Other lamps were contrived of driftwood hunks with shades made of maps, blueprints, and woven string. Up at the apex of the room we hung two large wooden boxes with tapered sides, painted white inside, each of which held four long fluorescent lights for general illumination. The kids promptly dubbed them "those baby coffins," a name which spelled their eventual doom.

Having considered the idea of built-in bunks, we decided that flexibility was better. So we built four low beds which could be rolled out from the wall for easier making or brought to the fireplace for warmth. We also made a long refectory table for eating, reading and games.

Between the kitchen and Great Hall we built a structure somewhat like a bar with a front of fir and a top made of an immense slab of maple given us by Polly Peirce from an old stable on her place that was being torn down at the time. A curtain wall came down from the peak of the roof to within three feet of this bar top. From the curtain wall we hung a Chinese matting screen that could be rolled down to cut off the kitchen area after meals. This bar top made a perfect serving area, with silver and linen shelves underneath on the kitchen side and dishes and glasses nearby. To complete our kitchen arrangements we made a series of shelves and work tops finished in Formica, between stove, sink and refrigerator, together with a small table which we gave a sheet copper top. This table could be rolled on casters directly to the opening of the grille or from kitchen to dining room with dishes, silver and food. And the grille, although I had laughed at the idea when it was first proposed by Fred, turned out to be perfect for doing chops, steaks, lobsters and fish, and marvelous for smoked mussels, which she makes as follows:

SMOKED MUSSELS

The mussels are steamed in a court bouillon of white wine, onions, carrots, celery, and parsley, then taken from their shells and laid on a fine mesh grille over a low fire upon which fresh green fir balsam branches are laid. The perfumed smoke from the balsam adds an indescribable flavor to the mussels already seasoned in the court bouillon. The smoked mussels are then packed into a jar of olive oil seasoned with crushed garlic and wild bay leaves where they keep indefinitely under refrigeration.

The only trouble is they are so delicious that we can almost never keep a supply for long.

Now, coming from Old Cabin through the woodshed and up the ramp into Great Hall, one had a curious sense of freedom, of expansion, of growth. Here where the forest had so lately been was a great room filled with light and space, which imposed its own sense of quiet, of order and proportion. The long high slope of the ceiling with its paired rafters, the huge gray fireplace with the rough texture of beach stones, the ample windows opening to a view of the sea through the fringe of trees along the bluff all seemed now that they had come together into a whole to invite one into a world which summed up and amplified the sense of enduring strength given by the forest, the water and the rocks. The building itself seemed as if it were not so much an interruption as a harmonic variation of the landscape. Its size was impressive to our family, used to the crowded conditions of Old Cabin, and to the village boys, too. As one of them said when he first came into the finished room: "Jee-sus Christ! Eff I ever see a bigger room than this, I'd jest like to know where 'twas to!"

In the kitchen, spatulas, forks, cups and other tools were hung on the wall above the sink. Erica, with her highly articulate sense of form, had hung the tools in a certain

order, perfect for her. Fredericka, with an equally exact sense of where each tool should live, had hung them in a different order. No friction, you understand — but each time one of these girls did the cooking, certain tools were quietly transposed. After this subterranean chess game had been going on for some days and the egg beater had been switched from what we boys called the "E" position to the "F" position for the umpteenth time, I took it into my head to draw a line around this tool on the wall at the "F" position and fill it in with a drawing suggesting a weird human figure. Lunch that day was to be an omelette-aux-fines-herbes, a dish at which Erica was particularly adept. Seeing the beater two-down-and-one-over from her favorite spot, she reached up and twitched it quietly from the wall, suddenly revealing the sketch. Peals of laughter! Everyone came running. Enchanted by the new approach, the whole family now got in on the act. Compromise decisions as to where the tools should hang were quickly made and a whole series of amusing symbols were created, each with the general shape of the tool which covered it.

"Oh, for some fresh thyme," said Fred one day. "Or just a handful of chives we could call our own! Or onions! You can do without anything in the world but the flavor of onions. Let's try a little herb garden and see what happens."

In the clearing near the edge of the bluff there was a sunny spot, covered now with wild grasses. Ripping out the foot-thick sod, we cleared a little square about five feet on a side and filled it to the top with loam from the holes where we had been taking out stumps, and in it we planted mint, thyme, and chives.

That summer there seemed to be no time to do anything but build Great Hall, no time even to make doors.

But there was one thing we did which softened the pace somewhat. We found and bought a fiberglass boat, of a type known as a Cape Codder. Essentially a sailing dinghy, it was nine feet in length, and equipped with a sail and a centerboard. It floated like a feather, responded to the lightest breeze. At the end of an exhausting day of building it was marvelous fun to sail quietly around the Point, or to watch our children like Wynken, Blynken and Nod in this modern version of the wooden shoe, maneuvering on the waters of the bay.

Jon was mad for boats, and an expert young sailor by now. But his mother was mad for cars and loved to drive. Though incredibly skillful, Fred has one majestic flaw in her makeup. The family years ago dubbed it the Pussy Cat Syndrome. A careful driver in all ordinary situations, and on all regular highways, from time to time she exhibits a compulsive and breathtaking yen to drive a car — the lower the better — into old, abandoned, rutted roads, headlong into swampy areas, or barreling into forest tracks that lose themselves in inextricable tangles of roots, logs, upended stones, nasty hidden holes. Seeing the gleam in her eye as she comes upon a hundred-year-old ox trace ending in a beaver swamp, I will feebly cry, "No!" But with the iron resolution of a Sherpa about to ascend the North Col of Everest, as often as not she swings the car — casting a scornful glance in my direction — directly into the jaws of the trap.

That year we had as one of our two cars a fine old Plymouth station wagon, Limpopo III, which had been partially packed for the trip home, but we had decided to take an hour or so off to look at autumn foliage. Now on the way back to the Point, dusk was coming on, and as Fred, who was driving at the time, suddenly left the highway at Norwood's Cove, I felt a premonitory twinge. We seemed to be heading directly for the flank of Western Mountain, whose forest-covered slopes now stood dark and silent some distance ahead. "Hey, Fred, what gives? D'you realize we're almost packed to go? The car's too heavy for this kind of thing." I might as well have been speaking Choctaw: the gleam of Pussy Cat Syndrome shone in my beloved's eyes. "Do you know where this road goes?"

"Well, who cares? It's beautiful! And it's our last chance" — (bump, bump) — "our last chance to get deep into some real country before we leave!"

The road had now become little more than a paired track. I seemed to remember talk of an old CCC camp up here somewhere. Zoom! Down we raced into a mountain stream and out again. "For God's sake, be careful! You'll never be able to turn the car around. You'll have to back it all the way out again, and the road's getting worse all the time!"

"Don't be chicken," cried Fred, as the car careened round the top edge of an abandoned gravel pit. Branches whipped the sides, stones bounded out from under the wheels. And night was coming down. An eerie green twilight lit the sky. We were definitely creeping along one high flank of Western Mountain, whose enormous black mass now loomed directly over us.

BANG! CRUNCH! CRACK! Limpopo III had come a cropper. It had shot onto a sudden ridge of stones and gravel deposited across the road by a spring freshet, and there lay suspended, all four wheels still turning, while the odor of gasoline dripping from the split tank filled the night air with nauseating fumes.

I draw a discreet veil over the dialogue which followed. Suffice it to say that it took the next two hours to locate a wrecking car and get headed ignominiously back to the land of paved highways. But did this episode cure Fredericka? Not a bit. She still whips the car into.a tangle of swamp alders or blackberry vines at the slightest provocation. And the gleam of Pussy Cat Syndrome still lurks unsleeping behind those marvelous hazel eyes.

The car was repaired. Goodbyes were said. One more season had almost come to an end. The work had carried us forward into autumn with machinelike speed, and with autumn, the Highland cranberries were beginning to ripen on our Point. These are smaller than the familiar bog-grown cranberries of commerce, but no less delicious. Toward the end of August and the first days of September they suddenly seem to spring to life as they turn brilliant red and carpet all the open spaces with a spatter of fiery points which creep in sparkling masses up and even over many of the old stumps and half-buried log ends left from former cuttings. Our village neighbors take advantage of this natural crop and during the period of ripening can be found almost any day working at the cheerful red clusters. On one of our berry-picking forays during the last days of that summer I came across Old Ben sitting on a stump with a pail full of berries between his knees. Ben was a large, square, somewhat rough-hewn man who could be seen during lobstering season, if you got up early enough, hauling his traps just off the Point, and sometimes singing in a hoarse voice which echoed across the water in an unearthly fashion, especially in the fog, as if it came from the vaults of a cathedral. He looked at me, his sea-blue eyes set deep in a mass of wrinkles. "That you I seen dooin' and dunkin' in them long grasses this mawnin' as I come acrost the bay? That red shirt o' yours shows up near as bright as Bass Harbor Light! Your cabin stood right out, pretty as a picture postcard: by God, Challes, it was a lum good sight!" Munch. Munch. "Good berries this year, ain't they. Maw ses I'm gettin' too old to run the boat, so I have to spend some time berry pickin', just to ease her mind." Munch. Munch. "Ptew!" (Spits out a mass of cranberry leaves.) "Well, old age ain't no disgrace. But it's mighty unhandy. I had to get up three times last night jest to empty some water off my potatoes, if you see what I'm comin' at." Munch. Munch. "Been awful dry this year. Don't see how them berries filled out so good, but reckon it's the sea fogs. Down here you get a soakin' every so often, but up to home there's not even enough moisture to make mosquito piss." Munch. Munch. "Pretty, though, what with the goldenrod and all, and them gulls flyin' overhead."

"You know, Ben," I put in, "I like watching them, too — they fly so easily it seems there's nothing to it: I feel as if I could almost do it myself."

"Oh sure, Challes." Ptew! "There ain't much to it. All you need is a pair of wings, hollow bones, and a big tail. But the way I figger it, all you got is the big tail, so I'm afraid you'll never make it. Heh heh! But my missus is smart — keeps her feet on the ground. She knows how to grow flowers in that gardin we have up on the hill back of the house, though I don't holt with growin' posies myself — never did. I'm more for vegetables and such. I like to look at a pretty flower gardin though, if someone else was to do it."

"We'd like to grow flowers like some folks around here," I said. "Those eight-foot-high delphiniums, for instance, that I see in so many Maine gardens."

"Shucks," says Ben, "flowers like that ain't real! What I mean is, t'ain't just spadin' up that does it: you look

real careful and you'll find a dollar bill behind every one
o' them posies! Well, I got to get on home or I won't have
any cranberry sauce on my corn fritters tonight."

Cold nights! Short days! Time to think of leaving the
scene of our summer's triumph — I was almost glad it was
over. Triumphant, but for the moment emptied of our
energies, we boarded up the gaping doorways, arranged
with the plumbers to drain the pipes, and bid Great Hall
goodbye. It had been a glorious battle, the stresses and
strains of which I felt had been, for once, graced with
victory.

10

Touches Here and There

THE following summer, on coming back to the Point, we noticed that in the cut the forest was beginning to grow back, faster than we had dared hope. There were birches, maples, mountain ash, poplars, swamp alder, spruce and fir, together with magnificent blueberry and raspberry bushes everywhere. Some of the trees were growing as fast as twenty-four inches a year, leaping for the sun. Around the cabins and in the forest clearings nearby the wild grasses stood nearly three feet high, a source of serious concern to me, as one spark could set the whole mass ablaze if we had a really dry summer. Almost my first act after taking the winter shutters off the windows and unboarding the doors was to get out the scythe and cut down all the grass in the vicinity of the cabins. Then I breathed easier. This cutting revealed thousands of brilliantly red wild strawberries at the base of the grass stalks. Our miniature garden patch had all but disappeared — only one straggling mint plant showed. The wind had blown in thousands of grass seeds and the patch had simply closed in upon itself, like green quicksand. It was clear that if we wanted a garden, we would have to create one on a far grander scale.

Almost at once our gang of boys was back, eager to begin work on the two girls' rooms we had been unable to tackle the summer before. We had had to learn this curious fact, basic to life on the Point: not only did the ever-watchful gulls come out of nowhere to pick up bits of garbage jettisoned off the rocks, but nothing we did on the Point, it seemed, passed unnoticed in the village. This wasn't telepathy or osmosis even — it was lobstermen. Their boats, passing and repassing the Point all day long from three A.M. till dusk, were as much a part of the ever moving scene as the scavenging gulls. We had long since ceased to notice them, unless someone was in trouble or came out with a newly painted boat — but they hadn't ceased to notice us. Not by a jugful!

"Well, Challes, when I see you puttin' shingles to your roof last summer, I like to called out to you to ask if you wasn't afraid that boy of yours was goin' to fall off."

"Hey, Challes, how be you? Couldn't figger what you was doin' with that fancy rig down to the beach last summer. Forgot to ask. Thought about it most of the winter when I had nothin' better to do. Pullin' up stones, eh? Well, I ses to Sara only yestidy — 'The Childs is here: figger it's about time they got to work. Been here two days already, and don't see any new walls.' Heh heh!"

So our isolation was only a dream. On the level of physical fact, we knew that we were now always on center stage, and our frenzied activities on the Point had become an integral part of village life.

Compared to the enormous battle of Great Hall, this two-bedroom addition seemed like the sheerest fun. Over the winter we had all worked on plans: one room was to face the sea, one to face more toward the forest. There would be ample closet room for each girl as we had promised, and over the two rooms we would make a loft which could be closed mouse-and-squirrel tight by lining it with galvanized iron mesh. There would be more big windows resting on log walls, a door giving on the porch-to-be, a connecting door between the rooms and finally two separate doors for access to Great Hall, one for each girl. We had a familiar work gang, and we had developed a method.

No sooner had the first batch of lumber been unloaded than we were off with a whoop and a holler. The girls, by now quite decent rough carpenters, were in the thick of it. It amused me to see Rachel, who used to be so slambang as a child, now slapping up a nail with a series of accurate hammer blows and never missing a beat, all the while carrying on a kidding conversation with one of the boys. Erica, somewhat more of a perfectionist, was an excellent fitter and finisher. And Jonathan, to my intense pleasure, was not only a very fair young builder for his age, but was developing a curious flair as a kind of Yankee tinkerer, an ingenious solver of space and weight problems, often suggesting unusual and practical shortcuts that no one else had thought of. I came by degrees to rely on this quality of judgment and objectivity which I could sense beginning to develop in him.

Along with the girls' rooms, we now added a kind of porch floor or walkway about eight feet wide, running down the whole length of Great Hall and around the corner past Rachel's room, the one facing the sea. As it turned the corner, we narrowed it to three feet. It had an apron in front which came down to about a foot from the ground, making it possible to see the supports — peeled sections of tree trunks resting on pillow stones.

"Okay, okay — but no *railings*," said the girls. "Can you imagine how suburban we'd look! Ugh!"

"But, kids, I had in mind something like the railings I used to see in Japan — not like a picket fence — more like an abstract pattern."

"Never! On this we're adamant! You can have your damn walkway! In fact, we can see some sense to it — but absolutely *no railings!*"

"But a porch without railings is naked," I gulped.

"Then don't call it a porch. Call it a platform," said Rachel. "Come on, let's go fishing."

"Tell you what, Ricky," said I, "I'll just make a mock-up of odd bits of lumber to show you the idea."

"I know your mock-ups," cries Erica. "They have a way of growing into the Eiffel Tower when a person's back is turned. But okay, if you have to get it out of your system, go ahead. Only remember, *strictly temporary!* Just to prove how crazy it is!"

"Agreed!"

The girls leave.

Now, whipping out my design and buzzing like a bee, I slam into the mock-up. Oddly enough, there were not enough old pieces: I would have to use good lumber! At any rate, I wanted something substantial to do justice to my idea — which was a slightly over-scaled, rugged retaining wall or fence done in six-by-sixes for uprights and two-by-fours for the rest. Carried away by conviction and enthusiasm, and now sawing and nailing like a wild man, I built a most substantial mock-up along the entire length of Great Hall, leaving a nine-foot gap in the middle for a broad set of stairs which I felt should lead down to the level of the clearing. Just as I was putting the finishing touches to the work, the girls returned.

"My God, the Bald Eagle has done it again! The whole thing!"

"No!"

"Yes he has, all of it!"

"It's terrible!"

"It is not! Why don't you just look at it. You'll get used to the idea."

"Well, I think it's not so bad. Really rather nice, in a horrible way! Why didn't you tell us it would look like this?"

"I tried to, but there was this Greek chorus in the way, if you'll remember."

"But — what's that gap? Stairs? Oh no — not stairs!"

"But you've got to have stairs to get down to the ground."

"Who wants to get down to the ground?"

"I do, for one. You can sit on the stairs, too, and drink your morning coffee."

"Well," said practical Fred, "it isn't so bad after all. Actually, it's rather nice. Let's give it a few days to kind of mellow. And I think the idea of stairs isn't bad, either."

The next day our friends, the Paul Nitzes, arrived for lunch. "Marvelous! What a great idea! Look at this long gallery! What do you call it? A porch? Really beautiful. But where are the stairs?"

"Paul, if you'll help me after lunch, we can make some stairs, just to see what it looks like."

"Okay, then — let's *all* make stairs."

So, a lovely set of stairs was built that very afternoon, descending in a long sweep to the turf. Perfect for lolling. Ideal for drinks and conversation — and the porch, the railings, and the stairs are there still, painted now a soft celadon gray-green. The narrower part of the flooring that goes around the corner and past Rachel's room remains a walkway, without rails, ending with two big stones for steps off the end, now ten years later embowered in wild roses and ferns.

About this time we decided to give Jon sailing lessons. He was mad for boats — all kinds of boats — and could be found nearly every day, when the opportunity presented itself, out on the water, as likely as not with a homemade mast and sail on the skiff. But on this wild coast with rough waves and fast currents, he needed more instruction than we could give him if he was to cope successfully with the real dangers inherent in the situation.

We took him to Jim Willis's dock and boatyard in Southwest Harbor, where he began taking formal instruction in handling the "Bullseye," a fifteen-foot craft of fiberglass, light as a feather and marvelously responsive. This was a most happy thought, as Jon proved to have a natural skill that needed only regular instruction to give it a solid base. And Willis, a sophisticated and delightful man who built and sold small boats and rented power boats to visitors to the island, had provided careful and considerate teachers. To make the taxiing problem easier, we combined forces with the Bob Riches (he of the boat-building family), one of whose two boys was just Jon's age. From that time on, for the next several years, the boys went over to Willis's together for instruction, taken and returned in turn by the Riches and the Childs. Thus, in the most natural way possible, Jon grew up as so many of the boys of the region do, handling small boats and, later on, power boats, till his skills became second nature. Now, seeing him zoom past the Point before a following wind, or tacking about here and there, we no longer felt that sensation in the pit of the stomach which most parents know when they feel warned of imminent disaster to their young.

From time to time we turned to the manufacture of doors for Great Hall, a delightful occupation which could be carried on inside on rainy days. The doors were made using a hollow core type of construction — a grid or "honeycomb" of two-inch-high strips laid on edge, fashioned so as to produce a mass of interior cross bracing. Fronts and backs were nailed to this interior grid. They were made of six- and eight-inch boards laid in strips, crossed diagonals and free-form patterns of squares and oblongs somewhat like the stones in a terrace. The floor of Old Cabin was painted a brilliant lacquer red about this time as a background for a handsome Chinese blue and gray wool rug that had come from Fred's mother.

It was beginning to be apparent to us that we might successfully combine elements from any part of the world together with the somewhat cruder things of our own manufacture, such as lamps, tables, beds and desks, if they were distinguished by vigor of design. Over-refined things looked out of place. No crystal ware, no porcelains, no silver, merely objects of basic simplicity and good materials. Bit by bit we added things: Japanese stoneware vases, a couple of simple Moroccan platters, wooden cooking spoons from Sweden, and some of my own fabrics, whose designs had been derived from regional elements, shells, moth wings, blowing leaves, waves. They all seemed to fit and to live happily together. Two little Italian peasant carvings from the hill region north of Venice came to occupy a space on one of the fireplace set-backs. We named them Mr. Lare and Mr. Penate. A copper water jug from Udaipur held branches and flowers at the broader end of the set-back. A great branch of driftwood which hauntingly reminded us of the antlers of a deer found an appropriate place fastened to the end wall, high over the girls' doors. Bit by bit the room was turning from an enormous wooden box into a warm inviting space for living.

Up the hill near the water tank we had thought there might be a good place for a vegetable garden. An experimental hillside plot with an area about thirty by forty feet had been plowed out for us by our friend, George Richardson, who, being Road Commissioner at the time, had tractors, plows and scrapers at his command. Early that summer we had had George put in a whole list of seeds for experimental purposes: radishes, beets, carrots, corn, lettuce, zucchini, tomatoes, cucumbers. The newly turned soil looked good enough to eat and we waited with watering mouths for the expected results. But as the weeks went by, to our dismay we found that this beautiful soil might just as well have been taken from the mid-Sahara. Spindling, piddling rows of half-vegetables, lackluster tomato vines, here and there a miserable lettuce leaf, were all our reward. We knew that the soil was acid and consequently had used some lime, but the truth seemed to be that in its present naked state, it just couldn't hold sufficient water. Fred figured for that summer with radishes almost the only thing that came up, each one had cost us in the neighborhood of $2.95. We resolved to add an immense quantity of lime to help hold the water and to further humectify the soil by adding to the mix about six cubic yards of hen manure, a product which is both abundant and cheap in that part of Maine. All of this, when it was turned over and stirred together by plow and harrow, we hoped would provide us with a stable base for growing things next season.

By digging into the hill and dumping dirt onto the lower side, we began now to widen our rather sketchy turnaround to provide more parking space. In the middle of this widened circle we planted wild roses, day lilies, veronica, and lupines, together with a European mountain ash for its brilliant red berries and a husky young Austrian pine to provide one dominant accent.

Emboldened by our great manure and lime program, we decided to put in a small flower garden right next to the new wing, where the girls' rooms set back about sixteen feet from the end of the long front of Great Hall. We were sure that we could conquer the curious problem of disappearing water as we had maintained both vegetable and flower gardens at Coppernose for years. Two long flower gardens and two vegetable gardens had been our standbys there for more than a decade, though we had to admit that this Maine problem was something new.

But now for the flower garden. After ripping out the sod over a square about sixteen by sixteen feet, we found that the soil at this particular spot was impossible to work without taking out an enormous quantity of stones. Such stones! We removed — hold your breath — one hundred

twenty wheelbarrow loads from this one little plot, and
having dug everything out down to the clay and gravel
hardpan below, we put back the soil that was left after the
stones had been removed and added one hundred wheelbarrow loads of earth from the hillside, every shovelful of
which had to be sifted through a one-inch screen. I could
just see those crunching, groaning glaciers which had done
so much to shape the coast of Maine, waiting till they came
past our Point to spew out this load of stones and gravel
just where we had planned to put the garden. Hardly a
single sharp-edged piece in the lot: all had been ground,
sanded, even polished to a satin finish. But of course the
elimination of stones and the addition of soil wasn't enough.
We now were fairly sure that this earth, if it was to hold
water once the sod cover had been removed, needed the
addition of lime and animal manure, so we added ten
barrow loads of lime and ten loads of hen manure, and
after hours of stirring and watering we began to plant a
mixture of perennial plants from a local greenhouse:
peonies, tansy, columbine, roses, thyme, delphinium, mint,
several kinds of lilies, phlox, eringium, astilbe, and tarragon, in order to see what would take. Now, having cast
our bread upon the waters, we would have to wait until
the following season to see whether it would come back
to us in the form of a half-loaf, or sevenfold, or perhaps
never come back at all.

In joining battle with the land, we had decided during
the previous season to plant a few apple trees. The local
apple trees — wind- and bird-planted here and there in the
vicinity — as well as man-planted trees — all seemed to be
singularly free from disease. We had written the local
county agricultural agent and gotten a list of varieties
which were suited to the climate of that part of coastal

Maine. And now seven little trees were set out on the high ground back of the cabin among the stumps of spruce and fir: Jonathans, Williams Early Red, and Golden Delicious. We carefully surrounded each tree with a kind of wigwam of poles covered with chicken wire in order to baffle the local deer. Since the whole island was off limits to deer hunters, these lovely creatures were abundant and tame, roaming freely over our land during winter and spring. And another thing: we could see that our problem was going to be not only the shallow soil and hungry wild creatures but perhaps most of all the shaking winds which often came swinging down with a force that rattled the very ribs of the land. But we were hopeful. If Johnny Appleseed could do it, we could do it.

But this wind thing was a constant problem. With a sense almost of impending doom, we saw that many of the oldest trees at the edges of our forest clearings were being blown down or beginning to lean crazily against their neighbors. The process was clearly irreversible, though in the long run these changes worked both ways. New trees were springing up everywhere as the ancients crashed or were snapped off by winter gales. The prospect of a lifetime of forest management loomed ahead. Was the old man, now gone to meet his fathers, smiling at our predicament from the safety of his cloud?

Seth had moved away. But George Richardson, our friend of the tractors, lived nearby. He had a real love of the Point and a deep appreciation of its beauty. And he was an excellent gardener, we found. We concluded an arrangement with him whereby he would plow our vegetable garden each spring and put in the seeds which we sent. In addition, he agreed to help in closing the cabins at the end of the summer — pulling up the boats, putting on winter shutters, draining the pipes, et cetera. "Tell you what, Challes," he said, "I do this for a number of folks and it would be a real pleasure to come down here to the Point and do it for you. I often come here anyway, when you folks are gone — sometimes I row my boat. Sometimes I jest walk around. It smells so good it makes a man feel twenty years younger. There's one thing, though, right out there on the end of your Point is the prettiest place of all. If I was you, I'd put up a nice flagpole there — dress the place up — maybe have a nice seat with an umbrella . . . and by the way, a little gravel here and there on that old corduroy of yours would help."

Well, why not gravel? Even though most of the half-mile road was not on our property, we should have seen the practical sense of this suggestion long before, and for once the financial situation was a bit easier. Accordingly we made an arrangement whereby the following spring enough gravel would be put down on the low spots to give us a reasonably solid passageway to the outer end of the Point.

Two new rooms, and two new gardens! A fine summer's work! The finished rooms for the girls were delightful, one looking out directly upon the little flower garden, for the moment in its autumn decline, and the other onto a bank of wild grasses where we had begun to scatter the seeds of lupine and columbine. Erica started a "stained glass" plaque to hang in her window: bits of colored glass found among the stones on the beach, most of it ground to smooth shapes by constant rolling, and possessed of an odd translucent beauty. She arranged these bits and pieces in a free design, and held them together with chewing gum for want of a better substance. Rachel wanted a desk, and we forthwith set about building one from some fine pieces of white pine we had left over from making a table.

One last feast that summer was especially good. A number of friends who had been sailing together up the coast came into Bass Harbor and descended on us unexpectedly. "It's marvelous, damn it all!" said Rachel. "Here we are letting all the food run out in the last few days, and these characters have to come by. What are we going to do — collect mushrooms?"

"It isn't that bad," said ever-resourceful Fred. "I'll scrounge around: we have some salad makings and a little bit of this and a little bit of that."

I knew that some of her most satisfying inventions in the food line were apt to come at times like this. Here were six frolicsome and hungry people at the door. Luckily they had brought some salad from the boat, and we added this to ours. Fred found that we had some leftover lobster and a bit of chicken. Here's a dish she concocted by combining the two. Rachel called it "Licken Chobster." Its particular virtue is that it is a dish upon which a number of variations can be played, according to whether you have more lobster or more chicken.

LICKEN CHOBSTER

Here we go: Take the chicken parts and put them into a baking dish. Now make a sauce with the lobster bits, using white wine, dried or fresh mushrooms, tarragon, shallots or mild white onions chopped fine, and parsley. Simmer the sauce for 15 minutes and, if desired, thicken with a roux (butter and flour). Pour the sauce over the chicken, grate cheddar cheese on top, sprinkle with more parsley and a dash of paprika and bake in a 450 degree oven for about 10 minutes, or until the whole thing is thoroughly heated.

Speaking of lobster reminds me of crabmeat dishes. The local lobstermen find many a crab in their traps feasting on the lobster bait. Nowadays, instead of being thrown back into the water they are often saved and taken to a local fish factory where they are steamed, opened, and picked clean, ready for freezing or canning. Combined with homemade mayonnaise, garnished with chopped hardboiled eggs and the addition of a bit of curry powder they are wonderful served with a bit of green salad. Various sauces based on crabmeat make delicious pilaffs. The ones we like best usually manage to combine the crabmeat with onions — "always onions," says Fred.

CRAB PILAFF

Fry onions in a skillet with a bit of bacon fat and a crushed clove of garlic, together with a couple of ripe tomatoes or tomato puree. Now the crabmeat goes in. You can always add to this basic combination eggs to make a kind of stiff omelette, or a bit of leftover ham chopped fine. In Caribbean countries they pour dark rum over the mix. We often add a cup of white wine, and some finely chopped basil, which goes so beautifully with tomatoes, and let the whole thing simmer for about fifteen minutes. Calorie counters should not add heavy cream, but for a party a generous dollop or two won't hurt. This is served with a large mound of rice steamed till it is fluffy. At Old Point we often add lightly cooked garden peas, which add a bright note of color.

On that happy note the summer came to an end, and we said goodbye for another year. Departing, we felt quite smug, enormously healthy, and almost ready to go on building forever. What would our new gardens be like when we came back? And now that the girls had plenty of space, should we not think about making a room for Jonathan? Would the loft over the girls' rooms keep out the red squirrels? The answers to these questions would have to wait.

As we came in the following year we experienced a sensation of utmost luxury. The road really had been transformed. The corduroy, a temporary arrangement at best, had been wearing out, and now rolling smoothly over the partly graveled surface, we let out a whoop of sheer joy. Here and there a few exposed ends of the old corduroy still jumped feebly as we passed, but slithering mud and splashing pools were done with.

That summer it may have been sheer momentum, but we decided it was time to think of doing something about Jonathan's living quarters. The porch at the ocean end of Old Cabin was the obvious place to begin: always cool, and often cold, we had used it less and less after the completion of Great Hall. Walled in, it would make a fine boy's room. Accordingly we began by taking up the grayed and weathered boards of the porch floor and using them, turned upside down to expose the weathered surfaces, to double the ceiling. This gave it a lovely soft silvery sheen. We built a new floor and walled up the spaces between the log pillars, leaving places for three windows and a door. A big double closet for clothes and two beds completed the arrangements. With this change of function from porch to bedroom, Jonathan, as well as his sisters, had his own quarters in the very prow of the cabin, buffeted by shaking winds and facing the sea. It was a splendid room for a boy. At last Jon had a place where he could have his own books and a constantly increasing pile of tools, electric wires, radio parts, switches, boat models, and beach stones, and his own door, so he could shoot in and out without bothering anyone.

And now the flower garden at the end of Great Hall had decided to cooperate! It was alive with color. The lime and manure had worked better than we could have hoped.

"Hey, Fred! Look at that crazy columbine! I'll bet it has over a hundred blooms!" Almost unbelievable, it was a truly majestic plant, nearly three feet high, covered with an amazing mass of pink blossoms. This was a phenomenon completely outside our experience.

"Nonsense, Cha! Who ever heard of a columbine with a hundred blooms?"

"Maybe nobody, but just the same a quarter says there are a hundred blooms."

"Done, but you count them. I never earned an easier quarter in my life."

As I began the countdown, and skimmed by the hundred mark, I realized that this was indeed a phenomenal plant. There were, incredibly enough, three hundred and forty-two blooms all told.

"And what in the name of a name is *that?* Gosh!" It was the tarragon, now a great bush of fantastic green, big as an easy chair. And here were enormous white peonies, heavy-headed with morning dew. Everywhere a yield of beauty such as we had never imagined. Our enriched soil was magical, incredible. A dart of color — a flash of pure emerald — "Fred! Fred! Girls! Jon! A humming bird!" From that time on, our garden has been blessed by these fairy creatures. I wonder still how they ever found it.

Up on the hill the vegetable garden was a blaze of greens. Here too, the magic of lime and manure added to the virgin soil had worked wonders. Everything was coming up. But this time, everything! Yellow-greens, blue-greens, silver-greens, the rows sparkled in the sun. In the long days of early summer, with sunlight from four A.M. to ten P.M., one could almost see, almost hear, the plants grow. They unfolded, they struggled, they leaped into being, with the whole solar system pushing from behind. I wondered if

we would have to give them some top shade as they do in Greenland gardens, so they wouldn't go to seed before their time.

Often after dark one could look up and see the aurora borealis pulsing in the night. At such moments I was reminded of the icy breath of this northern world. Yet by the light of day the sun, with more than Mediterranean splendor, had flung out his bounty everywhere and had turned this land into a perfect Eden, alive with leaping green, with singing birds, with madly colored blooms. Everything hummed, everything sparkled, everything sang for joy.

Homesick letters from Paul and Julia, now stationed in France. "Tell us everything! What are you doing? What building? What new things has Fred invented? How are the gardens? Send us some photos of Great Hall. And what about that open space by the porch? Have you made it into a lawn yet?"

Following the precedent of a porch-turned-into-a-room, we decided to close in the cloistered or pillared side of the woodshed. Rain and wind were always a problem and rolling our tarpaulin curtains up and down was a nuisance. Another thing: rather to our surprise, we were learning by degrees that the side of the cabins and shed facing south and east to the summer sun was beginning to take a beating. The extreme difference in temperature between day and night and the howling winds driven in from the sea were cracking the logs. The cracks were filling with seeds and spores and soil which here and there had actually begun to produce miniature plants. And there was a curious orange fungus which, in dry weather, was as hard as rock, but which during periods of rain suddenly turned to a soft, hideous sponge. Now we could see that it was proliferating along the cracks, holding the moisture and rotting the wood as it went. The northern and western faces of the cabins which I had expected to see degenerate under the batterings of winter storms were as hard as steel.

But what to do about these southeastern faces? Cutting out all the rot, we poured Cuprinol, an anti-rot chemical, into the cracks. This stopped the rot for the time being, but we foresaw disaster ahead unless we undertook more heroic measures. Experimenting with various paint and chemical mixtures, I finally developed a combination of paint, aluminum dust, varnish and Cuprinol which looked exactly like weathered wood. This mixture I used to paint the entire surface of the cabins; and for decorative effect I covered the butt ends of the logs and the sides of the bottom two logs all the way round with a combination of creosote and black enamel. This, for the moment at least, stabilized the situation, but left me wondering whether the implacable weather would not bring the cabin to its knees in the end.

In the meantime, there were stumps to grub out, holes to fill and turf over, fallen trees to clear, and, from time to time, the inevitable onsets of unexpected guests. I recall one peaceful day when Jonathan was busy wiring up radio parts, Freddie and the girls were upended in the garden, their blue-jeaned forms rather like Grecian amphorae looming up in a row of charming silhouettes on the hill, and I was putting the finishing touches on a new bookcase, happy in my shavings and sawdust. Suddenly, from the ocean side came the unmistakable sound of a fog horn. What?! On a sunny day? And a banging of dish pans: of course — that would be a signal we had arranged with our friend, Dick B. Running to the shore, we could see his beautiful boat, a sixty-foot yawl named *Sea Witch,* just passing the Point, with four . . . five . . . *nine* people board! "Halooo! Can—we—have—dinner—with—you?"

"Yes! We — will — meet — you — in — half — an — hour — at — the — Southwest — Harbor — dock! Drop everything, chaps! Erica, you get some lobsters! Rachel, you set the table and do a salad! Jonny, go down to the rocks and get a bucket of mussels! We know what this means — get out extra towels and soap — they'll all want baths!"

And here they come. And here comes Erica. No lobsters! All sold out. Damnation! Well, by chance we do have a five-pound salmon, which has been poached in a court bouillon of stock, white wine, and herbs, then chilled. Fred recalls an old Catalan receipt for a kind of super-rich mayonnaise — just the thing! You rub a whole handful of garlic cloves into a wooden bowl till it reeks. Then, in the bowl, mix olive oil into egg yolks till it forms a stiff paste. Gar-

nish the salmon with herbs and this super-mayonnaise, adding coarsely ground salt just before serving. The salmon
and the mussels, together with a clear soup, a salad, and
fruit and cheese brought by our guests, the whole washed
down with a good California rosé, was a meal to remember.
Steaming pink faces from the bath, music from the Vic,
joyous conversation and laughter — a room full of happy
people, some sitting on the floor singing familiar songs, a
couple of small groups in the corners earnestly discussing
politics, three in the kitchen washing dishes — this was a
lovely sight. Great Hall had become alive and golden,
fulfilling its natural destiny. A huge fire of fragrant logs
throws dancing shadows on the walls. And now Figaro,
filled with tidbits, sinks to the floor, his nose toward the
fire. Then, at last, fond farewells, a lingering departure.

One day Erica and Rachel were busy making blue denim
covers for the beds. Jon and I were working out the design
for a desk for his room, and just for fun making a secret
recess in the wall, fronted by a sliding panel, in which we
could keep money and other valuables while we were away
on all-day trips. Fred was taking a walk up along the
western beach toward a part of the Point which we called
"Twisty-Turvy Land." Here some wrathful ice storm had
once twisted a whole grove of young trees into fantastic
shapes at a point where the steep rocky bank sloped down
to the sea thirty feet below. "Hey, chaps," said Fred, suddenly appearing. "Come with me. I think I've found
something."

"What? What?"

"You'll see. Come on."

We raced along the shore, hopping from rock to rock,
as the water was just about at low tide level. During such
times it was far easier to go this way than through the forest.

Just at the foot of the slope, Fred brought us to a halt, put up her hand and said, "Now, everybody listen." We could all hear it clearly: a steady gurgle of water. A spring! There it was, coming out from a fissure in the granite rocks. But, alas, *below* high tide. A lovely sparkling spring that for ten years has never ceased to run and sing, but, for more than half the time, is covered by six feet of salt water.

We went on improving things inside, but on the whole, that summer was the summer of the gardens. What a yield! Gleaming orange carrots, enormous beets, six kinds of lettuce, zucchini, cucumbers, summer squash, corn — only the tomatoes failed us. About halfway through the summer, cold nights stopped them in their tracks. But we actually had so much lettuce that Fred began to sell it in one of the local stores. This unexpectedly bright success gave birth to a new idea: why not have just one more garden, this time a kind of factory for flowers, raspberries, and strawberries, now that we had licked the soil problem. So, once more to the drawing board and the graph paper. We laid out another garden on the shoulder of the hill nearby, at the place where there were no rock ledges. It was to be about twenty-five feet by forty feet, fenced around with cedar posts for a wall of raspberry bushes. We planned to fill it with rows of annuals and perennials for cutting — everything from nasturtiums to lupine, from mint to African daisies. "Come on, you hummingbirds!" said Jonathan.

That summer another boat entered our lives. The old skiff was by now pretty well battered and scraped along its bottom. The skeg was worn down almost to nothing, and the lap-straked sides were roughed and gouged by endless draggings across the rocks. From time to time we had had misgivings about allowing the youngsters to use it. But one day it happened that we found for sale an excellent fiberglass boat, about eleven feet long, which had been used as an auxiliary craft for a larger boat. It was still in good condition and had a heavy stern designed to take an outboard motor. This would be great fun to use in conjunction with the sailing dinghy. George Richardson needed an extra skiff for his family, and upon learning that he would be delighted to have the old boat and put it in good condition, we gave it to him and bought the new boat together with a five horsepower outboard motor. Now we had a fine balanced fleet of two fiberglass boats, one with a sail and one with a motor. If the smaller boat got becalmed or there was an incoming fog, we could race out in the larger one and tow her in. And the motor greatly extended our range, allowing us to do things we had never done before, like scooting around the Point to the nearby harbor for lobsters. It also gave Jon the opportunity of racing with his pals in and out and up and down among the boats moored there. It was frightening, of course, to see him take off with a whoosh, his bright orange life-preserver gleaming in the sun, until the boat and Jon, now no more than a colored speck, disappeared in the direction of the old lighthouse at Bass Harbor Head, or toward one of the outlying islands, but Jon was fearless and skillful. And though we worried, we had come to trust him.

Using the outboard, Fred and I began a minute exploration of the nearby coastal region. The inlets and rocky islands, the little coves, the hidden harbors, were now all open to us. Ship Harbor, for instance, whose secret entrance is a strip of almost dry land at low tide: here the good ship *Grand Design* was wrecked centuries ago. And so many other places with alluring names: Seal Cove, Duck Cove, Prettymarsh. And there were days when from a position far out at sea we could lay to and watch the cumulus cloud castles pile up over the peaks of Mt. Desert. Nearer home we discovered deserted beaches and rock ledges from which we often came back laden with driftwood treasure.

From time to time that summer, we thought with longing of the low-tide spring at Twisty-Turvy Land. It yielded ten times as much water as our regular spring. There were periods during dry spells when even an overnight wait was not enough to half fill our spring house box. Hardly a weekend now that we didn't have guests, and the gardens had a constant need for water which we often had to ignore. Sometimes for a week at a time we found that we could pump no more than half an hour in every twenty-four. The spring never stopped flowing, but oh, so slowly! At times like this, we became experts at washing dishes with a minimum of water, taking the briefest of showers, watering gardens if at all only after dusk, but even so, our carefully kept daily record of water in the tower and water in the spring gave us clear concern for the future.

Now that the major work of building was over, there was more time for other things. Picking blueberries and raspberries was fun, and getting off the Point and exploring the interior of the island itself began to be a part of the rhythm of our summer days. There were many lovely mountain walks. Leaving the car at any one of a hundred points, one can use the mountain trails maintained by the National Park Service. These trails wind through the forested slopes of Mt. Desert, usually emerging at some grand escarpment or boulder-strewn hilltop overlooking a vast island-studded ocean view. There are caves in the sea cliffs, mountain lakes and ponds, immense ravines, dense slopes, miles of them. The Lippmanns were great lovers of these mountain walks. One walk in particular which we took together stays in my mind. Starting rather tamely hard by a local inn at Northeast Harbor, we walked through groves of hardwoods, rising by degrees toward forests of spruce and fir. The trail would go up, then suddenly dip down to a rushing mountain brook — then up again to emerge momentarily on the edge of a cliff with a breathtaking view — then into the forest once more, but always trending up and up till the forest itself gave way here and there to long open slopes of shattered granite with a few stunted trees where a cold wind always seemed to blow.

One may think of Walter Lippmann as a venerable columnist and sage, which indeed he is, but anyone who essays a walk with him realizes soon that he is following a man with mountaineer's legs. He has a slow but fearfully steady pace, sparked by delightful conversation. During this particular walk, we came to rest high on the shoulder of Sargent Mountain, where we debouched from a darkly shadowed evergreen forest whose trees stand among giant granite rocks, into a dazzle of light. Here suddenly one finds oneself standing at the verge of a beautiful little pond of clear spring water, across the surface of which dart great blue dragonflies.

During this summer we were invited to go out to Little Duck Island with Lawrence Newman. Newman, as much scientist as fisherman, used to work in the laboratories of a large telephone company. Upon retirement, being a Maine man, he decided to settle in Southwest Harbor, where he took up fishing, first as a hobby, then as a profession. Thanks to a combination of a rugged constitution and a great zest for life, he now found himself putting in, even in the foulest weather, the kind of day and the kind of hours that one could hardly imagine anyone fresh from

years in a laboratory even contemplating. A friend of ours who went out fishing with him and his son reports that having gotten up at two A.M. and having gone twenty miles out to sea and then having between them caught fifteen hundred pounds of cod and hake, all on *hand* lines, he staggered off the boat at the end of the trip, only to find that Newman and son, far from being finished, were starting in to clean the fish! Lawrence Newman is typical of a modern breed of fishermen who work the Maine coastal waters. They now employ all the latest scientific devices, such as fathometers and two-way radios, by means of which they can locate schools of fish and keep in touch with other boats and the home port.

Little Duck lies some miles off the southern shore of Mt. Desert Island and was given to the Audubon Society as a bird refuge. It has a remarkable atmosphere of the most absolute primitive wilderness: chest-high grasses, giant

nettles, wind-blown trees clumped impenetrably together against the gales, here and there a loner, managing to lift its head ten or fifteen feet above the tangle, and enormous tidal pools in free-form shapes, holding little worlds of marine life in their incandescent cups. Some of these curious rounded holes seem to have the property of lenses, whose parabolic shapes catch the light till they shine with a mysterious inner brilliance. And there are the birds, countless sea birds, wheeling, screaming, dipping, and, in the spring season, nesting in the thousands of rock crannies down by the shore. The noise of these birds as they wheel in sky-darkening masses is often deafening and can keep up for hours.

We came ashore through schools of seals, tame and curious even to the silver-furred babies, and made a fire on the rocks where we steamed a mess of lobsters and cooked one of Newman's favorite outdoor dishes — a large hake or cod, split open, laid on a grill over the fire and laced with strips of salt pork. Baby gulls with downy gray feathers staggered about or lay quietly, staring at us from hollows in the rocks. From Little Duck, one looks back at the bald peaks of Mt. Desert, looming up over the sea as they must have to the Sieur de Cadillac centuries ago and as they did to me as a youth, far away, romantic and compelling.

This was the summer when Rachel decided that her birthday, which happened in mid-September, was an invention of the Gods designed to make life more miserable for her, coming as it did just at the time when she had to return to college. But she wasn't going to take this one lying down. No! Never! It was just too unfair. So why not make it come at some other time? She therefore proposed that, like England's Queen, she could and would henceforth declare a birthday at a propitious time of her own choosing.

From that time on, Rachel's birthday would come exactly at the moment — usually in mid-summer — when the place was full of guests. "The So-and-so's are coming for the weekend? And we're going to have the X's and the Y's for Sunday lunch? Wow! That's a good time to declare my birthday! And I want salmon, edible-pod peas, and ice cream with meringue!" It was a fine invention, and since that time Rachel's flexible birthday has become a family institution.

This was the summer, too, when Jonathan, whose scientific interests were expanding in all directions, undertook to wire the whole place with loud speakers, placed at strategic intervals so that by an ingenious switching device, we could have music anywhere, from the kitchen to Old Cabin. Music everywhere, light where you want it, water with a turn of the wrist — yet sometimes the whole thing gave one pause. We had come to this forest in search of simplicity, and we had found it. A drink of cool water from the spring lying in one's cupped hands would symbolize it, but then the spring was enlarged to a great thousand gallon box. Next, there was the water tank on the hill, now filled from the spring by an electric pump, and the same water came today from a tap in the kitchen. Good? Yes — undoubtedly good — but somehow perhaps removed by something fine as gossamer from the perfection of the original experience. From tents to cabin to Great Hall, one could mark the same progression. From open fires on the beach to a gas stove, from an outdoor cooler to a refrigerator, from kerosene lamps to electric lights, from rocks to toilets, from corduroy to gravel, from forest to gardens, and from comparative isolation to a Niagara of friends. What gain? What loss? With all the overlay of these sophisticated elements, it still seemed to me that we had created an environment which, if no longer primitive, was certainly not decadent. It was direct, vigorous, simple, a place which sustained health and which had brought us, in our fifteen summers of struggle, a sense of family solidarity, and of enormous respect for nature, and many new friends.

Thinking back to my Washington days, I realized that the challenge of Government service to me had been of a kind to which one's best responses could only be routine. Brilliance and creative invention were certainly not wanted. On the contrary, the best one could do in that particular context was a careful, conscientious job of administration. This Maine challenge had brought the spectre of disaster on the one hand and the growth of certain skills on the other: extreme adaptability to sudden change, inventiveness under stress, physical prowess, a kind of grim determination never to be defeated by one's own ignorance, and above all self-reliance, inner-directedness.

Who could say that some of these more individualistic virtues had not been here and there built into the structure of our children's characters by this experience? Maybe we could snap on a dozen lights and take a shower to the sound of music, but such civilized rituals can be strengthening as well as weakening. The real point was that in one second one could face an emergency with the courage born of tough experience, and on the other hand could also command the possibility of being able to walk barefoot through a wild forest, whose intricate mossy floor and silken grasses made all man-crafted carpets seem rags by comparison. We had perhaps succeeded to a considerable extent in protecting ourselves from the worst rigors of nature here. My hope was that in the process we had not separated ourselves as yet from any of its life-giving strength and vital force. I felt that we had long since, for better or for worse, launched ourselves as a family upon a course and a way of living to which we were happily committed, whose ultimate end of meaning we might never be able fully to see. Yet as far as the immediate present was concerned, I loved every minute of it and day by day plunged along, hoping to create from a gorgeous chaos an even more gorgeous order.

11

The Fall of the Forest

I WONDERED sometimes if we were getting old. Non-sense! We were a few years older, true, but that little catch in the knees hadn't caught up with us yet. There were moments this summer, now that the riot and rout of building Great Hall and the girls' rooms was past, when it seemed as if our paradise, not content with yielding us its spiritual treasure, had begun to expose a more earthly side in a way that made us its prisoners. There was so much to do just to hold it all together. The ardor and joy of construction had given way bit by bit to a certain pedestrian need for replacement and repair — "barnacle scraping," my kids called it. The floor of Jon's room had a mysterious sag in one corner. There was a leak in an area of the roof, which dripped precisely down onto the bookcases, and no amount of detective work seemed to be able to disclose its origin. I recalled a conversation I had had with an old builder wise in the ways of construction. "Well, Challes," he said, "I know a lady had a leak like yours. Seems there wasn't anybody could find it. She tried three different men, and after each one had had a go at it down come the drops and smuck her best rug clean amidships, same as before. Finally, she got hold of a big contractor from up Bangor way and he come down and looked the whole thing over from stem to stern. Then he turned to her and said, 'Missus, the way I sees it, some roofs is just like that,' and he took and clumb down the ladder and went back up to Bangor."

True, we could sit on the porch after a delicious feast of lamb chops, garden peas, new potatoes and raspberries as big as *that* and listen to the hiss of swallows' wings as they raced over the roof and swooped low above the grass. But there were always those windows to putty up, the water tower to paint, and that hinge which had come loose on the front screen door. There were stumps to get out; the deer had gotten through the wire baffles around the apple trees; the wild rose fence we had planted around the flower garden was sending six-foot shoots into the middle of the annual clumps; two boards on the porch needed immediate replacement, and there were those fifteen fir and spruce Fred was anxious to have transplanted as windbreaks for the vegetable garden.

And it was a dry summer. Deadly dry. This was perhaps the crux of the matter. The Fire Danger signs were up in the National Park areas, and everything as far as one could see was crackling and shriveling. The summer grasses had actually turned to a faded yellow, the water in the spring was as low as we had ever seen it, and the logs on the south and east faces of Old Cabin were showing a whole series of new fissures. It was not just that the goldenrod was bursting into premature bloom everywhere. That was a bad sign. But there were those once-in-a-while thunderstorms which had wandered near, their trailing edges maddeningly dropping a few feeble splashes on our parched land. You could almost taste the dryness between your teeth. Staring at that wet salt potential ocean off the Point, I used to mutter, "Why in the name of God wasn't I born two hundred years

hence." There were lots of systems for de-salting sea water
— distillation, freezing, vapor-compression, electro-dialysis,
flash-evaporation. But these were nothing but eeny-meeny-
miney-mo to me: far too expensive to be practical.

One could forget all this landlubberly preoccupation
in the joy of sailing. Dry on land: glorious at sea. A gay
group of friends called us up one morning. They had come
into Southwest Harbor during the night and for the moment were moored to Captain Bill's dock for the purpose
of taking on some supplies. How about going for a day's
sailing? Life at the Point is distinguished by these sudden
incursions and we had long since learned that if we wanted
to make the most of it we must be ready at any time to
drop everything and go. Grabbing up a number of sweaters and a pair of binoculars we headed for the dock. Coming down to the place where the boat lay we could see a
cluster of small craft crowding in rather closer than usual
to the vicinity of the dock. Something was going on that
appeared to be attracting boats from all over the harbor:
we could hear music of sorts — voices, and a curious click-
ety-click — could it be castanets?

Among this particular group of friends there were two
sisters, one the wife of a learned college professor, and the
other married to a top Government official. Both were possessed of an outrageous sense of humor, held in check most
of the time. But at the moment, bored with waiting for
the preparations to be concluded, they had dug out two
enormous hats from somewhere below, a couple of long silk
scarves, a pair of castanets, and an ocarina, and were putting on a fine rendition of selections from *Carmen*. When
memory lapsed, free invention leaped into the breach, producing weird combinations of sound. And when all else
failed, there were gestures. At the moment of our arrival

the waving of scarves and the clicking of castanets had reached a kind of peak, and several other members of the group, now caught up in the rhythm, had hastily improvised an orchestral support, consisting for the most part of wooden spoons and dishpans. By degrees more and more boats drew near till the whole area around the dock was solid with grinning spectators. A kind of dance began to emerge as scarves and skirts and hats gyrated to the tom-tom beat of the steel-band orchestra, now augmented by the rhythmic clapping of hands as the spectators joined in. Hundreds of gulls, disturbed by the sound, wheeled and screamed overhead, adding a note of frenzy. But all good things come to an end and suddenly it collapsed. Unless we climbed into the rigging or jumped into the water, there was nowhere else to go from there. Prolonged applause! Cheers from the clustered boats. Our two prima donnas retired with a last flourish of skirts, and the gulls, now plainly bored, settled back into stolid lines on the roof of Captain Bill's dock.

This episode rather set the mood for the day. In fact everyone was a bit intoxicated with the mere fact of being alive. We sailed here and there among the islands and up the narrow fjord of Somes Sound as far as Valley Cove, an inlet lying at the foot of St. Sauveur Mountain as it drops off dramatically into deep water. Here a gigantic cliff rears up — at a guess about seven hundred feet high — a fine place for echoes.

A swim off the boat, a quiet lunch among the rocks of the cove, and it was time to head homeward, for the wind had shifted and was now blowing directly up the sound. It was clear that in order to get out we would be forced to tack against it. Back and forth, back and forth, we stitched our way from one side of the sound to the other. This sudden shifting of the wind occurs quite frequently, and gives a good skipper the chance to exhibit his skill, as the waters are so deep for the most part that one can run the boat almost into the cliffs before the call "ready about" signals the exact moment for a swift maneuver. Sometimes this can be quite nerve-wracking if the skipper hesitates, or if the crew is not at the ready. Every few minutes there would be a crash of blocks and a swish of the boom as the great mainsail swung over, shaking briefly till it caught the wind, our craft at the last possible moment heeling over in response to the tiller before heading for the opposite bank. Sun and wind dropped together toward the end of the afternoon and we slid into the dock on the engine in a dead calm, faces and clothes rimed with salt and the sound of waves still echoing somewhere in the inner ear.

Back at the Point the next few days seemed to bring tensions to the breaking point. The spring was almost dry. Dishwashing was at an absolute minimum. And our lovely gardens were crumpling under the sun. Of course, there was that hurricane down in Florida. It was dumping fourteen inches of rain onto Tampa, but it was so far away it might have been on another planet. I was mad at it for being down there, mad at the ocean for being so near, mad at the cabin for cracking in the heat of the sun, mad at myself for not knowing how to build a better structure, and mad at my family for seeming to suggest, if only by their silences, that I *do* something.

A carpenter friend gave vent to the universal tension upon seeing a new boat which happened to be passing by. "God-a-mighty! Who built that? I jest want to know! Who vomited on the top-side and then drew a line around it? Well, I guess that'd be J.D. Looks like his work. He talks a lot, and he builds a right smart o' boats, but he can't think any clearer than a pig standin' in a bucket of swill."

"The hurricane won't come here. It's too far off. But you know what? The radio says it's begun to head up the coast, and small craft warnings are out as far north as Block Island."

The next morning, looking up toward the month-old blue of the sky, we could see that it was beginning for the first time in weeks to be laced with high flying cirrus clouds. We wondered. Suddenly we were aware that all the insects had disappeared and that the birds were silent. And the tension had, if anything, increased. Uneasy gusts of air began to come over the Point. "Are we really going to get it?"

"Challes, looks like we might be going to have a breeze," said Bobby Rich, the boat-builder, who had suddenly appeared at the front door. "I thought I'd just drop over and help you haul your boats back up into the woods."

The radio was turned on: "Hurricane warnings have now been posted from Block Island to Machiasport. Tides are expected to be eighteen feet above normal. Repeat — eighteen feet."

"Look to the lamps and candles. Get those cars close to the cabin, facing the wind. Damn it, do as I say — there's no time to argue! Get all those garden tools inside and while we're at it, maybe we better bring in two days' supply of firewood."

The wind increased. Huge gray cumulonimbus clouds streamed in overhead. There was a smattering of rain. My heart gave a little flutter. "You know what, Fred? It's a lot of work, but I think we'd better put on those winter shutters. Who wants a face full of flying glass? Hey, gang, let's go!" In a way we were all feeling better. The moving air was easier to breathe, and a certain sense of being at the beginning of a great drama buoyed us up. We knew now that the whole Atlantic seaboard was in this together. The shutters went up one by one, screwed fast with three-inch screws — and just in time. They were hard to hold against the rising wind. We brought Figaro in, dripping water. He was uneasy, apparently responding like an aeolian harp to the sounds outside. With each increase of wind he would look at us as if for reassurance. He paced about whining slightly, but finally after looking about almost as if he were in a strange room, he chose a spot under the table where he could touch our feet with his nose, and settled down to the long vigil with an audible sigh.

The forest began about 6 P.M. to cry out with a weird keening and moaning. It was growing darker and darker as the wind rose rapidly toward gale force. And now the rain began in earnest, the rain we had been praying for — but it was not given to us, it was *thrown* at us! Such a rain! Roaring and bulling through the trees, racing across the roof with the sound of a passing express train, it came in irregular gusts, accompanied by war whoops of air. Still, so far we were in good shape. We had hot soup and tea in thermos jugs, and stacks of sandwiches. They would have to do for the next twenty-four hours, as we had turned off the gas stove and heater to avoid the risk of fire.

About eleven P.M. there began a terrible thunderstorm in the midst of the gale. Monster flashes of lightning burst upon us with demonic fury. Water poured down the chimneys and out across the floor, by degrees extinguishing the fire, the blackened ruins of which now belched ashes over everything. The fury of the winds increased, bellowing through the forest and around the cabin like beserk Vikings. Now everything shudders, shakes, creaks, groans. The cabin begins to vibrate like the skin of a drum. Zap! Out go the lights as a tree falls on the wires. I thought then of the old Negro spiritual which goes: "I went to the rock to hide my face but the rock he say, 'No hidin' place, no hidin' place down here.' "

Hurricanes produce strange sounds. As we sat there, huddled around our candles, munching sandwiches and listening to the nearby sound of water trickling across the floor, we were treated to a full range of noise outside — human screams, banshee wailings, monstrous gnashings and breakings. There were rippings, roarings, growlings, elephantine trumpetings, and the constant crash of falling trees, together with a bombardment of things hitting the roof, banging on the walls and swatting the shutters like falling baseball bats. We could see the glass of our windows bending in and out inside the shutters with the changing air pressure. It was monstrous, fatiguing, frightening, but at the same time, in some curious way, marvelously exhilarating. Here we were, far out on an exposed bit of land, cut off from contact with humankind, and the very keel of the storm was barreling down the middle of the Point, knocking our forest to bits and trying to unseat the cabin from its foundations. But strangely, though we were racked with tension, we loved it and savored the experience of being in the very midst of one of the great works of nature.

Through all this black howling madness, we began to be aware of a new sound — enormous combers thundering onto the rocks. After each of these super giants had crashed and splintered, in about a second's time there would be a thundering roar as the spray hit the cabin full force. There were moments when I felt that the bolts holding the cabin to the concrete piers might give way and thought of the mariners in *The Tempest,* who cried: "Mercy on us — We split, we split!" I wondered then how wise we had been in deciding to stay with our house and not seek protection further inland. But I knew that in nearby harbors, many a lobsterman had decided to stay with his boat, his only means of livelihood, and ride out the storm facing into the gale on anchors fore and aft, and I felt that our case was easier than theirs.

But now I decided that I had to go outside and see it. I wanted to experience the once-or-twice-in-a-lifetime sensation of being in the very midst of a titanic storm. Besides, it had a compelling fascination, not unlike the hypnotic effect of standing beside a waterfall and feeling pulled irresistibly toward the brink, or of standing at the very edge of a cliff and wanting desperately to jump off. Putting on my oilskins and lining the family up by the door on the leeward side, I rammed my way into the storm. Somewhere up above there was a full moon, I knew. Briefly I thought how majestic this storm must look from there, but here it was midnight black, lit now and then by great gashes of lightning. I crept round the cabin on hands and knees to face the full fury of the storm. Like a series of instantaneous photographs, as the lightning flashed, the Point would light up momentarily and then disappear into darkness. Cupping my hands around my eyes, I was able to look up during these brief moments to see monstrous waves rip into the lashing trees. Then I would duck as the spray came thundering by. But it was too much. Soaked, frightened, exhilarated, I crawled back and pounded on the door, which opened with a crash. The wind had veered slightly. It now took all of us to get it closed again, a kind of comedy operation with everyone pushing madly, all ten feet slipping on the wet floor. "What was it like? What was it like?"

"Like crawling under Yosemite Falls," I muttered toweling myself off.

About two A.M. there came a sudden diminution of

sound. The rain actually stopped and the wind died down. Only the enormous waves kept up their thunder. It was the eye of the storm. Taking a deep breath, we flung open the door. Brilliant silver moonlight bathed a scene of awful devastation. The forest seemed to have half disappeared, leaving behind only an amazing tangle of fallen trees, twenty feet thick. The words of the Bible came to me as I looked around: "Behold, he cometh with clouds, and all kindreds of the earth shall wail because of him." Chasms and gullies in the turnaround, torn by the rain, were still running water. The waves, clearly seen for the moment, were spouting many feet into the air as they smashed into the rocks. But everything else was quiet — dripping. And the air was strangely warm. It gave one almost the sensation of being in the middle of an other-planet landscape, whose weird horizontal trees were somehow running water.

We hardly had time to note that the top of the water tank had disappeared and that the silence after hours of screaming winds was rather hard to bear, when we saw that the storm was about to close in again. We drifted back inside, closed the door, and got out the mops for a brief cleanup. Then we renewed the guttering candles and trimmed the lamps. Now the wind came upon us once more, this time from the other side, like a wild beast lunging in for the kill. No thought of sleep. Who could sleep with gusts of wind at one hundred and twenty miles per hour making the cabin shake like a wet dog, to the sound of satanic roarings and thunderings? I more than once wondered why the roof itself was not sucked off the shuddering walls of Great Hall into the night. Plop! Nothing daunted, Wisteria, our cat, had caught a mouse and now calmly proceeded to eat it in the middle of the kitchen floor.

Toward morning we realized that the worst was over.

The wind was beginning to veer sharply and the rain had stopped once more. Poking my head out the door, I could see a sudden brilliant streak of green shoot through the sky. Rents were appearing in the storm and within minutes, it seemed, the whole enormous demon-mass had turned into long streaming wisps of racing clouds that slithered away toward the dawn and then more and more from the west and northwest. And here were silver stars, golden moon, a giant green arch where the aurora borealis radiated silently from the north and a rosy glow from the rising sun, still hidden below the mass of clouds in the eastern sky.

As dawn broke, we all streamed out to view an indescribable turmoil. One felt like an ant walking through a tangle of autumn grasses. Leaves everywhere were brown — the salt spray had been driven right through them like machine gun bullets. In fact, the whole landscape, what there was of it, had a bronze tinge. Figaro raced about barking and lapping rain water from the streams of water which were running everywhere. Up on the hill the gardens had been pretty well flattened but here and there one could see a beanpole standing upright, absolutely bare. Perhaps those Kentucky Wonder Beans would drop somewhere off the Grand Banks. Branches, leaves, salt were broadcast over everything. Thousands of trees were down, their giant shards sticking up into the air like supplicating fingers. The wind was still lashing and whipping the remaining trees. But the air was fresh, the newly minted sun was shining, we were all alive, and we thanked God that it was over. A strange sensation of catharsis accompanies an experience of this kind. It is not something you can command at will or even reasonably avoid. You just have to live through it and, having lived, you are renewed.

We were renewed, but our forest was torn to shreds.

Here and there young trees thrust up through the tangle — but how long would it be? How long before there would be a forest here again? The cars and boats, though miraculously unhurt, were sitting under tons of fallen timber, for the most part supported on its branches ten or fifteen feet off the ground. The road was gashed and gullied, the wires were down, the water tank was swimming with debris, the windows were frosted with salt, the beach was eight feet lower than two days ago and strewn with tons of flotsam and seaweed, our Eden breached and broken. Trees one hundred and fifty years old had been torn out by the roots or snapped off ten, twelve or twenty feet from the ground. How many thousand had gone down? Who could count? All we knew was that where the forest had been there was now a wilderness of crazy stumps, pancake roots, fallen trees, lying every which way as far as one could see. We were numbed beyond tears.

But the sun shone, the seagulls soared, the dead grass and the bronzed landscape sparkled with a billion drops and the sky, now bathed in perfect blue, was filled with scudding white clouds galloping madly after the storm in ragged wild-horse ranks.

The problem of where to begin was solved for us by a cheery "Hi, there! You all alive?" It was our friend Dick Goodwin, crunching through the tangle with a yellow chain saw and a can of gasoline. Dick was a great, strong Maine man, a woodcutter by trade. He was wonderfully handy with axe and saw and had occasionally given us a hand when we needed firewood in a hurry. He was always cheerful, seemingly never tired, and had arms ribbed and corded like the trunk of a cedar tree. "I come out of it okay, down in my holler, but I kept thinkin' of you folks and jest thought I'd drop over and see how you was doin'," he said.

"Hey, Dick!" we yelled with delight. "Could you help us clear the road?"

"Sure thing. T'ain't so bad. As I come in I noticed lots of your trees fell alongside, and I think a half-day's work will get her clear."

As Goodwin's saw roared to life, we went to work to clear the cars and wash the salt off the windows. We knew that our personal tragedy was no more than a drop in the bucket of universal waste. Dick's sudden appearance had given us a lift beyond price. We cleared the cars, hauled barrow loads of soil and gravel to the worst spots in the road, found the smashed roof of the tank a quarter of a mile away and effected a repair.

On the third day, a crew from the Bangor Hydro Company came barreling in on one of their cheerful yellow trucks and began restringing our fallen wires. And the uncaring sun shone, the birds sang, and we were alive! Alive! With a cabin still intact, power being restored, and possessed of a grim determination to make the best of it. We had been spared the tragedy common in that part of coastal Maine: roofs shattered by fallen trees, boats piled up in kindling on the rocks or hundreds of lobster pots swept away, but we were sitting in the midst of the vast wreckage of our forest, murdered in a single night. By great good fortune, we learned that Dick Goodwin's current contract was coming to an end and so we were able to conclude a deal with him whereby he would work for us nearly full time, cutting up the fallen trees for pulpwood and timber. For the next two years Dick was on our land almost constantly, felling and cutting through fall, winter and spring, gradually clearing away the broken trees, cutting and stacking salvageable wood, laying down severed branches to provide a rough mulch for new growth, and though prices were down, the income from the sale of this wood paid Dick's salary.

Now no longer hidden, the cabin stood out on the bare Point like the prow of a ship by day and a beacon by night, and the once embowered water tower on the hilltop could be seen for miles out to sea, gleaming in its coat of aluminum paint. We dynamited the worst eyesore stumps, cut others as close to the ground as possible and by degrees we could see that the amazing vitality of the land was beginning to cover the wasted area with bushes and long wild grasses. Raspberries, roses, blueberries, even cranberries sprang up like magic everywhere and thousands of new trees began to show through the laid branches. Here and there patches of forest still stood, giving a curious accented beauty to the land.

One effect of the virtual disappearance of our forest came as a splendid surprise. Now we had a glorious view on three sides. A vast openness had replaced our former meager glimpses of the sky, and the sunsets and sunrises in soft pinks, roaring reds and tawny oranges were superb, flooding the cabins with brilliant light or the soft nacreous shades of new day seen through ground fog. We determined then, and have kept to it since, to leave the whole end of the Point open and windswept, letting the forest grow back only on the upper slopes and gradually over the years transforming the area adjacent to the cabins into a rough meadowland with a wide lovely sweep down to the island-studded bay.

For the time being most of the forest was gone, but who could take away the sky, the sea, the rocks, or the sense of an immense life, constantly renewing itself? And we could see that even the forest would come back in time. It was there, latent in thousands of young trees and in seeds and sprouts, whose green tips like the heads of Jason's soldiers were already springing up everywhere. The worst terror was fire, which could not only blast everything left from the hurricane to cinders but bake and burn all the new young seedlings and most of the seeds to the point where a whole generation could come and go before one could see evidence of new life. A terrible fire at Bar Harbor some years previously had left behind it a moon landscape of this kind, in which it seemed that nothing could ever spring to life for at least a century.

The last severe drought and the hurricane itself had made us resolve to strengthen our defenses. We would manage the young forest as it grew to maturity by selective cutting and by creating access roads or trails for wood gathering and fire fighting. In time we would have to dig a deep well for a more adequate supply of water. And right now we could repair and strengthen the cabins where they showed signs of aging and rot. Examination of the underpinnings of Jon's room where it sagged at one corner revealed that certain sections of the log sills had apparently been softening and rotting for some years. These sills had served as partially exposed members of the old porch, standing out in the weather winter and summer, where the stealthy microbial sappers and miners could enter and destroy. I borrowed a screw jack from a local contractor and setting it up under the room on a cribbing of heavy timbers, I jacked the whole end of the cabin up till I could cut away the rotted sections of the logs and replace them with new pieces, this time soaked in Cuprinol and painted a weathered gray. The hurricane had driven quarts of sticks, stones, dirt, salt and grasses into the cracks. I knifed out as much as I could, even using the vacuum cleaner in places (a kind of miniature reverse hurricane) and treated the rest to Cuprinol and creosote.

From time to time I abandoned the battle of the cabins and took to my brushes. What a relief! These occasions were often given a certain tang by conversation with local folks who appeared on the Point at berry-picking time. "That yore paintin', Challes? Never see one close up like this before." I looked up on this occasion to see a friend from the village standing just behind me. He had a pail of blueberries in his hand and was sucking on a corncob pipe while he looked at a finished painting I had placed on a favorite rock where the sun could help dry it.

"Yes, it's my painting, and I put it out here to dry."

"You dry 'em jest like codfish, eh? Well, I'll be damned. When we dry cod down here it's usually all gone in two hours. Folks love it: just like chewin' gum. Bet yore's don't go that fast though. But it's all accordin' to where they're placed: send fifty pounds of that 'strip fish' up to Bangor and it'll be there two years — wouldn't know what to do with it. Where was you standin' when you done it?"

"Well, what I was really doing was sort of standing inside my own head, if you take my meaning, trying to remember all the best parts of this coast that I've seen these last two weeks, and then make 'em into a design."

"Yep. To tell the truth, I've often stood on my head tryin' to remember somethin' too, but somehow it never did quite come out that way! You get paid for it?"

"Not exactly. But when it's finished and framed I try to sell it. Like you say, it depends on where it goes whether they'll buy or not."

"Hmmm. 'Bout the same as the codfish, 'pears to me: all good, but some will like it and some won't. Now there's folks that say I'm an artist at my trade but to tell the truth

I've seen times when I wisht to God I was doin' somethin'
else. Day in and day out I see so much fish I can hardly
bear to eat it. And mebbe you look at them pitchers o'
yours so much you can't get the taste out of yore mouth
either. What I don't see is how a big feller like you can
sit there all day twiddlin' with them damn fool little
brushes. Come to think of it, t'ain't much more foolish
than spendin' a whole day pullin' in cod on a hand line.
There's one difference though: at the end of a day's work
I stink and you don't. That ought to count for somethin'!"

At about this time, Paul and Julia, just back from their
several years in France on a tour of foreign service, came
to stay with us at the Point for a few weeks. Julia had gone
through the Cordon Bleu school, had worked under several
leading Parisian chefs, had been elected a Chevalier du
Taste Vin and was currently conducting a cooking school
along with two French friends called l'École des Trois
Gourmandes. Now a full-fledged and skillful exponent of
la haute cuisine, she immediately took Erica and Rachel
under her wing and began to give them lessons in high-style
French cooking. The consumption of chocolate, butter,
wine, mushrooms and egg yolks went up by leaps and
bounds as the kitchen of Great Hall became the center of
a vast activity. Poulet de Bresse à la mode de Nantua, Lobster Archduke, lovely little cakes, moules marinières, bouillabaisse, sauce Béarnaise, flowed out in a never-ending
stream. And I let my belt out another notch!

Paul was out with his camera. What could the man take,
I wondered, that he hadn't already taken? But that ever-
perceptive eye, now informed by years of experience, always
found something new, or a better way of taking something
that had been taken before.

Rachel, who had developed a flair for original costume, created a fantastic hat for Julia, made of wild flowers, bed springs, wheat straw and ribbons, and crowned her with it on her birthday in mid-August.

Jonathan, by now an excellent sailor, had improved to the point of winning a good many of his races. He had graduated from the novice class and was teaching younger boys in his turn. When one of the races in which he took part came up Blue Hill Bay past Gun Rock, we would all run to the top of the beach slope, settle down in the long grasses and wave him on as he came by. But his blood was not all salt water. He asked permission to set aside a few acres of our land as his own private domain, undertaking the responsibility of clearing and cutting and shaping it to his own fancy. Thus began a fruitful and long continued battle and love affair between Jonathan and his acres, which has continued until today.

Walking about and pacing up and down around the brow of the hill and at the end of the cabins in order to choose the best location for "Jon's acres," the idea of putting a studio somewhere in the vicinity suddenly surfaced. I had used Old Cabin as a place to paint since the center of our life had transferred itself to Great Hall, but it was a nuisance to have to clean up at the end of each day so as to be able to come into a room neat and orderly enough to undress in and go to bed in, and then each morning, reverse the process. And with those banks of windows all round, the light was often confusing and had to be controlled by an elaborate series of sliding curtains so that it could be made to come from a single source. I wanted to be able to bring all my work in progress to the Point at the beginning of each summer and, without too much fuss or too many special arrangements, simply take up where I had left off. A small reasonably segregated workplace of some kind seemed to be the answer. But the question was, where to put it. Should it be hitched to the far end of our wandering house? Or perhaps up on the hill among the apple trees?

The previous summer we had begun a project in a small way which all the family had come to enjoy, and eventually it was this which determined the location of the studio. The project started as an effort to regrade the steep hillside bank just outside Erica's room. In the course of this work, we began bringing in and transplanting wild roses, lupines, columbines, valerian, deep red honeysuckle, white and blue veronica, in fact any plant that was sufficiently hardy to maintain its existence without further care once it had become established. To build a studio here would have destroyed this wild garden which we now intended to extend along the entire seventy-foot length of the bank immediately in back of Great Hall. Moreover, it would have cut off a portion of the ocean view newly revealed by the hurricane. A final decision to put the studio on the hill back of Great Hall was almost automatic. To start with, I built a series of stone steps up the bank among the flowers. Having all but completed what I thought was a magnificent (if rather steep) set of stone steps, I saw my wife coming along through the meadow grass. Standing back and proudly leaning on my shovel I awaited the accolade which I felt was my due. But things are not always what they seem. The view of the stairs from Fredericka's point of view was apparently not quite what it had been from mine. "It's a fine stairway, but from here it looks a bit like the Giants' Causeway. Perhaps you had a troll in mind? Or a chamois?"

"Well, that's funny. With all due modesty, I was just standing here thinking it was a minor masterpiece of the stair-maker's art! Look here: solid, substantial, easy . . ."

"That's just the point! Easy for whom? Not for guests with high heel shoes who come to visit your studio."

"Well, I'm damned — it seems easy enough for me . . ."

"Stop puffing yourself up like a blowfish — just stand back and look at it."

"Doggone it, I like it the way it is, and it's a heck of a job to yank all those stones out of the hill when I've just set them in. Tell you what I'll do: I'll build another set of stairs with little non-teetering steps for ladies' heels." So I did. Now at the end of another three hours' work the doubled stairs ran up the bank big and little together, hand in hand, like Baucis and Philemon.

"Okay now, come look, Fred," I said at the door of the kitchen, from which drifted a wonderful odor of grapes.

Fred came out, her cheeks flushed from the heat of the stove, and running light as a feather up and down the little steps, cried, "That's gorgeous! It's a real Chafred construction too, and worth all the extra trouble. Now as soon as you get cleaned up, come on into the kitchen: I have something to show you."

Laid out on the counter which separated the kitchen from Great Hall were slices of bread and a bowl full of a dark compelling substance from which emanated all the odors of autumn. "It's a new grape conserve — I got the recipe from a Quaker friend back in Bucks. I'm going to name it after her — Beulah's Conserve." Spreading an enormous helping on a slice of new-baked bread I slowly consumed a mouthful all warm from the stove. Marvelous! If you would like the recipe, here it is:

BEULAH'S GRAPE CONSERVE

Stem 7 pounds of Concord grapes, wash, and place in a large kettle without water. Mash lightly, bring to a boil, and let simmer till well cooked and juice free (about fifteen minutes). Put them through a sieve to remove skins and seeds. Measure the resulting pulp. To every four cups of pulp add three cups of sugar. Add 2 pounds of stemmed and cleaned white grapes, and 4 oranges sliced very thin and boil carefully and rapidly to jelly stage. Remove from fire, add 1 pound English walnut meats, chopped fine, and pour into glasses and seal with wax.

Here even operations as simple as making bread became meaningful or were invested with a quality of unusual pleasure. Fredericka, for example, developed a loaf that we all found delicious. It was promptly dubbed "Fatless Fred-Bread" by the family and it has become by now a staple article of our diet. Here is the formula, excellent for holding down weight, if you don't cover it with too much honey, peanut butter, marmalade and similar goodies.

FATLESS FRED-BREAD

Dissolve 1 cake of yeast in ¼ cup of lukewarm water. Add to the yeast mixture 2 and ¾ cups of water to which has been added ⅓ cup of sugar and 1½ tsp. salt. Now combine 6 cups of coarsely ground whole wheat or graham flour and 3 handfuls of the whole grains of wheat (Italian and Greek stores usually carry the latter) and mix with the liquid. Raise the dough 3 times and bake in a moderate oven.

Oh, the odor of that bread! It has the perfume of a wheatfield under the sun, or as Rachel put it, "It smells like health!" Coming into the cabin when Fred is cooking one of her mysterious somethings gives one the sensation of being greeted with sweet music — an arpeggio of odors both familiar and strange. And there is the charming conductor of this symphony, waving her baton-spoon as she deftly orchestrates another masterpiece.

After considerable palaver, Jon and I staked out a location for the studio which, as these things sometimes do, had grown now into a building which would be a studio at one end and a small shop at the other for maintenance and repair. This little building would be carefully oriented to take advantage of the summer light. We visualized a small structure, the studio half of which would be about sixteen by twenty feet and the shop half about twelve by sixteen, with a connecting door, and a separate outside door for each half. Building such a structure would have the effect of freeing the old woodshed-shop for future use as a possible laundry and storage center for household cleaning things. But as usual, one idea bumped another in a little chain reaction. This laundry idea in turn would only work well provided that we put up an outside woodshed.

Accordingly, back of the kitchen corner we dug the steep hillside bank out on a long slope leading up toward the two gardens near the water tank. This artificial slope or ramp was made about eight feet wide. The left hand half would have a long woodshed on it, going up the slope in a series of stepbacks. The right hand half would be reserved as a turfed pathway for people, wheelbarrows and tractor. This would make it easy for us to haul wood from the hillside area downhill directly to a storage place and in the other direction to have easy access to the gardens and the water tank. The back of the woodshed faced the turnaround and Fred suggested the happy idea that we build it of weathered driftwood boards, in effect a fence, also going up the hillside in a series of steps. Delighted with the color and sheen of the driftwood, we planted arborvitaes and lemon lilies against it for contrast. This move gave us a greatly increased store of wood in a convenient spot and freed the whole woodshed-shop, which now for the moment had become no more than a long empty corridor.

That winter I had a number of successful portrait commissions which helped to provide funds for the studio and, between jobs, worked happily at perfecting the plans. This kind of mathematical play, with its rigorous requirement in visualizing space and function, was not unlike the work of a lawyer in drawing up a contract. One visualized all the possibilities in the situation, then limited oneself to the really possible and practical, setting these requirements down in a series of clearly expressed symbols. But it could be done at leisure, with plenty of time for reconsideration, in contrast to designing fabrics, for example — a bread-and-butter operation which I was engaged in at the time, along with the portraits. Work of this kind has to be done against a hard and fast deadline. I enjoyed designing fabrics. With their abstract patterns and free use of color, they were to me not unlike lyric poetry. But in the highly competitive world of commercial art, each job has to be done to an exacting schedule, often requiring hours of nighttime work.

Life at the Point had seemed to all of us, and particularly to our young, in some respects perhaps more truly home than life at Coppernose. In winter, with girls away at college and Jon at school, home to them was predominantly a place where you did your homework or came on an occasional visit and where you had brief but not continuous contact with busy parents. But in Maine we were all together, with time for each other and time to invent family projects, like the flowering bank, and to experience the joy of direct contact with nature. The assimilation of skills and knowledge was not part of an academic process here but came directly and simply out of our life at the Point. It was a place that gave us the sense of having a purposeful control over our own destinies within a context that was beautiful and rewarding.

Who could be so forgetful, I said to myself, so city-bred or so insensitive that he could not respond to the instant appeal of this land? It spoke to one in many tongues. Who could fail to drink in the damp sweet odor of mosses and ferns underfoot, of fog-laden or sun-drenched evergreen branches, the perfume of ripened raspberries, or the taste of the piercing sea air? And who could miss the sound of birds, birds who not only sing and whistle and trill, but cry like babies and mew like kittens as do the herring gulls, or utter hoarse laughings and croakings like the monster ravens and black-backed gulls whose deep primitive voices carry easily across a mile of still air. On a higher register one is offered a perfect woodwind ensemble from hermit thrushes and wood thrushes, and more insistently the penny-whistle talk of the warblers seething through the trees in great flocks, then higher still the eerie whistling of an os-prey, or the minute snap-snap of swallows' bills as they snatch their food from the air. Almost at the limit of au-dible sounds one catches the leprechaun talk of humming-birds through the purr of their wings, and if one holds one's breath and leans to the grass or close to an overhanging branch there comes the aeolian strumming of insects, blend-ing at last into reaches of supersonic vibrations. And you, the breathing animal, listening, looking, tasting all at once, can sense that your body, far from being a stranger to all this, belongs to it, is a part of its essence, responsive to its shift of mood. Even your bare feet in the grass can become aware of an electric vitality. Now you can feel enchantingly alive. Something in you reaches out from your own life to all these other lives, from the smallest snail nestling in his dark, mysterious curve to the great spiral of the galaxy.

Life together on our Point gave to Fredericka and me the added pleasure of sensing in our youngsters the growth to maturity and that inevitable pleasure-pain which all parents know, of learning and relearning their own new roles as guides and friends rather than as arbiters of their youngsters' destinies.

Rampageous Rachel, now majoring in government and economics at college, had somehow learned to master her volcanic fires. But she always brought a pinch or two of mordant wit, objectivity of mind and flash and dash to the family potpourri. Erica, deft and subtle, delighted us with an unerring sense of form which found expression in a craftsmanlike ability to turn her hand with equal skill to cooking, sewing, drawing and design. Now graduated from college, she had spent the last winter taking a course in archaeology in Albuquerque, and in the art of working in silver and turquoise, under the instruction of a Zuni master-craftsman. Jonathan was a science buff whose interest in physics and mathematics was steadily growing. Yet no sooner had we typed them in these convenient grooves than we were forced to revise our estimates and to see that our children were paradoxical, like all maturing young people. New facets appeared daily. Smooth personality could turn in a minute to roughness; sudden unexpected insights were followed often by callow or outrageous moments. The great question, "Who am I?" was always latent in them. Yet part of the joy of parenthood, or so it seems to me, is just this experience, not only of helping to educate one's youngsters but in turn being educated by them in a loving struggle to revalue one's own values in the direction of flexibility and compassion.

12

Slow Growth

WE came back to the Point with completed plans for the studio-shop and a determination to master, if we could, the problems of wind, weather and forest growth. Attack! Attack! Now equipped with a Skil-saw, Jon and I tore into the work with a vast anticipation. A Skil-saw is a circular high-speed electric saw with a long electric cable. It is light enough to be carried by hand to any point on the job. It cuts so fast that it does the work of four or five men, and it never gets tired.

In its final form, the studio design was based on a module of four-by-eight-foot prefabricated wood panels, a product which enormously speeds up jobs of this kind. A grid of two-by-eight-inch planks was laid on poured concrete piers, sub-floor "underlayment" panels were put down, and the skeletons of the walls, constructed flat on the sub-floor, were lifted into place with record speed, except for episodes here and there which held up the work momentarily. I remember one occasion of this kind which gave a hearty note to the day. We had laid out and partially built a section of wall flat on the floor, ready for raising. In the middle there was an opening for a window. "Okay, up she goes," I said. Now just as we were struggling to heave the section into

a vertical position a sudden blast of wind came over the Point and the whole section of wall took off, landing some distance away among the tall grasses — right over Figaro, who had been sitting there quietly discussing a bone, neatly framing him in the window opening.

"Woof woof!" cried Figgy, leaping to his feet and jumping about as one who would say, "Hey, kids, what kind of a new game is this?" Then suddenly getting bored with the episode he picked up his bone and made off across the meadow in a series of majestic bounds, appearing and disappearing over the tops of the long grasses rather like a wooly brown boat in a wooly green sea.

Slap-slap-slap — the roof went up. A red rubber floor covering went in, a cannibalized thing of holes and patches from the kitchen at Coppernose, but more than adequate for my small studio when recut and repatched to fit the new floor. Standard hollow-core doors were hung, and in the shop a heavy carpenter's bench and a series of shelves were built. For outside sheathing we used a kind of rough lap-siding available in the region. Its edges are not cut straight in the usual way but still have the natural curves of the tree trunks. This time every exposed surface was

Cuprinoled and painted as it went in and before you could say "Studio be built!" it was finished, sitting on the hillside at one end of our orchard of seven trees.

Hammers, saws, axes and other small tools were moved into the shop, and painting materials into the studio. The whole experience had been grand fun — almost hilarious. There were no logs this time — no felling, no peeling, no shaping. Only the buzz of the Skil-saw, signaling the end of an epoch.

Jonathan was an excellent working companion. Through long association we had developed an almost instinctive method of teamwork so that for hours on end we could saw and hammer together with no more than a word here and there or a glance to indicate what the next move should be.

Jon had grown and changed to the point where if we happened to be working together at a task of this kind, I felt more brotherly toward him than fatherly. He had developed his own methods of attacking a problem, and his own pace: somewhat slower than mine I must admit, which no amount of pressure ("Charlie fall-out," he called it) could alter by one jot or tittle. He could bring me up short, too, like his mother. "Cha! Stop making those animal noises and listen to reason for a minute: if you'll just turn that board the other way, damnit, and cut *across* the grain . . ." Now joking, speculating and telling tall stories, we raced along rarely needing to mention the work itself, which seemed that summer to go forward at relentless speed. In fact, a long spell of fine weather had allowed us to keep building almost without a break. Everyone was in a gay mood. We had been through a Valley of Shadow and had now come out into green pastures.

Perhaps this was just as well. We were entertaining more

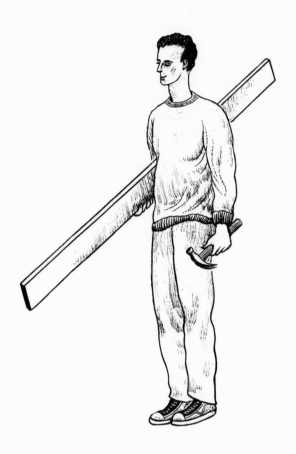

guests each year and were often in turn invited out for tennis in Northeast Harbor or at the Lippmanns, for delightful picnics and swimming with the Desmond Fitzgeralds, friends from our Washington days, who had a particularly lovely spot on Somes Sound, or again for excursions by boat or by car to the favorite haunts of other friends. There were those marvelous lonely island beaches every-

where where one could picnic, bathe, explore or watch for
an occasional eagle or osprey. There was fishing, which
bored me but delighted the girls. They could spend hours
in our little boats, bobbing up and down off Gun Rock
or on a dock a few miles away from the end of which one
could often land enormous flounder and eels, not to mention the rather uninteresting harbor pollock which were
caught primarily for the cat, Wisteria. She adored them
and, tipped off by the smell of the fishing tackle, would
eagerly await the return of the girls, pacing to and fro along
the beach, drooling from under her whiskers and, as Fred
remarked, "rubbing her paws together in anticipation. I
know cats are supposed to be aloof but ours is about the
un-aloofest cat I know!"

Rather than fish, I liked to stand on the edge of the bluff
and look out over the water, from which there might rise
the enormous unexpected form of a black fish, spouting at
the top of his rise, or more commonly a seal or two, and
here and there the fast-moving silhouettes of the "shags"
(cormorants) zipping over the surface of the bay so low
that the tips of their vibrating wings seemed to kiss the
water with every beat. Guillemots, little black diving ducks
who have brilliant red legs and white wing-patches are
common here, too. Both these birds seem to prefer to fly
just off the surface, perhaps to take advantage of a thicker
layer of air lying low over the water. It may be that this
curious habit results in an optical illusion, but their speed
seems incredible. One could easily judge it to be sixty miles
per hour. The cormorants in particular are fascinating
creatures. Able to swim under water faster than fish, they
disappear in a flash, only to appear some moments later
in an unexpected direction. They can also sit absolutely
immobile atop a channel marker or a rock, their water-

logged wings outspread to dry, in this position looking like heraldic figures made of cast iron. Cormorants are gregarious, and have their favorite foregathering places, usually on some lonely off-shore ledge, where they line up by the hundreds, preening and talking like a crowd at a cocktail party.

Standing and looking can be fun, but not as much fun as painting. I started a portrait of the darkly beautiful Mrs. Fitzgerald about this time, using the sea and cliffs of the fjordlike Somes Sound as a background, and began a series of drawings of plant forms to use as a basis for some designs in cut glass which I was working on. The studio had come alive.

But I had to learn to discipline myself. The view from its big window up there on the hillside was distractingly beautiful. "Well, Challes," said George Richardson one day, on coming into the studio, "I know what you're goin' to do. You're goin' to sit down on that big arse of yours and stare out that window at the boats passin' by, and them gulls and all, and you jest ain't never goin' to do a goddamn thing!"

But this wasn't strictly true. My studio with its clean white walls and its sense of quiet gave me the opportunity of continuing a piece of work just where I had left it without having to go through the complicated business of preparation. It seemed in some ways to complete, or make it possible for me to sum up, the whole meaning of life at Old Point. Here, where time moved at a different rate from the pace of winter, one had time to think, or dream, and the release of tension, the absence of deadlines (they sometimes called me Deadline Charlie!) often helped me produce work which seemed to me to have a special quality derived from relaxation and delight. I loved my trade and was happy in it, even in the midst of doing dull jobs, as often as not. But here, in this very simple room, with a somewhat limited set of tools and colors, and especially with no interruptions, I was being thrown back upon myself, and finding myself on another level.

An artist's brush, I reflected, was an ancient invention — probably some cave dweller chewing on the splayed end of a stick first found it useful. Yet it has remained a simple thing, merely an extension of hand or eye, like a chopstick or a hammer. The real tool of the artist is the artist himself, whose constant refinement of physical ability is extended by refinement of the mind. The best brush in the world, and the most brilliant pigment, are no better than the creature that uses them, and of no more account than the tail of a donkey if they are not given direction by skilled sensibility. Happy accidents in mixing and smearing are for children. They don't make great art, or any chimp were one with Michelangelo. The challenge, after an artist has mastered the technical side of his craft, is always himself, i.e. content, or realization, greatly presented. Nothing less will do.

Struggling through the brambles, bushes, rocks and fallen branches of our land about this time, we began to lay out a series of trails through the areas where the forest was coming back, using long stakes dipped in bright yellow paint to help us visualize the pattern. The brilliant color of these markers was highly visible across the slash and among the growing trees. It occurred to us that here was the solution to a minor problem that had annoyed us for years — the mysterious disappearance of tools, apparently left in plain sight, as when some sudden call to the telephone or the unexpected arrival of guests caused us to leave them propped up against a stump or rock in what seemed to be plain sight. We got out axes, saws, scythes, rakes, shovels, crowbars, and painted the whole galaxy, even the wheelbarrow, a brilliant yellow. Glorious! Then we hung them in a pattern on the back wall of Great Hall just where the steep slope of a hill came down, and behind each one painted a slightly darker yellow silhouette on the wall. This device indicated not only the proper place for each tool but which tools might be missing for the moment. The spread of yellow tools on the gray wall made a splendid abstract design which pleased everyone enormously.

And there were those winds, our constant problem: fierce shaking squalls would rush down on us from nowhere, lashing and hissing and striking like invisible serpents. Our first crop of forty apples was ripped off the trees in a few seconds. There would be thunderstorms, accompanied by icy winds and hail which could tear through the heart of a hot summer's day, hurling all the ripe raspberries to the ground or cruelly shredding tender green leaves. Plants like corn, pole beans, sweet peas and tomatoes, not to mention annual flowers, could all be bent and broken just as they were coming to perfection. Probably there is no final answer to such upsets if one chooses to live on the end of a point in a boreal climate, with no forest to break the force of the winds. But we did the best we could, transplanting rows of small arborvitaes and spruces to the windward sides of the gardens and encouraging and feeding the growth of wild vines among them as thick natural fences. For the rest, we wired and guyed and staked everything that could be held in place but it was clearly a battle we would never completely win, unless we or our grandchildren could sometime float a plastic dome down over the whole point.

One day after one of these stormy winds had finally blown itself out, we went down to the rocks to see what the sea had brought. Around on the other side of the Point we made a discovery. Wedged among the ledges of the eastern shore lay a great square raft, twenty feet on a side. Underneath it, as floats, there were lashed seven metal barrels. The eighth had evidently been torn away in the gale. The incoming waves were already lapping at one edge, causing the raft to rock to and fro in its water-floored prison. We could see that, with a mighty effort, we might just be able to float it over the rocks and bring it around the Point to our swimming beach. "What say, gang, do we try to pry it loose?"

"Why not? What can we lose?"

Running back to the cabin, we consulted a tide chart to fix the moments of highest water. It might work: the tide was nearing the flood and the waves, thanks to the storm, were unusually high. Digging out two spare tent poles, we raced back to the shore.

Now began a mighty struggle. Standing in icy water up to our armpits, we heaved and pried, timing our efforts to the incoming waves. Twice we gave up and lay gasping on the rocks. Twice we returned to the battle. Jonathan eventually secured victory for us by rushing off and bringing the outboard around. Now with a heavy line lashed to the raft, the outboard exerted a steady pull and as succeeding waves came rolling in, each heave of the poles inched our find across the rocks toward open water. With an audible sigh, as of some great animal giving up the struggle to defend itself against the attack of a pack of hungry wolves, the raft finally slipped off the last intervening ledge. We towed it around the Point, and having tied two heavy stones to ropes fixed to opposite corners, we moored it in the waters of our swimming beach. Then we came in and Fred and I had a drink to celebrate, for which she whipped up the following creation, called Sesame Canapes. Don't ask me how Fred ever invented this one. It just came! But it's delicious. And different!

SESAME CANAPES

To each (large) package of cream cheese, add 4 tablespoons of sesame seeds, roasted in a skillet for a half-hour or until browned lightly, 2 dashes of Worcestershire sauce, 2 dashes of tabasco sauce, and ½ teaspoon of garlic powder. Fred says, "Mess it all round together and roll it into little balls with your sticky hands. Now roll the balls in more sesame seeds till they cover the surface and make them easy to pick up." Rachel adds, "If you want to be nice Nellie about it, put a toothpick into each ball." Serve with drinks.

The raft stayed there most of the summer, far enough off shore for a one-minute swim. We had just decided to paint the top surface with two resting mermaids, and the tentacles of a giant squid coming up over the sides, when one night a sudden squall came down the bay, ripping it from its anchors and sending it wallowing off in the direction of Spain, or perhaps back to its unknown maker. At any rate we never saw it again.

At Coppernose, near the Delaware River, we had gotten used to the idea that a river is not just a river, a flow of water which never changes. Some years it was up, some years it was down, now purling, now raging, it changed almost from hour to hour. Our seacoast in Maine has the same character. Everything here changes, everything fluctuates. Storms could pile up windrows of flotsam miles long or could scour out our rocky beach to sudden amazing depths. Boulders as big as pianos would disappear by the hundreds over the winter, or the whole beach could rise suddenly from its previous level and inundate our childish human arrangements, such as stone fireplaces and seats, for three or four years at a time, then as suddenly reveal them. Some years a mysterious green seaweed that we called Mermaid's Hair would appear, clinging at certain levels to the ledges. Then it would fade away. Was this the result of a temperature change? A new source of nourishment? We never knew. There would be years when the corpses of great storm-racked trees could be found here and there, wedged into rocks seemingly with the weight and precision of a steel girder being locked into a concrete foundation. But they never stayed. Parts of old masts or smooth logs bristling with nails or twined with bits of campers' ropes, even sometimes with lanterns attached, provided constant evidence of the presence of others not too far away. Smashed lobster pots — dead and dessicated gulls — parts of glass markers and wooden buoys would suddenly appear. And the very fabric of the beach itself would undergo a constant and mysterious change. Some years it was all pebbles; other years these tilted shoals would be overlain with a coarse sand formed of the familiar broken mussel shells and the remnants of sea-urchin spines. The following year everything would be gone, revealing the very backbone of the land, the deep-lying, seemingly unyielding rock. But even this changed as it was split and splintered by winter storms.

So everything moved, everything changed, from Figaro, who used to bound and caper from his bed and now liked to have his paw held in a solemn morning ritual before stirring his aging bones, to the trees, which grew and fell, the shifting beach, the circling stars, the mysterious Mermaid's Hair, the embattled cabins, the struggling gardens, our growing children and, of course, Fredericka and me. We were not quite the enthusiastic youngsters of former years. Through all our joy we had often to face fear in one form or another. For example, there is a kind of ancient fear or dread which our forebears felt and recorded and which one can feel still if one penetrates any distance at all into the dusk and silence of these old forests. The atmosphere is somehow alien to humankind, one would almost say resentful of intrusion. There is life here — overwhelming life — but it is incoherent, timeless, and seems to suck one into the morass of its billion branches, which if they could think would consider a human being no more than a bit of something to be digested.

In our own more open domain we were naturally enough not without some more ordinary fears. These were the logical daytime fears of sudden trippings and fallings, the chance of broken bones, or the possibility of being lost in a fog at sea. Such fears one might consider the guardian deities of alertness: they are the necessary and helpful accompaniment of life in a situation such as ours.

But there were also more subtle and more powerful fears that had to be faced. They came by night, and were born of fatigue and self-doubt. They were not the fears that one learns to accept as the concomitants of sanity. They were of a different order, harder to combat. It took me some time to realize that they were not objectively "real," though real enough to wound, as they came in on the night wind like shadowy owls looking for an object into which they could sink their talons: fear of failure, of sudden illness, of the unknown future, of misunderstanding, even the fear of being itself. When one's mind is entrapped in the cobwebs of half-sleep, it remains supine in the face of such shadowy attackers. Too drugged with fatigue to wake and resist, too near the borders of the subconscious and the irrational to apply logic, one can lie there in his wakeful bed for hours — a prisoner of weakness.

But energy and hope accumulate, too, in some mysterious fashion, and more often than not, as the sun rose upon these midnight visitors, their half-seen shapes of terror would collapse and shrivel like dead bats, and be left behind with hardly a backward glance.

"You know, chaps," I said one dewy morning, as we all sat on the porch steps eating Irish oatmeal and honey, and watching the seals sporting off the rocks, "now that we've gotten out all the stumps and all the big stones from this clearing here and I can swing a scythe without denting the blade, I can't really see the sense of letting it all grow so tall."

"No!" growled Old Bear: "We know what you're up to! I can read that mind of yours like an open book. I can see grass seed in your eyes. Confess! Confess! You want a lawn — a real, honest to God damn suburban lawn!"

"A lawn? Who said lawn? I didn't say anything about a lawn! I just think it would be . . . practical, say, to borrow George Richardson's power mower from time to time and keep this cussed hayfield down as long as we're here. Now I ask you, what's wrong with that? Look at your legs, Old Bear: they're covered with mosquito bites. You should be the first to want to do away with this full-time mosquito refuge."

"Well, I suppose we've got to let him try it. He'll do it anyway," they cried in nearly perfect unison. "But remember, no *lawn! Absolutely!*"

Well, I did try it, setting the mower as high as possible, and it did look better. A sort of rough not-quite-meadow, the cut stems of the wild grasses visible for about four to six inches, then going down into an impenetrable springy mass that seemed to have no bottom. The effect of this, and subsequent more or less regular cuttings, was that the whole sweep of turf inside the embrasure of the cabin wings turned by degrees a brilliant emerald green and became finer textured. You could call this a "lawn," but we never completely tamed it, nor do we want to, and to this day it remains, now extended around the cabins, a rough, heavily textured wild grass carpet which even a powerful rotary mower is hard put to it to handle. Flocks of robins, ranks of parading cowbirds, sprinklings of sparrows love to settle on it and explore its depths while hummingbirds and swallows weave their swift skeins overhead. Thus, a grace note of gaiety and motion has now come to enrich the quiet melody of dappled green.

With the girls on their own and Jonathan headed for college and army, our life was less child-centered than it had been. I had sold a large picture of boats in a Maine harbor to the New York Hospital and other Maine-derived pictures in Washington, which pleased me very much. Even though I was busy now with two more portraits, freedom of choice as to how we would spend our time from here on loomed up as more real than it had been for years. But flexibility and freedom are nothing in themselves, without being hitched to values. As summer approached, Maine and our land called to us as insistently as ever. For the moment there was where the supreme value lay. Like certain wines and cheeses that can never be exported without loss of flavor, there were things we could do there and intensities of experience which we felt could never be exported or duplicated elsewhere in exactly that form.

13

Foggy Mornings

THIS time on coming to our land we brought along two cats as well as our haystack-shaped dog. There was Wisteria, the fish lover, and with her her side-kick Mary Margaret McKitten. The goings out and the comings in of these critters became such a complex operation that we built them their own private door, a panel of Masonite swung from a piano hinge at the top by means of which, with the push of a nose, they could either enter or leave. A game of King-of-the-Castle, with one cat on each side of the door, became a favorite pastime.

A vast osprey nest had been built that year on top of our light pole, an enormous ragged platform of sticks and branches, but a storm or the presence of humans had apparently caused it to be abandoned. However, the osprey family had moved to a more suitable location atop a dead tree not far away, and at the time of our arrival Mama and Papa were busy teaching a great flopping baby to soar. Booted out of the nest, with a great flapping of wings and piercing screams he would elbow himself aloft up the ladder of the air, then essay a circling glide with his parents overhead egging him on. Apparently not yet used to the new posture, he would ignominiously go into a power dive or a side slip and break once again into the flopping and flipping routine amidst screams and whistling calls from Ma and Pa. Oops! Down he would go. Flop-Flop-Flop-upward again. Then, ah — the glide! Then, oops!! We felt for him.

The old cut, now a young forest, was beginning to obliterate the acres of blueberries which had sprung up there. Over all our hilly point we could see real trees pushing up from the branches laid down by Dick Goodwin. Some of these young trees were now high enough to obscure our yellow stakes. If we were ever to clear those trails, this would have to be the year.

The weather worked for us in bringing back the forest, in growing magnificent vegetables and flowers in the gardens, but at the same time we were conscious that the fight against the encroaching trees would be endless. This summer, as I had so many summers before, I now went to work repairing and replacing — shingles here, warped and cracked boards there, and paint — forever paint. The roofs of the northwest face, as usual, did better than those of the opposite side and, I noticed, were now being gradually covered with a soft fuzz of gray-green sphagnum moss. The outside doors were repainted in brilliant lacquer red, the windows were reputtied, the woodshed replenished, and I began again the everlasting summer job of grubbing out stumps, this time up in the orchard area beside the studio-shop.

Erica and Rachel, having managed to get their vacations at the same time, came for a fortnight and with their appearance life took a fine swing toward youth. Young men began to appear, and the sound of guitar music, dancing feet and young laughter was heard in the land.

Our own friends, too, came crowding in. The Paul Nitzes, who had been coming quite regularly to Maine

with their delightful family, had decided that summer to buy a place in Northeast Harbor. Our friends, the Duran-Reynalses, came often and brought with them the art of distinguished conversation, tinctured with a Catalan accent. Francisco Duran-Reynals was a specialist in cancer research, a pioneer in the theory of a possible virus connection. And Madame, a brilliant pathologist and researcher in her own right, had a vivid sparkle. The talk would range far outside the field of their own professions into nuclear physics, politics, cooking, travel.

In fact, one of the best things about our summer life was the constant and casual dropping in of friends. There would be good talk, a pickup lunch, or a leisurely tour of inspection around the Point. There was always something going on: the doubling of a floor, rocks to get out, a bit of painting or repair. And people loved to help. Dressed in a pair of our dungarees or shorts, they would willingly join us for an hour or two at some necessary task.

New ways of doing fish were always popping up on such occasions. Friends often say, "Have you ever tried this one? No? Let me show you." Here is one which is basic to

Peruvian cookery and was brought to us by a friend who had lived in Peru for a time. It is perfect as a first course for dinner, and is called Seviche (pronounced "SayVEE-chee").

SEVICHE

Fillet enough very fresh white fish, such as flounder, to make 3 pounds. Pick to small pieces while still raw, and shred as fine as possible. Over the shredded fish pour 1 cup of mixed lemon and lime juce (fresh) mixed in the proportion of ⅔ lime to ⅓ lemon. Mix juice and fish thoroughly with your hands. Add one cup finely chopped red onion, and a good sprinkle of cayenne pepper, or, if you have them, very finely chopped hot red chili peppers. Allow this to marinate for about 6 hours or better still overnight in the refrigerator. The juice of the citrus fruits is said to "cook" the fish. The Seviche is served cold on a platter of fresh lettuce leaves, surrounded with a ring of black olives. Some people add cold steamed corn on the cob, broken into two-inch pieces. Adds my friend: *No* dressing — this is *not* a salad!

But some of the best times came when we were able to drop everything and plan a monster picnic with two or three families cooperating. Each group would contribute something: fruit, wine, cheeses, lobsters, and as the cars rolled in, the place would fill up with laughter and song, and the woodsmoke odor of an outdoor fire. How lovely to see a score of little children gaily running over the grass, or the older youngsters flying kites, rowing about Gun Rock, or playing ball, what time their elders, covering our long porch with color, gossiped and sipped their drinks or got in each other's way in the kitchen while they piled up stacks of sandwiches to take to the beach. A favorite meal on such occasions was fish chowder. The virtue of chowder is that it is full-bodied and hearty and just as good — some say even better — on the second day or the third as it was to begin with. There are those who say that you can't make it without tomatoes. Some say you can. But no Down Easter would be caught dead with a tomato while making fish chowder. In any case, everyone has his own perfect receipt for this New England bouillabaisse, which is of course superior to everyone else's. Here is our receipt, which comes from Camden in nearby West Penobscot Bay, where some of the best fish chowder in the world is made.

FISH CHOWDER
(for four hungry or six ordinary folks)

Boil 2 or 3 pounds of cod or haddock in salted water. When cold, bone. Fry 4 medium-sized sliced onions with ½ pound of cubed salt pork. When golden brown, break up enough water biscuits to soak up the fat. Boil 1 pound of potatoes, sliced thin, in 2 quarts of milk. Have fish very hot, in enough of its own liquor to cover. Add to potatoes and milk. Both should be boiling hot at time of adding, so they won't curdle. Now add onions, pork, and biscuits. If liked fairly thick, add a little flour made into a paste. Serve with toasted water biscuits. Some guests like to add cracked pepper.

One sport which was great fun on these picnics was shooting at bottles thrown out into the fast-moving currents off Gun Rock. With a couple of .22 rifles, a crowd on the bluff to cheer and jeer, paired contestants would take turns trying to see who could sink the bottles with the first shot. Women are quite as good shots as men, and the competition was keen. Empty bottles thrown out in this way take on a certain amount of water at the first plunge. As a rule this makes them sink so that only their necks show, wildly bobbing up and down in the trough of the waves as they pass the Point. Bang-bang! Another bottle goes. Someone throws out three bottles at once — blurp, blurp, blurp: Bang — bang — bang — bang . . .

Now the crowd settles down to the feast like a flock of brightly colored birds among the rock hollows surrounding

the outdoor fireplace. The gulls soar about overhead, waiting for tidbits. An occasional lobsterman putt-putting
round the Point gives a friendly wave. Then the gathering disperses for walks or games. The soberer members
curl up cozily in Great Hall, smoking and talking till it is
time to leave. After such good times the whole Point often
seems to simmer and vibrate for hours with a curious happiness.

One day our old friend George Richardson regretfully
announced that he had taken on a full-time job with a
large family group on a nearby island. This new situation
required him to move away, but in the courteous and
thoughtful manner of so many of the Maine folk we had
come to know, he had found someone who could take his
place. This was a man named Roger Stanley, a lobsterman by trade, who was knowledgeable in the matter of
gardens and handy with every sort of tool. We liked Roger
Stanley at once and after a bit of palaver, we concluded
an arrangement with him, satisfactory to both parties. He
was highly intelligent, had a diverting wit, and a nice way
with words. For example: "I'll be glad to upset your garden." (Spade it up.) He has proved to be, as George Richardson was, an estimable friend and a fine co-worker.

George performed one last unexpected service just before
he left. "Challes," he said one day, "I put a couple o' ton
o' gravel on your road just about where she comes up over
the hill. There was an awful soft spot there and when I
hit it, I like to have stove in my cah."

"Where did you get the gravel?" I asked.

"You know, that's a funny thing," said George. " 'Bout
eleven-thutty one mawnin' I was pokin' and pryin' round
amongst your trees over there lookin' for a place to eat
my dinner. ('Dinner,' amongst the locals, comes at midday.)

Well, sir, I thought I see a mess of gravel peekin' out at me. Shore enough! When I put the shovel to her, she turned out to be 'bout as good gravel as a man ever see. Hardly any stones to it. Smooth as mother's milk, and packs down like a dance floor. Come on, now. I'll show you where it's at."

Sure enough — there it was — a large scoop of golden brown that looked like a gigantic bowl of Grape-Nuts. Squeezing it in one's hands, one could compact it almost instantly into a hard, slightly resilient mass. This was real riches. If it held out, we could repair our road from our own land, and so save the costs of screening and hauling. Most of the local gravel had stones and even boulders in it, and had to be pre-screened before it could be used. This naturally ran up the cost. If our supply were really big, we could use it to cover the forest trails which we were planning.

Jon and I now began to hack away in the next few days along the series of yellow stakes we had put down the year before, in order to clear and smooth a roadway from point to point, beginning at the water tank and running up over the hill to the region of the Magic Forest, most of which had escaped the full fury of the hurricane, then around the shoulders of the land, down to the swampy area by the eastern shore, past the gravel pit, and thus back to our own road. Swatting mosquitoes, sweating, up to our ears in brambles and rocks and beefing like Boy Scouts on their first hike, we pushed ahead foot by foot. The going was exceedingly rough and after two days of this, I realized that hard handwork was just not going to do the job. At the rate we were going, it would be years before we could call it finished, and I wasn't about to spend the rest of my summer life battling trees if I could help it.

I was confirmed in this conclusion by Jon, who had been tackling a particularly ferocious mass of logs and roots. Scratching a mosquito bite on the end of his nose and shooting a speculative look at me he said, "Look, Cha, this just isn't very scientific. We're not getting anywhere. Too much like Robinson Crusoe."

"Got any ideas, Jon?"

"Well, yes, I have. I think we ought to change our tactics — just clear sight lines from one stake to the next, so a man on a dozer" — here he paused to gauge the effect of this last word — "would be able to see the direction of the paths."

"Okay I think you've got something there. Let's do it!"

So we now changed our tactics, merely clearing a narrow sight line from one stake to the next, about three feet wide, so that a man on a dozer would be able to see the intended directions of the pathways. By this change of emphasis, we managed to make fair progress, and in a week of off-time labor had finished laying out the entire system of roadways and foot paths.

Paul Nitze had found a place ample enough to house both his own family and that of his brother-in-law, James Jackson, who decided to come in with him on the venture. Jackson had a beautiful family and a motor sailer which could be brought up from his home near Boston and based on the fine harbor at Northeast for summer cruises. While we were looking the place over, the idea of a mural decoration for the dining room came up and Paul asked me if I would like to do the job. This proposal was made more natural by the fact that a few years previously I had done a similar decoration for his house in Maryland. We agreed that the mural was to be light and happy in mood and suggest the rocks, trees, boats and mountains of the Mt. Desert region, and with this in mind I started a series of sketches to provide the raw material for the design — a synthesis of memories and sharply renewed observations of the various elements around me — wonderful old work boats, cloven rocks going down to the sea, driftwood, sea birds, storm clouds — a delightful alphabet which I hoped could be fused into a meaningful statement.

We began about this time to hack away at the steep bank back of Great Hall according to our long-range plan, planting it to wild flowers as we went. This was an operation which we surmised might take a couple of years to complete. The hard clay and granite underlayment at this point came close to the surface and it was going to be necessary to change the whole character of the soil, by degrees cutting back into it about three feet, then replacing it with top soil and turf to provide a proper bed for growing things. It was boring but rewarding — the kind of job one could do for an hour or two each day, just enough to sense progress as the new bank slowly emerged and began to take on its eventual character.

One day and night another gale swept over us. The whole Point moaned and shuddered like a whipped child. During the early hours of the storm, at about sunset time, we were going into our now familiar routine of battening down the hatches, putting on shutters, gathering up tools and preparing for the siege. Suddenly an enormous bald eagle glided by, not fifteen feet from where we were working. He seemed contemptuous of the wind and having balanced his way forward on the breast of the gale, he lit in a nearby spruce, calmly looking us over from his lambent yellow eyes like a king who was master of his domain.

About two A.M. the sky suddenly lit up with a tremen-

dous orange glow. Fire! Lightning had struck something
a couple of miles away. The storm had kept me awake,
and now Fred stirred in her sleep, then woke suddenly —
chuckling. "I was just dreaming about open-faced sandwiches — but what's the light?" Hastily dressing, we ran
out of the cabin and up to the water tower. The wind at
seventy miles per hour was scything over the Point with a
kind of furious glee. One could see miles of billowing
clouds lit from below as from some orange and yellow hell.
One of the old wooden resort hotels of the region had
caught fire and was burning like a torch.

In the returning light of morning we saw that in the
gardens most of the plants were flattened or leaning crazily.
And everywhere there were trees whose green leaves had
turned to bronze under the bombardment of salt spray.
Out came the chain saw. Dozens of our remaining fringe
of trees were downed and must be cut. The salted windows had to be washed, fireplace ashes blown all over the
cabin by gusts coming down the chimney had to be cleaned
up and the boats brought back to the shore, and now we
must see what could be rescued or propped up in the gardens. This salt spray reaction is selective. Some trees look
as gray as pumice, others are browned here and there, still
others remain quite green. All the apple trees were the
color of cocoa, however, and the apples were gone. The
corn was flattened beyond help, but the sweet peas growing at the edge of the garden over a stout chicken wire
fence were blooming bright and clear as if there had never
been a storm, and wonder of wonders, there was a hummingbird!

The days following gales are often wonderful — sparkling
seas, heavenly skies filled with innocent little clouds gam-
boling like lambs, sea gulls skirling overhead and flocks of

terns just off the point, wheeling and diving into the trough of the waves in an intricate dance of sheer joy or, more likely, sheer appetite, as they dive for a passing school of herring. But if you look back up the hill you can see that all the gold and purple of goldenrod and asters and the pink and green of the roses have turned a dismal mud color as if someone had suddenly turned off a light, leaving even the daytime landscape in semi-darkness. But everybody waves to everybody, from car to car, from boat to boat, and everybody stops to talk to everybody, including the birds and squirrels scampering and chattering in the scrambled branches.

We were in the mood to get out and about after this last siege and the horror of the fire, and we took an all-day trip around the south side of Mt. Desert, running as close to the shore as we dared, in and out of marvelous little coves and under the lee of beetling cliffs to watch the great seething waves beat and burst into the sea-caves and to sense that our whole island world was athrill with the sweetness of renewed life. To top off the day, the girls baked a great cake. In the course of the evening it all disappeared except for a few crumbs which we scattered on our rumpled lawn for the birds.

Still in the mood for exploration, we went island-hopping the following day near the western extremity of Blue Hill Bay. Here in a cluster of smallish islands lies Opeechie of the beach picnics and the clam feasts, now for the most part a tangled wilderness of forest and rock. Like many another island hereabouts, Opeechie had once been inhabited. But now time and weather had all but obliterated the furrowings and scratchings of the early settlers. The shallow waters off the eastern shore of Opeechie must have been a perfect feeding ground, for they were once teeming with fish. So much so that the family which lived on the island had built a weir across the natural inlet which forms a little bay or harbor here. The fish, coming in with the tide, were led into the weir by means of a series of open passageways which could be closed at high tide, impounding them in the little body of still water at the head of the inlet. Then a purse seine was lowered and by degrees pulled into an ever-tightening circle which concentrated the fish into a great roiling mass near the shore where they could be gaffed and thrown into the boats.

Sailing over to Opeechie with some friends, we came into the inlet at about high tide, and looking down into the clear water we could see the tops of the posts which had formed the skeleton of the weir. Back some distance from the shore we could just make out over the tangle of the woods the dry bones of a house or shed sagging down into the bush. A couple of iron bedsteads and a few fluttering rags were all that one could find to remind one of humankind except that down by the water on a high ledge there lay a great iron pot surrounded by the traces of a black overflow of tar whose rivulets had run out over the rocks in all directions. Here the family must have tarred their ropes to keep them from rotting under water as they held the bushes and branches which formed the walls of the weir between the posts.

Pushing our way inland toward the center of the island along what seemed to be the trace of an old road, we came out after a half-hour's walk into a great meadow about thirty acres in extent, where a series of granite ledges lay so close to the surface that only grass and brambles grew on the thin soil. Here and there this meager covering disappeared entirely, leaving enormous bare slabs of lichened rock lying open to the sun. In the midst of this open area there had risen a mansion sometime after the close of the Civil War built on the proceeds of the fishing at Opeechie, which Maine legend has it was once called the Golden Shore. It had been the most splendid house anyone had ever seen, with turrets and towers and curlicues and great overhanging cornices. One of our friends remembered being taken there as a little child, but as with memories of a dream, there remained only unconnected snatches of recollection — a line of people in rocking chairs on a vast gingerbread porch — a highly varnished set of cellar steps down which he was taken for a sweet pickle, given him by the lady of the house from a jar on the shelf — and a horse: some kind person had put him on the horse for the ride up to the manse. This had been the supreme experience: all else had faded.

Now we stood looking at the dessicated and fallen shards of the old structure, sadly bleaching in the sun. It was the usual picture once more — a few holes in the ground, here and there a sagging timber, and the last three boards of the old cellar stairs, gray and rotten, ready to fall away at a touch. Apparently the fishing had given out, the enterprise had slowly failed, and the discouraged family had moved back to the mainland, taking the best parts of the building with them. The Mayans and the Khmers in their pride had successfully fended off their surrounding jungles for a time, only to be overwhelmed in the end. But the hardy Maine folk must have had a similar battle against the rigors of the fierce unyielding climate, which never sleeps, never gives up, is never completely subdued.

Hundreds of people had once populated these islands and for the nonce must have been able to make their peace with the forests, the gales, and the snows. But if for any reason they left, their dwellings and all their works were inexorably bitten off chunk by chunk, chewed up, swallowed, and finally digested. Unlike the dry southwestern mesas where the seemingly fragile yucca-fibered artifacts and wooden ladders of the cliff dwellers have lasted in a remarkable state of preservation since the dawn of recorded history, these wet northern "jungles," with their alternating rhythms of intense heat and icy cold, had completely overridden and obliterated the handiwork of the early settlers, so that now hardly a trace remains after the passage of a mere hundred years.

Coming away from sad and beautiful Opeechie by moonlight, we had now to skirt most carefully the posts of the weir which at low tide were standing some six feet out of the water. Looking back along the phosphorescent wake of our boat, we could see them ranked there in long lines of skeletal black silhouettes fingering the night in a monotonous and slowly fading rhythm.

It had become our custom as each summer drew to a close to go over to a swamp on the edge of Walter Lippmann's land, where a series of secret springs come out of a tangle of stunted forest. Partially dammed up by a great natural sea wall along the shore, the overflow finally bursts through and down to the sea in a narrow rush of tea-colored water. By degrees the swamp had been formed into a natural cranberry bog whose brilliant red berries and tiny bushes lay among their waterways in a series of richly textured carpets covering a space of several acres between the ridge of the sea wall and the forest. As the berries turned crimson with the advance of autumn, we would come here to gather a few quarts of these little rosy-cheeked wilderness fruits which made a delicious sauce for Thanksgiving. "Turkey with Old Point sauce," said Fred. "Yum! What a tang! That's something no supermarket will ever have! The Indians here must have used this very swamp. I feel like a flea-bitten old squaw myself — whew! These mosquitoes are fierce. But nothing that a good layer of dirt and bear's grease wouldn't prevent. Too bad we're so civilized."

As for Mary Margaret McKitten, she had had a fine summer. A gay, irresponsible young cat, she spent most of her time chasing butterflies or sitting for hours on end on top of a stump, immobile as an Eskimo at a blow-hole in the ice, waiting for a mouse to pass, or sometimes leaping among the long grasses in a wild abandon of pleasure. Now she appeared to be fleshing up a mite and, suspecting that she might be in a family way and possibly might abandon her brood, we offered fifty cents for any kitten that might be found. Wisteria, meantime, feasting as usual on pollock, began to look more and more like a soft furry football gradually being inflated as the weeks went by.

That year Jonathan, Erica, Fredericka and the dog departed on schedule, leaving Rachel, the two cats and me for a few extra days. I was in the midst of making sketches for the mural and needed a bit of time to wind up the work, and Rachel, whose vacation still had a few days to run, agreed to stay, particularly as she was in the midst of a lovely creative splurge, painting a series of gay watercolor sketches of the cabin interiors. Finally, everything was packed and put away and the station wagon, laden nearly to the roof, stood at the turnaround ready for departure. That last night was icy cold. Rachel had retired to her room and I was dashing through the last chapters of a book.

As I lay reading in Great Hall, I heard what I thought must be Mary Margaret McKitten yammering just outside the window, but strangely the sound seemed to come in chords. I made for the door and looked out. There in the moonlight was Mary Margaret, accompanied by a mass of gorgeous kittens. They must have been nearly six weeks old and they looked exceedingly competent, if somewhat scared. "Rachie!" I yelled. "Come here! We have work to do!" The proud mama now scooted in through the open door, followed by a clump of six of the wildest and scaredest kittens I have ever seen. Mother McKitten said to me as plain as day, "Okay, Dad, here they are. You take it from here." Scampering and racing all over the place, the kittens were almost impossible to grab. One of them got wedged behind the kitchen sink, too far for hands to reach, and had to be pulled loose with the fire tongs. Biting, scratching, dodging and twisting six ways, they were finally collared one by one and put into the wagon. Heaving a vast sigh of relief, we fell into bed.

Promptly at five A.M. the next morning, as we were tak-

ing a last lingering look around, Wisteria came out of
Erica's room, where she had been incarcerated for the night,
looked up at me and without so much as a by-your-leave
produced a kitten. Seizing it in her mouth, she raced down
the ramp and shot out the cat door and up the hill behind
the cabin. A wild scrambling chase followed, ending with
her eventual capture in the long grass under the water
tower. Then into the car kittens mewling and puking,
mamas crying, and Wisteria giving birth to four more
kittens on the way. At two the next morning we arrived
at Coppernose with all thirteen animals intact, but the car
looked and smelled like a charnel house. I recalled then
a conversation Fredericka had had with a wise old woman
of the region. "What is it about Maine that seems to make
our cats have so many kittens here, when at home they
have only two or three?"

"Why," replied the beldame with never a change of
expression, "it's the foggy mornin's, dearie, the foggy
mornin's."

14

Marriages and Murals

THAT fall Fredericka and I were both deep in community work and I was preparing for a one-man show in the spring and gradually assembling a coherent design for the Nitze mural. Living in one place for years as we had, one weaves a thousand threads into the fabric of community life and associates oneself, in the familiar American way, with the work of a school, a hospital, a co-op, or some other local enterprise, to the point where an hour or two of quiet life at home seems to take on a rather special quality. And so, breasting the familiar current of work, we saw another winter loom up.

Erica had had a number of suitors during the last few years, but though she had kindly given the principal ones a careful scrutiny and had made good friends of several, she had seemed on the whole well satisfied with things the way they were. But now on a weekend visit to Coppernose she let it be known that she had found the right person. Hector, the young man in question, was one of three brothers, sons of old friends of ours. Hector, and Anthony the next brother, had both come to New York to work, and our girls had found them excellent company. Together with a cluster of their contemporaries, they had come frequently to Coppernose in the last few months for country weekends.

Hector and his brothers were vigorous lads, as different from each other as Erica and Rachel. All three had dark hair. All three gave the impression of energy and masculine vigor which closer acquaintance did nothing to dispel. Hector, who was the oldest of the three, had a noticeably clear quality of intellect, and like Erica, was rather precise in his approach to most questions. He had attractive hazel eyes, verging toward green, set in a good square American face of open aspect, distinguished by a high forehead, dark curling hair, and a generous mouth, the whole animated by a constant quiet sparkle. He had the quality, so rare in many young people, of balance, and an almost judicial turn of mind, which with its analytical and penetrating quality made him a delightful companion and a good raconteur. He gave the strong impression of breadth and staying power, and I felt that Erica had chosen well.

Anthony, the second brother, like Rachel, was a creature of boundless energy, enormous physical vitality, a man of quips and japes and wreathed smiles. Dark hair lying straight over a face that might have been hewn from wood, gave him an air of enormous power, emphasized by a pair of glowing eyes, and a most engaging smile.

Richard, the third brother, was about Jon's age. Away at school most of the time, we saw very little of him, but like his brothers he gave the impression of latent power. The three brothers arguing a matter of politics, for instance, could fill a room with raucous laughter, bellows of mock rage, cutting remarks, skillful sallies, all delivered at lightning speed.

Now with the announcement of Hector and Erica's engagement, we realized that we had again crossed one of those invisible but real dividing lines which both distinguish and separate one group of years from another in the life of a family.

On a brief visit to the Point the summer before, Hector had quietly and naturally slipped into our life and its basic outdoor activities of wood chopping, transplanting and repair, along with tennis, sailing, swimming, mountain walks and bird watching. In fact it was he who, with the enthusiasm of a recent convert, had spent longer hours than any of us at "birding." Peterson's *Field Guide* in hand, field glasses over his shoulder and notebook at the ready, day after day Hector would slip out at five A.M. for a couple of hours' quiet stalking. And it was he who had begun a systematic compilation of all the birds seen in the region of the Point, something we had never done. To celebrate this happy initiative I sent him a bit of doggerel, which since it embodies the entire list of birds he had seen during his stay, I append herewith:

THE MIRACULOUS OBSERVATIONS OF
HERR PROFESSOR DOKTOR HEKTOR
or
"Mein Kampf Mit Der Birds"

General refrain:
O buckle on my trusty glass
My pencil, pad, and I'll amass
A list of Old Point birds that go
Before my eyes both high and low!

(*Sea and water birds*)
Vat's that, a Loon?
Mein Gott, zo zoon!
Am I in luck!
Und there's a Duck —
T'is black — no ornament
Perhaps a Double-breasted Cormorant!

(*Wading birds*)
Hardly had I started on my errand
Before Tch-Tch! A Great Blue Herrand!

(*Shore birds*)
Who needs a catalog from Spiegel
To spot from here a great Bald Eagle?
An Osprey who iss holding a fish
Chust seems to answer mein dearest wish,
Und yiper!
There goes der Semi-palmated Piper!
Und, if I'm not erring,
Vir haben Gulls; type Herring.
Now, in der lull, a Black-backed Gull,
Und believe it or not, a Guillemot.
Ach! Birds to burn — der Diving Tern!

(*Forest, marsh, and grass birds*)
Now quicker und quicker iss flying der Flicker,
Zo joyous I write as I pridefully snicker.
It's going like eating a box of marshmallows
As I flashes my glasses at all kleinen Swallows:
Barn, Cliff, und Tree, allen at last!
Und Hummingbird vöglein iss chust flashing past.
Now Belted Kingfisher, chust diving für bait:
There's hardly a moment for writings — but vait!
Till Blue Jay und Crow pass over mein head,
Und schön little Nuthatch mit bosom of red,
Then Craven der Raven ist haunted by Crows
Und Redbreasted Robins now lined up in rows;
Ein Flycatcher, olive-hued, catching a bee.
O wunderbar! Choy! Iss this really me?
Ja Hektor, true, but now you must hush
To hear der faint flute of Hermit, der Thrush.
Und Olive Back too — It's ever so natch,
Efen ven spotting der White-breast Nuthatch.
Und Ruby-crowned Kinglets und Cedar Vaxvings,
Und a Starling who burples ven (thinks he) he sings,
Und Vireo Blue-headed, Vireo Red.

Yust call me Der Birdman before ich bin dead!
Und Varblers! Mein Gott — der Black-throated Green,
Der Yellow, der Pine, Ach zo! I haf seen
Der Myrtle, und Parula, they come thick und fast:
An American Redstart, aber he ain't the last.
Nein! Never! Now Cowbird, now Finch,
Both Purple und Gold, ist a three-legged cinch!
Der male Scarlet Tanager (but no Whippoorwill)
Yet I swear I chust seen a bright Red Crossbill!
Der crackle of Grackle, und two kinds of Sparrow:
Savannah, White-throated, flit by like an arrow.
Ein Zong Sparrow, too, I'm bractically sartin,
Und great jumping frogs legs, a real Purple Martin!
Und Red-shouldered Hawk. He's last, but not least
In der Wunderbar Wunderlich Avian feast!

O buckle on my trusty glass
My pencil, pad, and I'll amass
A list of Old Point birds that go
Before my eyes both high and low.
Chust call me birdman, feathers' friend,
Und may my birdsong never end!

The winter, busy as always, took on a special quality, with our thoughts turned inevitably toward spring and the approaching wedding. Erica and Hector were married at Coppernose in the month of May. Appropriately enough, it seemed to me, the ceremony took place out of doors, assisted by the singing birds and passing clouds of a beautiful day, which was given brilliance by masses of flowers that come into bloom at that time of year.

During the summer that followed, everything about the Point seemed to exist in a new light. I had often thought sadly of how I had blundered in building the cabin; window sills that didn't throw water properly, those cracking softwood logs, that sagging corner, the leak in the roof which nobody could find, and all the rest, but now I was

in a mood to see its rugged beauty, and to realize that on
the whole our family enterprise had perhaps managed to
fulfill its function as a place of peaceful growth. Never
mind those seven little nails sticking down through the
ceiling where some childish hand had blundered. I was
kind of fond of them by now. And don't look at those
hundred dozen stumps. Time had stood still here for won-
drous moments and sophistication, circling back upon itself
like the osprey, had often found simplicity.

Drought came again with the coming of summer. Shallow wells everywhere on the island were beginning to go
dry and it was a common sight to see folk on the roads
carrying buckets of water from wells which still had a supply. Our friend Bobby Rich, the boat builder, who lived
on a magnificent granite ledge overlooking the harbor of
Bernard, and who for twenty years had depended on a
rainwater cistern for his supply, was quietly desperate.
"There's got to be water down there somewhere," said Paul
Scribner, the deep-well driller, to Bobby. "Most deep wells
around here come in at about seventy-five feet, which isn't
too bad, and if you got a gallon a minute you'd be in a
lot better shape than you are now. So where do you want
me to put her?"

"Oh, hell," says Bob, "what's the difference, anyway?
It's all granite from here to China and back again. Just
set her over here by the kitchen where I can ease a pipe
in under the frost line without too much extra expense."

Scribner has a drill that doesn't thump but cuts by turning round and round like a screw. Its diamond teeth eat
through granite like a barracuda tearing into the flank of
a victim.

The rig was set up and the drilling began. At about
seventy-four feet there was a trickle of water, "hardly

enough to launch a cake of soap," as Bob put it when telling me the story. But at seventy-six feet there suddenly came a strange rumbling sound from the hole. "What in the name of Tophet is *that?*" cried Bob.

"Don't know," said Scribner. "Never heard anything like it before, but I think mebbe we better stand back some."

With a terrific roar, up came gushing water, mud, stone chips, pipes and cable, geysering to the top of the second-story windows and sweeping Bobby off his feet.

"Hey, Mildred!" he yelled to his wife as he climbed clear. "Go git the gin and some glasses and let's see what she tastes like!"

For twenty years, carefully husbanding every drop of cistern water, Rich had been sitting directly over an underground river, the original flow of which through the casing, until they got it properly controlled, was estimated at more than fifty gallons a minute, or about seventy-five thousand gallons a day.

"What are you going to do with all that water?" I asked Bob.

"Tell you what, Challes," he replied. "I never did want to be a millionaire, and I didn't figger to get feudin' with my neighbors, so I didn't go into the water business. Now Mildred wants to have in a few friends from time to time and be able to wash up the dishes afterwards without worrying about rinsing off the suds. You know, if you can jest throw a few duds into the washin' machine without waitin' for a rain to come so's to fill the cistern, that's real luxury if you've never had it. I may be settin' right over an underground river, like you say, but as far as I'm concerned all I ever need out of it is a bunghole and a hose, so I can have a couple drinks before supper and a damn good cup of coffee in the mornin'!"

Spurred on by this remarkable episode, we decided to have Paul Scribner dig us a deep well, but there seemed no logical way to determine where the best supply of water could be found. Perhaps the only thing to do was to put it in some convenient spot not too far from the tower where the drill rig wouldn't be in the way while the digging was going on. Or we could find a dowser. Of course the water might be brackish — we were surrounded by ocean on three sides and in all probability would have to go some way below sea level before we hit a substantial supply. It was an interesting problem. Scribner came and traipsed over the land with us. "I've dug a heap of wells all over Maine," he said, "some just where dowsers said to dig and some not, and I'm stumped if I know whether they're any help. In this part of Maine you'll always get water if you go deep enough. Somewhere around one hundred feet ought to give you a nice supply. But it could be salt or you could get iron stains or sand. You just never know. Taking one thing with another, if you want to use a dowser, I don't see how it could do any harm. But my schedule is so full right now, I'm afraid you'll have to wait till next summer."

So we signed a contract for a deep well, and with the prospect of an increase in our water supply, we decided to transform the one-time kitchen area in Old Cabin into a bathroom. This would give us parents in effect our own private wing to which we could retire when the place was pre-empted by the younger generation.

I built a shower with a free-form mosaic design of polished beach stones to stand on and had the plumbing installed for sink and toilet, which included digging a hole for the necessary septic tank. One of the men digging the hole was about the most taciturn critter I ever had anything to do with. Seamed and weathered, he almost never spoke if a grunt or two would suffice. No one, it seemed, could get more than a word at a time from him and then it appeared as though it came out with an effort. I mentioned this to the foreman who told me the following tale:

"Old Harry there? Awful good worker — steady as a rock. Don't say much, though — never did. Fact is, I never knew a man could say so little. But mebbe that was his wife. She never give him much practice: she was wuss 'n he was. Harry used to have a little farm . . . lived there alone with this sick wife that never said nuthin' from one day's end to another. Heart, they said. I lived nearby at the time and once in a while I'd come in and see her lyin' there on that sofy of hers while Harry was out in the kitchen doin' the cookin', though I always did wonder some just how bad it was. Well, when she was took with a spell, she'd ring a little bell, and Harry'd come a-runnin'. When he had to work down in the lower meadow he'd arrange with a neighbor woman to answer the bell. So come a day when she was took real bad for once and hardly had time to ring the bell before she passed on. The neighbor come but t'was too late. She laid the body out nice and easy on the sofy and went outside and rung the big farm bell. I heard it and come over to see what the trouble was. Well sir, I was standin' there in the livin' room with the Dear Departed when Harry come leggin' it up the hill and in the front door. He seen her lyin' there with a newspaper over her face to keep off the flies. He went over, lifted up the newspaper and took a good long look. Then he straightened up, heaved a nice long sigh and ses, 'Well, that's more like it!' "

Fred found a delightful little Franklin stove which we put in the corner back of the chimney just where old John Henry used to be. Now at last we had our own quarters in which we could entertain our guests. Here we could foregather in front of the fire and discuss Hispanic architecture with the Kublers, bird watching with the Fitzgeralds, viruses with the Duran-Reynalses while listening to the distant sound of music and dancing from the region of Great Hall.

It worked like a dream and brought to all of us a new sense of flexibility and freedom from constraint. Now there were times when Fred and I could simply loll by the hearth with a languid cup of tea of an afternoon and casting a glance seaward, watch those intelligent and laudible chaps, the porpoises, or give a passing thought to the adorable orange bumblebees in the garden, the darting terns, the creeping mists slowly swallowing the islands in the bay, or to tomorrow's project, like those stone steps we were about to install at the old woodshed door. It might be true that every eleven minutes six hundred and five new United States citizens were born, but here the sense of space and calm and peace were paramount. We had time to watch rain trickling down the windowpanes and to be reminded of all the world's waters: the mighty flow of Amazon, Volga, Mississippi, dew falling from a petal, reflections in a mountain pool, liquid lustre of an eye and wet, blue distances. Or seeing a little seed ooze down the pane inside a rolling drop be reminded of the endless forests of Maine's yesteryears, the leagues of grasses, billions of flowers, Himalayas of wheat and corn and the infinite and as yet unstaled variety of the American wilderness.

Our friends George and Betsy Kubler, just back from Spain, came on for a weekend. One afternoon while the others went for a long ramble about the lower slopes of Western Mountain, Betsy and I got a short ladder and some paints from the studio and, singing lustily for sheer pleasure, painted an impromptu mural on the white plaster wall above the kitchen grill: there was a livid green octopus at the bottom, whose tenacles reached for the tools above the sink, sundry rainbow-hued fishes, a dock midst dancing waves and then as one looked further up, gulls, a balloon filled with laughing people, and at the very top just at the apex of the roof a splendid yellow flying saucer. I am glad to report that our mutual effort was received with wild cheers of enthusiasm by the returning wanderers.

A recent squall had brought down one of the remaining trees right across our old tent platforms. It had been some years since we had last put up the tents which now lay moldering in the loft of Old Cabin. This seemed a good moment to cut up the tree and get rid of the platforms at the same time. Gray with age and now sagging and splintered under the fallen tree, the battered old platform still recalled vividly to us our first magic moments under the tents as we rolled into our blankets so many years ago, slightly unnerved by the hum of mosquitoes. Thinking of Erica, now a glowing young woman, I heard again faint and far a child's voice saying sleepily, "Charlie, do you suppose the trees are talking?"

The trees did talk. Everything talked. And the storms *yelled*. But there was another language, a language of whispers, and the shift of iridescent colors, which often had a more profound effect in the long run than the dramatic bombardment of coastal storms and great winds. These messages from infinity came on days of pearly silence, when all of nature seemed wrapped in mysterious sleep. Beyond the fringe of trees on these days the water stretched out and out endlessly, reflecting the hazy opal light so that it seemed as though the sea and sky had blended into a single element which had no beginning and no end, truly days of mystery when it seemed as if the rude sound of a hammer might shatter the dream. On such days one felt almost compelled to walk on tiptoe and speak in whispers. The thought of time was meaningless: there was no time; one hung suspended in a magical Now. Soft air, sweet perfume, the caress of quiet, and above it and through it the wonderfull nacreous light were the gifts of such days. If one yielded to their spell — and who could resist? — one could be brought again for an hour or two into the innocence of childhood, without thought, without plan or care, and could experience that rarest of all human emotions, beatitude. On such opal days the bay seemed to be floating in nameless light. Who would want to work on such a day? The thing to do was to get into a boat, give ourselves utterly to it, and let it take us where it would.

I recall a day of this kind, when we decided to drift over to Black, an island a few miles across the bay. It was one of a group of low-lying forest-covered mounds which accented and gave a certain rhythm to our ocean view: Great Duck, Little Duck, Black, Gotts, Placentia, Swans. They lay in a long line, half seen through veiled mists in the early morning or suddenly standing out bold and clear, for the most part covered with a shaggy coat of trees down to the water's edge. Black had once had a famous granite quarry which contributed stone of excellent quality to a number of public buildings in New York. The old quarry, now totally engulfed in a thick forest of spruce and fir, had stood silent for years. It was a romantic reminder of the age of windjammers and four-masted schooners, which conveyed the stone down along the coast to New York and Boston.

We set out for Black Island on this particular day with Bob and Mildred Rich, who were luckily in the same mood. Bob had just completed work on a boat, which he was now eager to test out with a number of short shakedown cruises before delivery.

"What a beautiful day on the water!" said Bobby Rich. "Don't see how anybody can live huddled up to them skyscrapers. Last time I was to Boston I couldn't hardly hear myself think: noise all over and everybody in a hell of a hurry. If they bump you off the sidewalk they just turn on you and say 'Humph!' That ain't no way to live. A man has to wash his hands thirteen times a day just to get off the bugs and the air stinks like a sewer. Down here on the bay most of us don't get rich — lots of the women have to cut up old dresses to make aprons and all — but money won't buy good air. And the ocean's still free, and there's plenty of room to maneuver. Now look at that little island out there: I've passed that island mebbe five hundred times all told, and every time I look at it it looks different, and always pretty as a picture. I don't know too much about art, but if I stick with you I might pick up a few crumbs here and there. So I make bold to say if you done it quick with those colored chalks o' yours, 'pears to me that island would make a fine little painting. I don't understand this 'modern' art, though. Looks like a lot of artists are just puttin' their private confusions out to where everybody can see 'em, or else they imitate children's doodles because some lily-livered museum man tells them it's the thing to do. It's like them crazy hats wimmin buy and throw away after a couple weeks. T'any rate, if you live here you got it made: God paints new pictures for you every day and it don't cost a penny!"

As we came toward the shore we could see the remnants of a grand old dock hardly more than a jumbled and heavily lichened pile of square-cut rock standing some way out into the bay. Here one must anchor a good distance out and row in in order to avoid the hundreds of sunken granite blocks which litter the bottom. At the top of the slope, we came across two rusted iron rails and a few desiccated ties, a sort of miniature railway by means of which the dressed stone had apparently been delivered from the quarry to the waiting schooners. In a little dell still within sight of the water stood the skeletons of two ancient apple trees, covered with bearded moss. Someone here had felt the need of apple pie!

We began to follow the metal rails through the forest, gradually ascending a long rise. "Somewhere up there there's a lake or a pond," said Bob. "Used to be a hotel there, too, they say." The rusted tracks of the railway by degrees disappeared but along its entire length one could follow the trace by means of hundreds of squares of dressed

stone covered with green moss which had evidently fallen or
been tossed aside during the descent from the quarry and
now lay half submerged under the spongy surface of the
forest floor. Beaver had been at work here too. Gnawed
lengths of tree trunks lay all about, the beautiful scooped
hollows where the beavers' teeth had cut quite clearly visible. The forest began to open as we advanced. Suddenly
we saw the lake, if it had ever been one. It was now a great
hummocked swamp, laced with narrow waterways, and open
areas from one of which rose a flock of black ducks with a
roar of wings. At the edge of this swamp on a little rise of
ground we could see the remnants of the hotel, now no
more than a series of square hollows faced on the inside
with weathered stone and choked with enormous blackberry
vines, wild roses, day lilies and swamp alder. Sad but beautiful, a gigantic lilac bush still stood at one corner, its clustered seed pods showing that it was blooming still, after its
fashion faithful to the hand which planted it. Eerie silence.
Whitman's lines came to me as I stood by those rather
mournful hollows and gazed out over the swamp:

> *O death, I cover you over with roses and early lilies,*
> *But mostly and now the lilac . . .*
> *Lilac and star and bird twined with the chant of my soul,*
> *There in the fragrant pines and the cedars dusk and dim.*

Someone kicked a pebble down the remnant of a rotted
stairway into the cellar hole — plop, plop, plop — as if to
introduce a human note into the unhuman calm. "Well,
this old place ain't no more use now than tits on a rain
bar'l," said Bobby Rich. "Let's go on up there and see if
we can find the quarry."

Uphill once more toward the center of the island, after
a fifteen-minute walk, the trees began to thin out and fall

away. The buried rails suddenly emerged again onto bare rock lying in tumbled masses at the foot of a series of cliffs. Here was the quarry. Its granite had formed the walls of the New York Public Library, or so it was said, and were now spread along one of the busiest intersections in the world. Hard to relate that glittering confusion and throbbing noise to the uncanny emptiness here, seldom disturbed unless by the shadow of a passing hawk. Looking down, one could see that the uneven floor of the quarry was partially filled with pools of rain water, now and again lightly touched and rippled by the moving air. We did some climbing and heard our voices echo once or twice from the surrounding walls. But there was a kind of sadness here, marking the end of the era of hand tools, of primitive engines and the hardy men who sailed on the New England waters.

Black Island had been romantic enough but somehow we always returned to Baker, which was a bit further out to sea. It had a certain wildness, an indescribable peacefulness that always drew us back at least once a season. Toward the end of that summer there came a great bull-roaring day filled with the energy of sea-spume and tossing treetops. Off the Point the water heaved and sparkled where a hundred terns, uttering high-pitched cries, were diving into the waves, their silken wings flashing in the sunlight. There had been a storm at sea some days before. Now subsiding, it was still sending sea-swells crashing and shouting onto the beach. This was a day made for Baker Island! Hopping to the telephone, we managed to collect a group of eighteen children and grownups, arranged for a boat, and in a fine furious mood began to pack knapsacks and canvas bags, each family contributing something according to plan. There were the makings of salad: lovely purple onions, lettuce and tomatoes damp from the garden, cheese, fruits, bottles of wine and soft drinks. Then came heavy woolen sweaters, dark glasses for the sun, cameras, drawing pads, bathing suits — all hastily stuffed into the nearest bag. At last a look-around to see if anything had been forgotten and we were ready to go. Figaro, catching the spirit of the occasion, danced about barking madly, eager to be taken along.

Down on the dock waiting for the boat we started singing folk songs and dancing slowly round and round a large square opening which gave upon a wooden tank filled with live lobsters, who were swinging about in a free-form dance of their own. In the midst of this gaiety our boat slid to the dock and we all piled aboard. Figaro, not to be left behind, plunged forward at a gallop and straight into the tank, rising like Venus from the wave with six lobsters clinging to his coat.

During the forty-five-minute run out to the island in a heaving sea, we sang again, trolled for fish, towelled off the dog and gave him a bit of bread and cheese to re-establish his dignity. The old abandoned village lay basking in the summer light, deep in its waist-high meadow of blowing grasses and sweet fern, through which we made our way uphill past the lighthouse. One of the buildings had been given a desultory coat of red paint by some recent occupant, perhaps a writer in search of solitude. Peeking through its faded curtains one could see a skeletal bouquet of flowers withering in a vase set at one end of a kitchen table. Otherwise there was no sign of life. The village itself was quietly withering away too — gray and salt-encrusted, its chimneys covered with orange lichens, its shingles curling in the sun, here and there a tired board dropping off the walls into a mass of goldenrod. One of the boys, eyeing an old chain draped across a sagging door, touched it idly, whereupon it suddenly gave way, its two ends swinging in descending arcs till they came to rest with a patter of rusty crumbs across the granite threshold.

We filed now past the empty lighthouse and into the woods beyond, where the path wound downhill toward the open sea. If one stopped to listen one could hear it faintly booming and sighing, though the forest itself held us in its own stillness, broken now and then by the faint twitter of a warbler, and the reedy lisp of cedar waxwings, a flock of which seemed to be accompanying us as we drifted among the trees. As the forest gave way we had a sensation which we had often experienced before: with dramatic suddenness the darkness melts between one footstep and the next and one steps out into blinding sunlight, moving air, a sweep of pink granite slabs reaching away on either hand, and the sight of enormous green combers rushing in to spend themselves in gouts and fountains of silvery spray.

Breaking from darkness and silence we ran shouting for the rocks, this other lighter world where everything sparkled, everything shone, everything sang and tumbled, advanced, retreated, and at once caught us up in an overwhelming sense of fierce compelling life. Here was the open sea!

Eighteen bodies on a beach like this are no more than a few grains of colored sand, easily dispersed and soon almost forgotten. It was a vast impersonal universe of primitive forms and giant motions whose hypnotic rhythms and outerworld repetition of rock upon rock induced forgetfulness and brought on a trancelike feeling of not belonging any more to a world of familiar things but at once having become a wild keening wind-borne something, or no-thing, released from time, but alive in a strange fourth-dimensional Now. There is a rapture-of-the-depths, a kind of drunkenness or nitrogen narcosis known to divers who go too deep or stay down too long. But this was a less danger-ous rapture-of-the-sea-strand, a rapture of wind, sun, and waves. We all felt it in our several ways. The young-est children, like the sandpipers and plover which darted around them, ran shrieking among the rocks, or lay en-chanted by some tidal pool gazing into its Lilliputian shal-lows where waving fronds and jeweled pebbles made ex-quisite fairy landscapes that lay spread out a few inches be-low the surface as if seen from a balloon.

There were rock-leapers and driftwood-gatherers, and there were sitters-around, fire-makers, and a residual group of practical parents busy making sandwiches. There were strollers and sketchers and dreamers, and here and there a solitary philosopher asking only to be left alone. And there was Figaro, lapping water from the overturned cover of an ice bucket.

But hunger brought us all to earth. Frozen chowder was heated over the fire, the vin rosé began to flow, a gorgeous green salad was shaken from wet cloths and marinated in olive oil and lemon juice. Purple onion slices were arranged between slabs of Freddie's homemade bread covered with mayonnaise; piles of fruit, hunks of cheese were laid out. Then with a smacking of lips and a licking of oily fingers the feast began.

How pretty modern beachwear has become in comparison to that worn when I was a child. As if it were only a mo-ment ago I can see my quite beautiful mother coming from a ladylike dunk in the sea draped in a bathing costume more appropriate to a hippopotamus: long black cotton stockings, black bloomers, middy blouse complete with dicky, and over it all a stout skirt that went swish-swish as she walked, the whole topped with a fearful bathing cap made of some substance like jellied rubber. But this gay company was all rainbow colors and lovely tanned legs, the mothers for the most part in halters and shorts, the young-sters in briefest butterfly-hued bathing suits, and two or three of the youngest completely nude, as pretty as little ripe peaches: the men more soberly garbed in shorts but nearly as bare as Greek statues. Everything spelt simplicity, health, and the elegance and purity of bodies exposed to the sun. "It took two thousand years to get back to it, but here we are," I thought.

A walk along the slanting wall of giant pink slabs brings one to that southeast-facing point where the rocks jutting to the open sea catch the full fury of winter storms. At this turn-of-land the forest gives way, yielding a little to form a smallish amphitheater back of the wall of granite. This acre-sized spot is filled ten or fifteen feet deep with drift-wood tossed over the wall year after year. Great baulks of timber from forgotten ships, tree roots, bits of deck or mast, smashed lobster pots, barrel staves, old boxes, pilings with iron hooks and ringbolts still embedded in their scarred sides — helter-skelter, all lie there inextricably entwined like the bleached bones in an ancient elephants' graveyard. A group of us swarmed here like ants exploring the skeleton of a dinosaur: skittering, prying, peering and running out to the ends of trembling half-balanced logs. We fell into sudden looming pockets and tugged futilely at bits and pieces of driftwood too tightly wedged to move. But the sea dominated the day and it was not long before we were all back over the sea wall again, slipping and sliding down the slopes to meet the thundering surf which was now advanc--ing over the ledges with the incoming tide, filling the half-emptied pools and running in under tilted rocks with a satisfying roar.

Here Fred found a marvelous piece of driftwood which

must have spent years as a homeless wanderer on the face
of the waters. It was about four feet long and a foot wide.
Scoured and shaped by wind and water and sand, it had
five holes rather mysteriously piercing a seamy carapace of
ancient ringed oak. It was stained here and there with
traces of orange rust and spattered with barnacles. This old
slab had a curious grace which gave one the feeling that it
might almost have been made by some Chinese artisan to
delight the eye of a mandarin. Now shaped and reshaped
by years of erosion, it looked almost like a bird, almost like
a hand, or like a fish, or almost like a piece of garden sculpture by Henry Moore. Three enormous square jade-green
bronze pegs protruded from its surface. This thing, then,
had once been part of something which had been worked
and shaped by a brain and a hand for a purpose whose
nature had long since become obscured by long reaches of
time. But it was not mute. It spoke in the language of
rhythm, color, silence.

I tried sketching rock plants and sea birds for half an hour but it was impossible to concentrate. My mind kept wandering out to sea and losing itself there half dissolved in the roar of wind and the steady downpour of blinding light. My penciled scrawls seemed to make no sense, for the delicious impression came over me that I was gradually spreading out and out till I had become the rocks and waves and light.

A faint cry brought me into time again. A distant semaphore of arms from the picnic place signaled that it was time to gather up our things and be off. The shadows were beginning to lengthen over the slabs, bringing a breath of chill to the air. Along the horizon a stealthy fog was uncoiling like a serpent, slowly digesting the outer islands. And suddenly I realized that my feet were wet and somewhat cold. By degrees our little tribe was drawing together, forms appearing and disappearing over the tops of the rocks, voices gradually getting louder. Then a hustle and bustle of departure as sweaters were put on and the gear was repacked. Once more, as so often in the past, we cast regretful clinging glances back along the magic shore, now for the most part lying in deepening pools of blue shadow. But it had been a day to remember. And as if to end it with an appropriate gesture, Father Neptune at this moment disclosed to us the solemn back of a whale some distance out, momentarily crowned with a jet of steam.

As we left the island, its tiny gray village slowly retreated into the gathering fog. First the lighthouse disappeared, then the forest, then one by one the encrusted houses in their dimming golden meadow. For a second the little red house stood out clearly from the rest. A few moments later, as we huddled down in the boat listening to the softly chugging engine, we could see it there slowly fading: the last ember of a dying fire. Gradually it turned to darkening pink as the boat drew away, blurred, became gray like something infinitely old, then as with a retinal image which is both seen and not seen, its shape by degrees became less and less distinct till one could hardly tell the moment when it began to exist only in the memory.

We did not see Rachel that summer till the month of September. She had been away in Europe, partly on vacation and partly on an assignment from British Information Services. But now having returned to this country, she flew in to the Bar Harbor airport for the Labor Day weekend together with Anthony. Joy everywhere. Radiant faces. There was music in Great Hall and dancing on our ruffled lawn. It was a tumultuous time in which the activity of the moment made no difference: everything was marvelous. Rachel and Anthony were in love! But now, having waited nearly a year to make sure, and Rachel's absence having only served to confirm it, there was no more waiting for them. They wanted to be married that very fall at Coppernose, married with autumn decorations, a great Harvest feast, ruby wines and a roast suckling pig. We were elated by their decision as we had been by Erica's and Hector's. The weekend went by like the flash of a hummingbird, and on Sunday, all in a rosy glow, they took once more to the air, which seemed just then to be their natural element.

One day toward the end of the season I dropped in on Wendell Gilley. Things were apparently going well. Beside his house stood a garage, now converted to a workshop for his carved birds. Gilley greeted me with a smile and a firm handclasp. Here was a happy man. Bronzed, muscular, his hair now turning silver, he was dressed in a checked hunting shirt and gray slacks, over which he had fastened a workmanlike blue denim apron. Wind and sun had given his face the fine patina of ruddy copper, and his gray-blue eyes twinkled through steel-rimmed specs.

The shop consisted of three rooms filled with the paraphernalia of his craft — carving tools, saws, jars of paint, hunks of driftwood, brushes, and birds in all stages of preparation from raw blocks of basswood to the final product, mounted and painted with exquisite skill. "See this?" he said, pointing to a small dark-brown object on the top shelf of a cabinet set against the wall. It looked like a child's attempt to whittle a duck from a piece of firewood. "That's my first bird. Did it about the time I put that old second-hand sink into your cabin — must be twenty years ago now — but it got me into this business, so it's a kind of lucky charm, and anyway, it's a good measure of how far I've come. Hardly believe it myself. Isn't it fierce? Now look at this — just finished it this last week for a customer out in Ohio." He pointed to a beautifully finished pair of Canada geese.

"Those are marvelous, Wendell," I said, "and your paint work is pretty sophisticated too."

"Yes, I've learned a lot since the old days — see that sheen? That's air brush work. I use several kinds of paint, one over the other, to get the right effect. Basswood to begin with: I buy it green, by the cord, and air dry it here. You can carve it in almost any direction without splitting it, for one thing. Now take a look at these gulls." We walked over to his workbench, where there was a pair of herring gulls with outspread wings just settling delicately onto a piece of driftwood. They had not yet been painted: the honey-colored basswood forms were wonderfully satisfying just as they were.

"You know, I almost like them better this way than when

they are finished in color," I said. "It emphasizes the purity of line and in a way simplifies the whole design."

"Well, most people want them in color," he replied, "but now and then I get an order for them this way. I have orders for two years ahead right now!" He slapped a bulging order book. "But when I get too many orders I sometimes get to feeling put upon. So I just quit and go fishing. Good for the soul. I've shipped out over five thousand carvings all over the world, so now I just work for the fun of it, and the heck with the pressure. I figger I make better carvings that way. Even took time off to write a book * on how to do it and that's brought me a lot of new friends, and a good deal of correspondence with folks who are just as crazy as I am." He grinned, his face breaking into a hundred fine wrinkles.

"It's a far cry from lying under a sink trying to keep the grease out of your eyes," I said.

"Yep," said Wendell Gilley, the happy man, "but the principle's the same: now it's sawdust, which I admit smells better than grease. Oh hell, that's beside the point. What I'm trying to say is if you work for quality and not for money you may not get rich, but it feels pretty durn good down inside."

At the very end of the summer, the Nitzes and the Jacksons having returned to Washington and Boston, I gathered up my painting materials and the final approved sketch of the mural and went over to the empty house to set up some lights and go to work. Nothing more provocative than a series of empty walls! Just here was where those reddish

---

* *Bird Carving — A Guide to a Fascinating Hobby,* by Wendell Gilley. D. Van Nostrand Co., Inc., 1961.

rocks would go — and there a clump of forest with an eagle like the one we had seen at the Point — now a bit of the bay with a suggestion of stormy sky, and perhaps a flock of ringed plover. And past the door to the hall I would put a little fishing village with a white steeple on the hill, some docks, and a cluster of boats in the harbor. A cormorant or two on these rocks in the foreground would be fun, and perhaps a couple of happy bathers and a few black-backed gulls. Further in the background there would be mountains and at last the sea with a fairylike simulacrum of Baker's Island in the distance, some twenty-five feet from my starting point. And here, to finish, around the corner and over the fireplace, a whirling flock of terns.

As the days went by, whirling like the terns, the mural began to take on an existence. Friends of the caretaker came to look from time to time, a number of them bringing their children. There were moments when, seized by the conviction that I was not alone but more nearly assisting at some public function, I would turn around to see six or seven of the local folk to whom an artist actually at work painting a mural is a wonder as odd as a uranium pile in the dining room. "Hey, Jerry — you see what he just done up there? Real as life! Them's gulls, ain't they? Look! By thunder — there's old Harvey's dock! Well, dumfound me if he ain't made them rocks so natural you could paralyze your backsides. Hey, Challes, how about a few shags on them rocks? Hardly a rock around here ain't got a shag to it. Now look! He's done it! God created the heavens and earth in about six days so the Good Book ses, but seems like you're even quicker!"

One gets used to this sort of thing. It is rather friendly. For years, sketching in many of the plants of the Bethlehem Steel Corporation in the course of preparing their adver-

tising material, I had had to work somewhat deafened by
noise and surrounded by moving ingots and slabs of red-hot
metal, and almost always in the midst of a group of curious
and friendly steelworkers. The early period of invention
is when one needs most to be alone. Actually in painting a
mural, one can often work at what might seem to the lay-
man to be tremendous speed. By the time one gets to the
wall, most of the hard work has been done and one is so
steeped in the theme-and-variations that the wall itself is
nothing but a catalyst serving to precipitate the material
into final form.

I took a series of color shots of the finished mural to
send the Nitzes. During the process, Fred wandered in, as
she had been doing throughout the course of the work, and
suggested that I paint on the boats in the design various
names corresponding to the members of the Nitze-Jackson
entourage, the Phyllis N, the Jimmie J, and so forth. Delighted with this charming conceit, I did so, adding at the
end a rowboat drawn up on the beach upon which I in-
scribed the rubric "C loves F." "I like it," said Fred. "It
doesn't take itself too seriously and it seems to enlarge the
dimensions of the room. The four walls have thinned out
and one finds oneself in a magic world which is not quite
Maine and not quite Nitze-Jackson-in-Wonderland. I think
food will taste better here."

Turning my back on the little world of my invention,
and hoping it would look as well when I saw it with fresh
eyes the following summer, I packed my tools, returned to
the Point to put the cabins to sleep for the winter and
then prepared to whiz back to Coppernose to prepare for
Rachel's wedding. The ceremony took place in October
in a setting that reminded me somehow of Breughel's painting of a wedding feast. The suckling pig was there in all

its glory, charming toasts were offered, and guests wandered through a house glorified with chrysanthemums and autumn foliage. No sooner was the wedding over than Rachel and Anthony took off for the Point to spend a brief honeymoon. And so it came about that Anthony and Hector, the brothers, married Rachel and Erica, the sisters. "Well," remarked Jonathan, "if Richie (the third brother) had only been a girl, how much simpler it would have been for everybody."

Fredericka and I took off for Maine with the dog to spend a few days of quiet after the fine but exhausting hurly-burly of the wedding. Rachel and Anthony had just gone and had left the place open for us by previous arrangement. The weather was cold, the winds howled, the maples and the rowan trees had lost their leaves by the time we got there, but after all the excitement and the stir, Fredericka and I enjoyed a week of utter peace, punctuated by frequent trips to the woodpile to replenish the fire. It was a moment of vast content. The next summer would surely be a time of working on the land, finishing our forest roads, digging the well, and perhaps we would have time to finish the long transplanting job on the bank back of Great Hall.

As we ate lunch one day, each cozily reading a book, I glanced across the table at Fred. Those red curls of hers, when I stopped to think of it, showed a few silver threads here and there, and what was left of mine revealed the approach of winter, too. But Fred could sparkle like just-opened champagne from hour to hour, or more often quietly bubble with a marvelous sense of the ridiculous. She never seemed so young and gay as she was at the moment, lolling back in her chair with a smile of amusement at whatever it was she was reading. Touch Fred and you touch life. "Well, look at us," I said aloud. "Two middle-aged people sitting across the table from one another, and each with a book — I guess we've slowed down some."

"Oh nonsense, Cha, I *like* being middle-aged," she shot back. "It has enormous compensations. I wouldn't be sixteen again for anything in the world. I've never been as old as I was at sixteen. Now I feel like something ripe and

ready to feed people. We've got Jonnie and the girls, and they're all still part of us, so we're more than we were. We aren't just Chafred any more: we're connected in all sorts of ways with the people here, for instance. We're Maine, too! And it's us! You know, if you don't put down roots somewhere you just don't grow. Maybe that's why so many middle-aged people seem so adolescent. I wonder why animals always seem to mature so successfully as they grow older? I suppose Nature pushes them into it since the element of free will is missing. Figaro, for instance: Yes! I'm speaking of you, baby! He's old, but he's wise: a Schweitzer of the doggy world. Gosh! I've been preening my own feathers a bit, haven't I? Forgive me! But you look pretty good yourself: you're kind of big and square like the cabins, and some of the bark's still on — weathered around the edges a bit, though."

"Oh, come on, now," I said. "I feel as young as I ever did. I'll admit I don't stay in that icy water as long as I used to. I just don't have to prove anything any more."

"That's just it," cried Fred. "We don't have to prove anything — we are what we are, whatever that is. The exploration is more inner than outer now. That's the only difference. Well, what'll we do this afternoon? But maybe we don't have to do anything — I call that progress!"

True, just now there was nothing much we could do. In a sense we were out of connection with the land, which had gone into partial hibernation for the winter, and we too, sitting in a place built only for summer occupancy, were in a sense hibernating and glad enough to go when the week was over.

15

Home at Last

THAT winter and spring, with a number of portrait commissions on order and the financial responsibility for the girls now dwindling toward zero, I felt that whatever the cost of the deep well and the forest trails might be, we could manage. I might even hold a one-man show in Maine where we now had so many friends. With this in mind, I began work on a series of paintings based on my Maine sketches.

Fredericka and I went up quite early that next spring with a carload of pictures, staying only long enough to greet a few friends, unload the wagon and get a good night's rest. It was almost like being asleep, then upon opening one eye briefly and seeing familiar surroundings, dropping off again. The land in its late April aspect greeted us drowsily. Long windrows of snow lay all about. The deciduous trees were still asleep and the soil of our gardens was cold. A few weeks later when we returned to Maine in a more stately manner, with both cars, both cats, the dog, and all the regalia that accompanies a summer stay, everything had come alive once more. The carapace had burst, releasing a flood of color and birdsong.

After we had been at the Point a few days, a local road

man came to look at the gravel. "Yep, she's good gravel all right. Fact is, it's better than anything we have over to my place. If it holds out, we could do all your trails in a few days' time. I'll just put the dozer in here and rough out the roads where you put them yeller stakes. Then we'll use a power shovel and a couple of trucks for the gravel, smooth it all out nice and fancy and before you know it, that red-headed boy o' yours will be scootin' around them roads like a wolverine."

Two days later, the dozer came onto the Point and began to march down the lines of yellow stakes, in the process crunching through bushes, trees and rocks, filling in gullies, smashing out stumps and leaving lateral moraines of wreckage on either side of a strip about eight feet wide. Next, on crawler treads, came an enormous power shovel that could fill a truck as if it were an ice cream cone, with just two scoops. It began to tear at the gravel pit, grunting and bellowing. The two dump trucks swiftly laid the gravel and gradually firmed it as they wallowed over the roadways in the course of the work. In three mighty days, the whole thing was done. Our golden gravel had held out, though the pit was now sixty feet long and ten feet deep. "My God! What a hellish hole!" I cried when I first got a really good look at it.

"But what a swimming pool," murmured Fred.

The roads would have been ten years' work for a man, but for a few machines and an intelligent crew, just three days or a little over one thousandth part of that time. Like retreating dinosaurs, the steel monsters slowly rumbled off.

Timidly now, almost holding our breaths, we piled into the station wagon and putting her into gear began floating quietly onto our system of forest trails. It was almost like being in a gondola in Venice. A dreamlike experience, this coursing quietly up over our hill and round and round and down again where before — was it only three days before? — we had pushed and stumbled through a tangle of laid branches, rocks, and new forest growth. Of course there was plenty more to do. Those windrows of shattered junk piled up along the sides, for instance. They would take some years more to eliminate. A good deal of the stuff could be stacked in heaps for winter burning. The rest could be dragged off or sawed up into bits and pieces. We hoped that in time those silken forest grasses and shimmering mosses which we loved so well would creep in and cover them with green. Then a cutter-bar hitched to the tractor and run through once or twice a season could give these ribbons, which would in time be shadowed by tall trees, the appearance of rippled Chinese Tribute silk, or happily the rougher but more appropriate texture of a millefleur tapestry.

About a quarter of a mile from the gravel pit, down toward the eastern shore where in former days the forest had stood so thick that it was always dusk, and where among the alders the deer had found their secret spring, we had asked the road men to make a turnaround. We or our children, we thought, might some day have a larger power boat, and a little landing place here where the water was ordinarily not as rough as on the other shore would come in handy. Now pressing along at this spot, the dozer had first uncovered a large perfectly flat rock ledge, ideal for a turnaround in itself. But in enlarging the area it had suddenly tipped off one end of the ledge into a great soft mass of almost coal black loam. No harm done: it crawled out again, after a few minutes' backing and filling, leaving a kind of crater filled with a mass of material which looked like peat or lignite but was remarkably soft. Crumbly in dry weather, rubbery in wet, it had a sweet nutlike odor, and was simply and wonderfully the best loam anyone had ever seen — apparently hundreds of yards of it at least three or four feet deep. Whatever divine or natural agency had formed it, we were grateful. At Coppernose, we had labored for years to create adequate compost piles, but here a mass of perfectly composed compost was being handed to us on a platter as big as a football field.

And this was to be the year of the well. We had found a dowser, or "water witch" as some folks called them, in a most unexpected quarter. It was Mrs. Jim Willis, a most sophisticated young lady indeed, who had been born and raised as a city girl and had therefore discovered only much later and quite by chance that she apparently possessed the curious power of "divining" the presence of underground water. Having been enchanted by several tales of her prowess, we asked her if she would be willing to come over and try her skill on our land. After all, we had nothing to lose: as far as telling where water might be under the great jumbled and tilted body of granite and other rocks which constituted our Point, one might as well have shot an arrow into the air and started digging where it fell. She readily agreed to come. So on the appointed day, armed with a few freshly cut forked twigs of swamp alder, our delightful friend, in her new role as a water witch, arrived ready to go to work.

Up and down and round about we went, trailing after our cicerone. Holding the twig by its forked ends, with the point forward, she picked her way among the rocks and brambles and young trees. Occasionally the point of the stick would dip uncertainly. But in two spots it positively lunged toward the ground. We put a couple of our yellow stakes at these spots for future reference. Both Fred and I

tried it, of course. Rather haphazard in Fred's hands, the
fork plunged so hard in mine it tore the bark off the twigs.
It was a strange, rather compelling sensation, which either
did or didn't "mean" something. I didn't quite believe it
even when it happened, as one's own volition appears to
have nothing to do with it. But one must leave the door
open to mystery: dogmatists have so often been proved
wrong. The sensation is one of having an invisible hand
reach up suddenly and pull the stick toward the ground as
you pass over certain areas.

Of the two "good" places, one was difficult to get at, but
the other lay at the far edge of a temporary turnout or
parking area we had made years ago in the course of road
building. This particular location would allow Scribner
to bring his drilling rig in along the principal road and to
begin drilling just off to one side, with hardly any extra
trouble.

The next day the rig came in and was set up, towering
above the little trees along the road. When working, it
made a sound like a growl that never ended, loud enough
to make one shout close to, but not unpleasant, as the diamond bit bored its way down through loam, hardpan and
rock which at that point came up within a few feet of the
surface. Now it was rock, pure rock, nothing but rock, hard
and black, probably one of those volcanic intrusions or
dykes which are common on the island. The diamond bit
is backed by a series of hollow steel pipes which are fastened end to end as the hole gets deeper. Water and compressed air are pumped through these pipes down to the
working face where they flush away rock chips and dust and
carry them up the sides of the hole into the open air.

A day passed, then another. An endless goo of rock-dust
and water the color of gun metal came out of the hole.

Fifty feet. Seventy-five feet. Gray goo was spreading all over the area. Eighty feet, ninety feet, one hundred. Still nothing. One hundred and fifty. The stock of our charming water witch was beginning to decline rapidly. And what was all this confident talk among the wiseacres about wells coming in at seventy-five feet? We were more than twice that deep now and the damned hole was as dry as the bottom of an Egyptian tomb. On the third day, at one hundred and sixty feet, we got a feeble squirt — perhaps a quart per minute. The men at the rig, since they were not paying for it, exhaled an air of hardened confidence which Fred and I found ourselves unable to share. All that digging for something no better than a leaky faucet? Never! "There's water down there, all right. We'll strike her yet! Might have to go down a bit more, though. Why, we dug a well only last week up at Carl Smith's place at the head of the sound and *that* one, she didn't come in till two hundred and fifty feet — but we found water!" Shades of our diminishing bank balance! No use to try another hole: we were in this one now up to our necks, and way beyond.

As luck would have it, on that day we had to go out to lunch, and we left with more than a slight sensation of dryness in the throat. After lunch, which tasted strangely like well water mixed with mud, we were coming back along the road to the Point, and from a distance we could see the rig and hear the familiar growl, this time with a slightly softer cadence. This meant that the men were testing the flow. Screeching to a stop, we were met by broad grins. "We hit 'er! Right on the nose at one hundred and sixty-five feet!"

Water! Pure water! Limpid, liquid, looping, lovely water! It was pouring out over the top of the casing in a steady stream, and the first measurements showed we were getting a flow of more than six gallons a minute, or about ten thousand gallons a day. The pumping went on at our request for at least two hours more. We sat around the wellhead munching cookies and drinking coffee with the men, watching and watching the steady flow till we were well nigh hypnotized. And we had a water-tasting ceremony in which all gulped in turn from a large pewter pitcher. "Marvelous! Let's try it on the doggy!" Quickly filling a basin, we called to Figaro, who came over willingly enough and seeing what was wanted dipped his shaggy head into the basin and treated us to the friendly sound of lap-lap-lap-lap. Hooray! He likes it! It must be good! It was pure, clean and cold, and in it not a trace of salt or gypsum or sand. A quick telephone call to Martha Willis. Were we to congratulate her? Can a water witch's prowess go that deep? Or was this blind chance? Who cared! We did congratulate her and were congratulated in return. Then back to the well to bid goodbye to the men and their marvelous machine.

During the course of the next fortnight we installed a submersible pump and ran a line of pipe to the tower. Inside near the top we put in a float valve which by rising and falling would keep the water in the tower at a constant level in this way: the pump itself, sitting at the bottom of the well at the end of a polyethylene cable, cut on and off automatically, actuated by an electric switch controlled by the rising and falling float. Jon and I built a little house over the wellhead in which to house the switch, the fuse box and a small pressure tank. We smoothed out the depressions where the heavy drill rig had stood and covered the whole space with a few inches of fresh black loam from our newly discovered loam pit.

That loam! Fred and I rolled down to the eastern shore

in the station wagon, and Jonathan took the tractor with its wagon behind. Filling both big and little wagons with loam, we would come back up over the hill and dump and spread it in strategic spots. In the course of the summer, we brought up ton after ton of loam, putting it on the orchard, around the studio, over all the gardens and on the forest roadways in the vicinity of the cabins.

Thus our domain had yielded us in its bounty, logs from the forest for our walls, rocks from the beach for the chimneys, fish and mussels from the sea, vegetables, fruits and flowers from the gardens and now both gravel and loam from the earth. The whole thing reminded me of the recent mural in a curious way — all these elements, all these raw materials, once disparate, latent, and as yet no more than potential, had been brought together over twenty years into a new focus. In their present relationship to each other they had now produced a coherence which was not quite that of nature alone, not quite that of nature dominated by man, but seemed to me to represent more nearly a marriage of man and nature in a collaborative effort.

One day the wheel of my lawnmower came off. "Take her right down to Uncle Abner," said the local storekeeper. "I don't know whose uncle he is, but that's what everybody calls him. See that little neck of land sticks right out into the harbor? That shack on it is his shop. If he's in a bad mood he won't so much as give you the time of day. But if he feels like it he can practically build you another lawnmower while you wait."

I found Uncle Abner standing in a thicket of lathes, welding machines, engine parts, boxes of wheels, bars, cast-iron bits and pieces. He was covered by grease and grime all the way from a pair of what seemed to be cast-iron

shoes as far up as two startling blue eyes that peered at
me from behind a pair of gold-rimmed glasses. "You in
trouble, bub? Mower, eh? Yep, I'll fix her. Never see a
mower yet I couldn't tame. T'won't be wuthwhile, though.
Them things is more of a toy than a tool nowadays. You
take that wheel now — steel's as thin as tissue paper." He
gives it a tremendous wallop with a light sledgehammer.
"See that? Hardly touch her and she's ready to give way.
I've got a good mechanic, but he's off sick — information
of the larnyx — so I'm a bit short-handed. Last time I seen
him he was so thin you could split him with a hair. Hand
me that wrench. Now you see that lathe over there? When
he was in good shape, that mechanic of mine, all he had
to do was walk in the door and that lathe would lay right
down and purr like a kitten. Now I'll just true up this
bushing. Where the hell did I put them calipers? Yore
threads is worn: probably hit a rock with that wheel, and
like to stove it in, thin as it is. See the way this lathe cuts?
Swear it's got it in fer me. That's why I wear glasses. Eyes
is good, but them metal chips fly right up and feel like nails
drove into yore eyeballs. You see that cuttin' tool anywhere? Here jest a moment ago — can't seem to locate it.
Ah! There t'is! Now I'll jest weld this to the old piece.
Goddamn it, who took my weldin' rod? Can't keep a
thing around here. Oops! She's melted a hole clare through
the wheel, just like it wa'nt there — but I'll braze it acrost.
Where's my glasses?" (The phone rings.) "Yep. Yep. I
don't care if yore fire engine *is* broke down. They're
standin' over me six deep here, and I can't get away for
at least an hour." I look around the empty shop appre-
ciatively. "Now we'll put the wheel to her — feed her a
drop or two of oil. There! Ain't that pretty! Two dollars."

Great news! Paul and Julia were back from Norway and

were coming to the Point. Julia, who with her colleagues had been working on a cookbook which was now in the final stages, would undoubtedly spend most of the time correcting proofs.* That would give Paul and me time to indulge in just one more glorious "folly," accompanied no doubt by the snapping of Paul's ever-present camera.

The gales and the cold of the previous winter had been severe. A lobsterman friend had said to me only a few days before, "When I come past your Point after that big storm last February, the ice off the bluff here was about twenty feet thick. A man could of drove a span of oxen halfway out to Gotts Island on that ice and she wouldn't have let go. But, come spring, it just up and took off one day and carried along quite some stone from your beach."

It was true. The beach had changed shape once more as it so often had in the past, and nowadays one could see about sixty feet out, and revealed only at low tide, a great stone which I had never seen before that summer, and no wonder. It had been buried under six feet of overburden which now the ice had removed. The stone had an enchanting hand-worked shape and was about five and one-half or six feet long and two feet thick overall, curving here and there in a series of slopes and buttresses. In color it was not unlike old Korean pottery, a slightly grayish jade-green, into which was mixed in whirls and swirls like twisted sea foam, a lacework of white quartz. A marvelous stone. I dared not think what it would weigh but I was determined to have it. What a front step it would make, right under the lacquer-red surface of the big front door! And now with Paul coming, and if he would help, it might just . . . be . . . done.

* *Mastering the Art of French Cooking,* by Simone Beck, Louisette Bertholle, and Julia Child. Alfred A. Knopf, 1961.

Well, one folly leads to another. Here we were, at it again, laughing like hyenas at our own jokes, and glad to see each other after a long absence. We spent about a day analyzing the situation, debating every possibility. Though one can never visualize everything ahead of time, one tries to reduce the "x-factors" as far as possible. We first fashioned a double track of heavy planks, edge up, which went on a long slope up along the buttressed face of the rocks from the beach to the meadow which surrounded the cabins. We braced and counter-braced this track or inclined plane with heavy timbers. However, it was obvious that the crux of the problem lay on the beach. I felt that if we could move that stone just one inch, we could master it. Using a method employed by the natives of Easter Island in lifting their heavy statues without machinery, we first managed to lift one side of the boulder about two inches by means of crowbars and tree-trunk levers twenty feet long. Under the lifted side we got the girls to edge a mass of small stones, one by one. But lifting one side had depressed the other. "Goddamn it, Cha, we're for it. Look what we've done: the bloody stone is digging itself in like a clam on the far side. Mmmmm. Tell you what: we'll have to let it down again, then we can dig trenches under both sides and put in two lines of flat stones — big as possible." Painfully and slowly we dug the mushy sand out from under first one side and then the other and using the heavy sledge, hammered home two lines of large flat stones to support the weight of the two edges as the stone was tipped. "There! Crissakes, if that doesn't work we'll have to give up." Puff puff. "No use waiting, though. Might as well begin again." Heave. Grunt. Groan. "It works! Now gals, quick with the little stones. Wedge 'em in tight as you can." One by one the little stones went in, and this time the other edge held. Then we went to work on the other side, slipping in little stone by little stone as we heaved. In this way, very gradually tilting first one side and then the other, we got our boulder up about six inches off its ancient bed. Next we began very carefully to remove the little stones one by one, first along one side, then along the other, and by degrees (working toward the middle) we drove a series of two-by-fours under the boulder and spiked them together with strong cross-members at front and back. Now the boulder was resting on a kind of platform. By repeating the whole tiresome process once more, we put three tree-trunk rollers under the platform. Then a third time: barring the ends of the rollers up, we slid and hammered two long two-by-eight planks under the whole contraption. Now at last, we had a boulder on a platform, the platform on rollers, and the rollers resting on a track. Each time the tide came up we had to retreat, and see our stone disappear under eight feet of water, hoping that no sudden storm would come and bury it once more. Luckily the weather was in a mood of silken calm, and as the tide receded again each day we would slog down to the beach and go to work. Three days passed in this way. But now on the next receding tide, we were able to run heavy ropes over and under and around the stone and under the platform in a spider web of cross-braced knots. This would keep it from slipping off the platform as it was being hauled up the ramp.

The next morning we hitched the block and tackle to a stump at the top of the bluff at a point toward which the ramp was headed. We eased our captured friend along the planks a distance of about thirty feet to the bottom of the ramp and then up upon it. The ramp's lower end hav-

ing been constructed on a very low gradient, the stone went up onto it more easily than we had expected.

But, to save material, we had built only twenty feet of ramp. So each time the stone reached the top of its twenty-foot run, we tore down the bottom ten feet and rebuilt it up ahead, changing the shape and length of all the legs and braces as we went in order to fit them securely into the various crevices of the rock ledge. About halfway up the slope there was a point where we knew we might be in for trouble. Here the inclined plane, although we had tried to equalize the gradient all the way, was forced to go up at a somewhat increased angle for about ten feet. Our engineering had not been sophisticated enough to take this sufficiently into account. The operation ground to a halt. There was the great stone in the middle of the slanting ledge on its twenty feet of ramp. Nothing up above, nothing down below. It looked rather silly clinging there like a giant green bug with ten-foot legs fore and aft.

"Well, if I ever see a pair of damn fools, you're it!" cried a hearty voice. "I knew all along you was both crazy, but this beats a trip to the monkey house!" It was Bobby Rich, nosing his big black boat close to the shore to get a better view.

"Listen, you sea-going tenderfoot," I yelled, wiping the sweat out of my eyes, "if you want to give us a hand with this pebble, we can just about make it over that hump. But personally, I don't think you're man enough to do it!"

"Well, bub, I dunno as I want to lend myself to such goin's on," said Bob, "but if you was to bust a gut and have to leave the Point, I wouldn't have any more stories to tell the boys down to the boat shop. So, I guess I'll have to give you a hand."

Anchoring his boat, he quickly rowed ashore. Now with

the addition of Rich's enthusiasm and strength, we just managed it, squeaking over the hump inch by inch, blocks, ramp, rollers — everything — protesting with squeaks and nasty little sagging motions.

"Now," said Bobby, with a pleased expression on his face, "I'm just as crazy as you are." And going down to the beach, he rowed back to his boat and sped away.

The total run from the beach to the front door — all uphill — was about one hundred and fifty feet. Including lifting the stone and building the platform, which in some ways were the hardest part of all, we made it from beach to door in five days of glorious battle, and at the very end found that we had to use our curious *aku-aku* method once again, this time in reverse, in order to lower the boulder slowly down upon its shaped bed. But it worked! Bellows of masculine triumph! Howls of laughter! All our grunting, swearing, and heaving now forgotten, we christened the rock with a stream of water from the hose. Nowadays, lying quietly in its bed and seeming to grow out of the surrounding green grass, it looks as if it has always been there, glacier-carved and sea-polished, and might be there still one hundred thousand years from now when the cabins and all our other miniscule works have long since vanished.

Our general approach to the gardens, after the early difficulties with wind and desiccation, had been first to change the proportions of the mix which made up our soil in order to strengthen its water-holding properties, then to baffle and break the force of the winds by means of transplanted trees and vines. This program, though it had taken some years to get properly underway, was now beginning to look as if it might work quite well.

One came into the hillside gardens these days with a real sense of triumph. Our closely planted windbreak barriers,

those long walls of wild roses, spruce and fir, mountain ash,
wild raspberries and shadbush, were in some places more
than six feet high and eight feet thick, and everywhere
presented an impenetrable mass of interlaced growth that
protected tender growing things from the shaking winds
which so often raced down Blue Hill Bay and swept over
the land of our Point. Here was the ravishing ice-blue of
arctotis nodding in the slightest breath of air; here were
tall blue spires of veronica and lupine, the incredibly delicate salpiglosis whose flower heads reminded me of butterflies' wings, gentle blue phacelia, white baby's breath, Greek
valerian, and Iceland poppies balancing on their delicate
stems — all of these and many more were growing now in
the shelter of our natural barriers. Of course, a fifty-knot
gale could bring the giants down if the stakes were not
high enough. We were growing Russian sunflowers and
their hybrids with mahogany-colored heads and deep purple
stems, together with other tall flowers like the Olympic
strain of Regal lilies, aconite, and blue and white delphinium, all of which were more than six feet high. Even supported by stout bamboo stakes they sometimes snapped.
But perhaps this was not too high a price to pay considering the day-to-day delight. The gardens were more radiant
in the sun than stained glass windows, and somehow life-
giving, like a great work of music perfectly performed. In
fact, I often thought of these gardens of ours as visible
music, pulsing with rhythms which constantly changed,
and girded about with chords of color. The wild rose
hedge around the little flower garden next to Rachel's room
was three feet thick and nearly head high and covered with
blooms and pollened bees. Its running roots which had in-
vaded the garden had been conquered by digging in a wide

plastic strip all round just inside the hedge. This acted as an underground fence or baffle.

A wall of raspberry vines fastened to posts now ran all round the periphery of the upper flower garden, and the tangle of vines and trees on the windward side of the big vegetable garden was six feet thick and ten feet high. And the addition of loam, hen manure and lime to the soil had helped to keep it in a gratifying state of health. We could cut armfuls of flowers now and hardly see where they had been taken.

There were always more vegetables than we could use and the surplus was being given to friends, not to mention the sale of lettuce in a local market, which paid the entire cost of maintenance. Two kinds of sweet corn, turnips, carrots, beets, large white onions, magnificent potatoes, dill, radishes and pole beans all had come in with a rush — all except our reluctant friends the tomatoes, which were still green, slow to ripen in the cold air of evening and morning. In wet weather, slugs were a constant menace. These we attacked by heavy liming, with a bit of poison here and there and by simply picking them off the juicy leaves by hand. For the tomatoes, we had constructed a long arched tent of polyethylene sheeting, held in place over the rows by a grid of wires. This acted as a miniature greenhouse to hold in the daytime heat and moisture through cold nights. But it was only partially successful. Winds and hail were constantly at work shredding the fabric. Now we were seriously considering a row of stout cold frames as a possible answer. We had been told on a number of occasions: "You just can't grow good tomatoes out of doors here on the island," but we were determined to try.

Strangely, weeds were no problem. Although they loved the soil as much as our garden plants, we could pull even

the biggest weed out by hand. Their magnificent root systems proliferated in the loose textured soil with incredible
speed but came out whole and clean with a single pull.
And now that we had a constant supply of water, we could
use the hose even in times of surface drought. We rejoiced
in these triumphant gardens which sparkled so with health
and lustre. They were rewarding our labor a hundredfold.

The great stone was at the door, the tank was full of
water, the forest trails were already showing tiny green

grass fingers here and there. It was a kind of new beginning. I thought of Erica, who was expecting a child that coming September — another beginning, full of bright promise. Then there was our shaggy dog, Figaro, just now lying over there in the shade of Old Cabin scratching his ear with a massive paw. Figaro was slowing up a bit. His nose was still keen but his eyes weren't what they used to be, and his hind legs sometimes got a bit out of sequence if he tried to run too fast. He seemed to belong to the Point somewhat as did the few old trees that remained: he was part of our present, yet even more a part of our past.

As for Fredericka and me, the almost-grandparents, I had to chuckle: I couldn't pull us up out of our native ground to see how we were doing. It seemed to me, if I thought of it at all, that in the middle of our circling years, we were still reasonably rugged, maybe even still full of sap. The roots of our lives having entwined themselves and embraced in a thousand ways, we were dual but one. A merry whistle from the kitchen interrupted these meandering thoughts. "Hey — Cha, who was it that promised me some tarragon half an hour ago?" Of course! Of course, life goes on.

There was a sudden interruption as a voice cried, "You folks want to go clammin'?" It was Josh, a fisherman friend. "Tide's makin' out and I got a real hankerin' for a nice mess. There's that place I told you about where them two islands come together — don't think anybody else knows there's any clams there. We ought to be able to pick up a nice mess and be back for dinner."

"Great, Josh," I said. "Just wait till we get a couple of clam forks and a basket, and we'll be with you."

Josh's stinking old boat pulled away from the rocks, rolling slightly in an oily swell as we made our way across the bay. "Now Dick here," said Josh, pointing with his thumb at a friend who was standing at the gunwale, "he thinks he's the best goddamn clammer this side of Monhegan Island, but I can beat him at it any day."

Dick, a large quiet man of forty-five or so turned a pair of ice-blue eyes upon Josh and spat reflectively overside. "Time was," he remarked in a deep booming voice, "when you wan't as old and crooked as you are today. I could of beat you then with one hand tied behind my back. Now it's positively pitiful: I could dig 'em out with my bare toes and still lick you all holler. After all, years make a difference!"

I glanced at Josh. A bit seamy perhaps, now verging on sixty, but hard as granite. His face had a rocklike quality, chiseled in deep furrows. A large bulbous nose which had been broken at one time and was twisted slightly to one side gave it an odd quality of wit, borne out, I noticed now that I was examining him carefully, by the expression of his mouth, which seemed to be set in a permanent smile. "We'll see, we'll see," he said, almost to himself, chuckling slightly.

The two little islands were really one, separated at high tide by about sixty feet of water. But when the tide was out, as it was now, one could cross from one to the other on a spit of coarse gray sand, which I noted as we came in, had formed a land bridge between the two little masses of rock and scrub spruce. Dick crossed over to the other island and set to work. We stayed with Josh. The clamming was excellent, the sun was warm on our backs, and for a while the only sound was the crunch of the iron forks biting into the gravelly beach.

"Hey!" cried Dick from the other shore. "I got a good mess! Tide's makin' in fast. Come over here and git me!"

Sure enough, the land bridge had disappeared and Dick was stranded on the opposite shore.

"Can't do it, Dick," cried Josh. "Clammin's too good over here and not much time left: go on — if you want to get over here so bad, wade acrost. Yore young — remember? You can make it."

"Will not!" cries Dick. "You got the boat."

"Can't do it," says Josh. "Haven't filled my basket yet."

"Listen here, you old sculpin," Dick cries, "who do you think I am, the Holy Sperrit?"

"Might be!" says Josh, now finished and enjoying his friend's predicament. "So why don't you jest put on yer Jesus boots and traipse over — you won't sink!"

"Well, God-a-mighty!" thundered Dick, wading into the inlet up to his waist in ice-cold water. "Must say, this ain't no way for a man to shrink his hemeroids!"

"Tch, tch, I wouldn't do that for a thousand dollars," cried Josh admiringly, "or even for twenty-five cents — but don't quit now! If you do, I might have to use the boat, and t'ain't hardly wuth it, considerin' yore condition."

Dick, now safely across, grinning hugely and pouring sea water out of his boots, made shift to reply: "I guess I need more religion! I prayed some on the way over, but I still got kind of low in the water!"

"T'ain't lack of religion," said Josh reflectively, glancing at the large wet fundament of his dripping pal, "jest too much keel!"

On the way back Dick disappeared below and reappeared shortly in an old pair of Josh's dungarees. "At that, I beat you, and it would have been wuss if I hadn't spilled some clams on the way over," said he.

"Well, mebbe you did get one or two more than I did," replied Josh with a sly smile, "but a feller who can't do an hour's work without wettin' his pants shouldn't boast about it!"

The date of my exhibition was approaching. For the next two weeks I saw very little of my family. I was holed up in the studio, painting furiously on the last of seven designs I had been working on at Coppernose. Announcements and invitations were sent out and on the appointed day Paul and I hung the show in the gallery at Southwest Harbor's Causeway Club, a beautiful room created from an old barn.

"Challes," said a local friend, staring at the assembled pictures with a somewhat baffled expression, "used to be hay in here in the old days. Then it was square dances. Now it's pitchers! Don't know whether you call that progress or not. But I will say one thing: them pitchers o' yours is a lot better lookin' than a row of cows. I like that one of the boats in the habba at sunset real good. I've seen it a hundred times in my workin' life and most of the time I was only thinkin' of catchin' a mooring. But you come along and the first thing you know you've turned it into art! That's one thing you've done for me — disturbin', kind of — now I see pitchers everywhere, and like to think I could of took up sketchin' if t'wan't so late in life. Don't see what you was gettin' at in that one though — the one you call *Arrested Motion*." (This was a design, slightly abstracted, of a bird poised on a branch.)

"Well, Ab," I said, "I was trying to suggest that everything in nature is on the move and even a painting can only catch a moment in time, which will change before you can quite grasp it."

"Yep," says Ab. "Catch the moment! Well, you can't catch it, no more than you can stay a big fish from goin' through a small net, or in my case a ten dollar bill: it goes through my hands so fast I can hardly feel it. Now that bird up there — if it is a bird — he's free. He don't know you've caught him in the act, and I dunno as you have, either: it's more like the echo of a bird the way it's painted. 'Pears to me like you left the paintin' unfinished, some way."

"But that's just it, Ab," I said. "The artist tries to make the viewer finish the work in his own mind — it's a kind of collaboration between painter and viewer."

"Hmmm, never thought of it that way," says Ab. "Here I was cussin' you out in my own mind for bein' lazy, and all the time you had me in the net, puttin' me to work! But I still like them boats better, though you didn't finish them up so good either, come right down to it. So I guess you got me caught whichever way I turn!"

The show turned out to be an agreeable experience and quite a success as these things go, yielding me a modest financial return and the experience of being surrounded by both old friends and new. Perhaps I had better plan to do it again another year.

In fact, the range of possible friendships was one of the most surprising and rewarding new aspects of life in this part of Maine. I thought back to the time when my wife had said to me, "You've done nothing but cultivate your family, your cabins, your garden and your dung hill out here on the end of the Point for fifteen years, like the Hermit of Lonely Gulch — you may not know it from where you sit, but there are people out there." Well, it was true. But now I realized that perhaps I had been missing something, too. Any enthusiasm one had could find its counterpart in the region among dozens of people. As gardeners, for example, we had for years been exchanging seeds and plants with the Lippmanns, who might come to lunch with

a basketful of hemerocalis fulva, the orange day lily, or
several plants of feathery pink astilbe. In turn, we might
offer them a clump of the dainty thymus serpillum, which
seems to delight in rewarding the tread of a heavy foot
with a burst of fragrance, or oregano for salads, or tansy
for remembrance. Our bird-watching friends had by degrees come to share their secret haunts with us, and we
with them: we were wont to spend many a delightful afternoon together with these enthusiasts, equipped with glasses,
notebooks and the inevitable Peterson's *Field Guide* — "I
tell you, Ben, that was a Henslow's sparrow, not a chipping
sparrow."

"Charles, I had a great day today — up on the cliffs above
Jordan Pond I saw two Hudsonian curlew — (or such and
such a warbler, or a flock of semi-palmated plover, pine
siskins, cedar waxwings) and how's your list this week?"

From political scientists to lobstermen, from passionate
cooks to those who love lonely mountain walks or sailing
and picnicking among the islands, one could choose a hundred good companions. Jon, for example, was one of a
host of happy sailors, many of whom had grown up together, and was much in demand as a crew member on
racing days. He could speak in the peculiar jargon of the
cult, using phrases wholly unfamiliar to his doddering
parents. Sometimes, during an attempt to analyze a victory or explain a defeat, a look of bafflement would cross
his face as he realized that he had left his landlocked au-
dience far behind. There were tennis players who spent all
their time on the courts. There were the deep sea fishermen and the lake fishermen, the inevitable riders of the
cocktail circuit, and there were quiet folk with a little place
which to them meant time to read and write or to get away
from the constant ringing of the telephone.

Of course, in a sense all of us were getting away from something in the process of looking for something and yet for me the real value of "getting away," it seemed, lay not so much in the inevitable change of rhythm which can be either boring or creative, but in the rediscovery or one's self. Yet the deepest value of the self, I had come to see now, as I had not seen before, is always in the direction of its relationship to other people. The self by itself and within itself is meaningless. So, in a sense, having gotten away and having discovered something of ourselves in the process, we had now come round full circle: the walls of our Eden had long since crumbled; friends and acquaintances had swarmed in over the ruins, and our activities as a family had spread from a hermetic beginning in which we were forced to concentrate on the immediate and the special until now, on a new turn of the spiral, we were connected once more with the world outside ourselves.

And what about our children? Had they "discovered themselves?" "Can you imagine an oak when you look at an acorn?" I recall saying to myself one day as I stood over baby Rachel's crib. Those enormous unfathomable blue eyes under her copper-colored ringlets told me nothing then. But now, years later, having experienced the curious sensation of seeming to stand still while our children had grown and caught up with us, the might-have-been had vanished. An abundant reality had taken its place. Rachel, still with a hint of wildness, was unpredictable only in the sense that one never knew what direction her wit would take or in what direction her mind would plunge. But she was basically a disciplined, enormously capable young woman who seemed to shoot color and fire to all about her like a moving jewel. Erica, the self-contained, was less pungent — one could call her the perfectionist of the family.

She had more of moonrise, less of sunset in her makeup, and always seemed to be moving to inaudible music. (I recalled a remark once made by Paul in his curiously perceptive way: "Erica is like a cat: never out of balance.") Jonathan, our scientist, was, strangely, not dry and over-factual. It was he who had, more than the others, played the role of diplomat in the family, often moving to ameliorate angers and frustrations or to bridge differences of opinion with a skillfully turned remark. He had a deft and subtle wit, yet gentle, a glorious ability to get on with all kinds of people. Many a time Fred and I had exchanged a secret smile as we watched Jon handling us with a kind of humorous tact.

Now the family too had grown beyond itself. By degrees our children, who were no longer children, had taught us to see them and to treat them as emerging adults, to play secondary roles as spectators of their increasingly self-directed lives rather than as powerful mentors and guides. From time to time the whole group managed to come together: Hector and Erica, Rachel and Anthony, Jonathan, Paul and Julia, with Chafred playing the role of guardian deities. On such occasions, alas less frequent now, we were able to enjoy each other as friends, and often seemed to mesh and merge like the component atomic elements of a giant molecule, held together by some force which yet allowed full freedom of movement and of thought. "Well," I mused, "they are lovely souls who have learned to sustain and to respect each other and our domain has played a part in the process." And whatever the respective roles of the young people would be as time went on, I felt a serene confidence that its impact would be creative, although it was apparent that this structured environment of ours, even though at times it had seemed more master than slave,

by insensible degrees had become only a background to our
expanding activities. Building it was no longer the central
theme. It was simply there, dear and familiar. This kind
of home, I thought, is unlike England or France, where so
many places have stayed in the possession of a single family
for centuries. The American pattern was looser, more
nomadic, and one could sense that perhaps in a few years
the various members of our family would be dispersed to
responsibilities which would make it impossible for them
to return except at infrequent intervals. What would become of our domain then? When we were gone who would
take over? Anybody's guess. I felt a yearning at the thought.
Nevertheless, perhaps this was mere possessiveness and pride.
Our creation, like all other human things, would pass away,
leaving behind some sort of residue in various hearts and
minds. Was this residue, I wondered, this precipitate, the
only value?

16

The Launching

"I MUST be getting old, or something," Bobby Rich had said one day. "Here I have this new boat to build, and for some reason it's got me scairt. T'isn't as if t'was something I'd never done before, like a submarine, say. No, she's just a motor-sailer — a handsome Alden design too — sixty foot overall not counting the bowsprit, and fifteen foot beam: real rugged boat, which I'm modifyin' to some extent to suit the owner. Well, to put it frankly, the damn thing's so big it just about fits the whole boat shop and a little more — reminds me of a cowbird in a warbler's nest: the more you feed it, the hungrier it grows. I pretty near have to skin in sideways to get into the shop as it is, and damn it, the bowsprit sticks four feet out the front door. Now these last two weeks I've been puttin' the lead weights to her for ballast and I swear to God I woke up in the middle of the night the other night and got to wonderin' whether she hadn't sunk right down through the floor. You know how it is in the middle of the night? Finally I got so nervous I got up and snuk down to the shop. Felt real foolish, too. But no — she hadn't moved a muscle. Now just yesterday we finished puttin' her engine in: there she stands, twenty-seven tons on the hoof, and I don't know whether I can wedge her out the door. And," he went on, a sly grin coming over his face, "fact is, I'm goin' to have to lanch her before she's ready to lanch, jest so's I can see whether I *can* lanch her!"

Now at the boat yard looking at the *Lazy Lady* — that was her name — her bulk was impressive. The ample topside seemed only inches away from the roof, and her stern nearly touched the great double doors through which she would be launched. A crew of men were swarming over the craft putting the finishing touches on her decks and cabins. A grand odor of wood chips and paint filled the shop. Mahogany from the Philippines, teak from Siam, cedar and spruce from Oregon, all had come together here to be incorporated in one of Rich's well-built boats. In a second shop hard by lay the great spar of Sitka spruce ready to be stepped in place after the launching, polished now and gleaming, and subtly shaped in an airfoil design to take the Atlantic winds. "Next Wednesday!" said Bob. "That's the day, rain or shine! If I wait any longer I'm afraid she'll jest take it into her head to lanch herself without so much as a word to any of us! You got any red, white, and blue flowers in your garden? We could use a few for decorations . . ."

Tuesday dawned dark gray and gusty, and as the day progressed, the wind veered straight into the east, accompanied by a nasty rain which began to pelt the windows and roofs of the cabins. Looking out, we could dimly make out the firs and spruces at the end of the Point bending and swaying and the grasses up on the hill seeming to run in waves before moving air which had now increased its speed and strength to near gale force. I wakened several times that night to hear the roaring sound of wind and water.

By Wednesday morning the tail end of a hurricane was lashing the whole Atlantic seaboard. We wondered if Bob would go through with the launching of the *Lazy Lady,* and as we donned oilskins in preparation for the event we asked ourselves if indeed any more than a handful of people would get there. But we needn't have worried. Maine people are tough. A telephone call brought the information that there was no thought of delay. "If she can't take a little breeze like this," said Bob, "she's no good anyway, and I'd ought to be shot. But she'll do fine, never fear."

Coming down to the boathouse, we could hear the murmur of a crowd of friends who had gathered for the great event. Inside the shop the *Lazy Lady* had been carefully jacked and pulled on steel cables to the exact launching position, and now stood poised on her blocks, gay in coats of fresh paint, with a lovely blue-and-gold carving at the bow, where just aft of the bowsprit itself one of the crew had painted two jolly swordfish about three feet long, one on each side.

A stand with red, white and blue bunting had been erected for the launching ceremony, and a long table had been set up down one side of the shop almost under the curving sides of the *Lady*. It was sumptuously garnished with sandwiches, coffee, drinks, and vases of red, white, and blue flowers. The crowd — about a hundred persons — was in a mood of tense excitement, gay in oilskins, sweaters, peaked caps, and rubber boots. A couple of dozen children ducked and slithered among their elders chirping like sparrows. Shouts of greeting from the men and a perfect bellow of conversation echoed under the roof as the crowd milled about, gathered in groups and offered boisterous toasts to the crew of workmen now making final preparations for the launching. "Well, my old pipe-smokin' friend! I didn't know's you'd get here!" cried Bobby Rich, giving me a tremendous thump on the back. "Look at her! She can hardly wait! If that bowsprit don't take the roof along with her as she goes down the ways, I'll be lucky . . . figger she has about three inches clearance."

"Clearance!" bellowed a neighbor in oilskins and boots. "Clearance! Why he's got that bo't in here so close it's as tight as a bull's arse in June!"

"Drunk as a skunk!" muttered Bobby. "Here! Have a drink!"

The rain was now coming down in long silver streaks through the open door and spattering the stern of the *Lazy Lady,* whose newly polished bronze screw gleamed in the half-light. Through the doors one could see the grease-covered ways descending in a long slant toward a mass of green waves tossing below the boathouse. "Now you three men get up topside and be ready with the lines as soon as she hits the water. I'll have a couple of men on the dock to catch 'em. Okay, boys, loosen them chains. Easy now. And Chum, you be ready to saw through the chocks when I give the word." Bobby looks at his watch. "Two minutes to go! Tide's about full. Mildred, you get up on the stand and be ready to smack her good with that champagne bottle when I give the word. And for God's sake, don't forget to sing out loud and clear."

Now the owner, a large bronzed man, bare-headed and dressed in a leather jacket, mounts a ladder to the deck. An expectant silence falls, broken only by the hissing of the rain and the slapping of waves just outside the doors. "Laydees and Gentleme-e-e-n!"

("Hey, boys! Can the chatter: the owner's goin' to make a speech!")

"Ladies and Gentlemen! I'm glad you're all here for the

launching of the *Lazy Lady*. She's a beautiful boat, even now, without her mast. One of Bob Rich's best! And never mind the weather — she's built to take it and come up smiling!" Cheers from the crowd. "Now, if everything's ready, let's get going."

"Okay now. Saw them chocks. You ready, Mildred?" Mildred stands poised with a bottle of champagne in one white-gloved hand, smiling expectantly. "All sawed through? Take a little strain on that jack, Abner. Now where's that maul? Let her have a couple of taps. Easy now. Easy."

One of the men swings a heavy sledge in a series of taps, loosening the last wedges that hold the boat. The *Lazy Lady* gives a lurch. Suddenly, before one can take a breath, the great bulk takes off. A roar from the crowd drowns Mildred Rich's words as she swings the champagne bottle on its cord against the bow. The *Lady* shoots down the greased ways like a frightened cormorant, and hits the water with a glorious splash as she butts her way out into the teeth of the storm. The crowd surges forward toward the open doors. Through the rain I can see the *Lady* sizzling directly into the wind, somewhat slower now as she loses way. Suddenly two white streaks erupt from the ends of the boat as new nylon ropes are flung to the men waiting on the dock. The *Lazy Lady* is gradually brought under control, and seems to be the center of a milling crowd; a number of small craft have come in close and whiz about, bouncing gaily in the waves, their oilskinned figures carrying on some sort of animated conversation with the men on the boat, which the wind carries away, so that they appear to be a set of beautifully articulated mechanical dolls. Now, looking back, I can see the empty shop, delivered of its offspring, and it suddenly looks enormous, dark, its roof disappearing upward in a series of shadowed arches. Below, the crowd, momentarily caught and frozen in a picturesque lump of color, is straining to see the *Lady* brought back to the dock. "Jesus Christ! Wasn't that exciting!" says Bobby Rich. "Now I know how Mildred felt when she come out of the ether!"

The crowd of onlookers began to disperse. There were congratulations and back-slappings all round. The great double doors were swung to against the rain and fastened by a number of men who swarmed up the inner faces on a series of crosspieces. As I made my way out to the rain-swept deck I could see the *Lazy Lady* pulling gently against her ropes and riding rather high without the final weight of mast and fuel. Her long clean lines wedded now to her natural element, she seemed already to have forgotten the place of her birth and to be heading confidently toward adventure.

Back in the shop once more I could see a couple of dozen friends who had lingered on after the rest had gone. They had been invited for lunch. It was to have been a cook-out. But the storm continued to blow, so the suggestion was made that the party be transferred to Old Point where the meal could be prepared in comfort on our indoor grill. A few minutes later they all began piling into Great Hall, talking and shouting and shaking the rain from their slickers. The room was suddenly filled to the vibrating rafters with a great stamping of boots and a hullabaloo of voices and laughter. We put a stack of records on the Victrola, lit a charcoal fire in the kitchen grille, a larger fire in the big fireplace, and began pouring out a round of drinks. A chap who had had some restaurant experience offered to cook the eighteen pounds of prime steak, a salad was assembled, there were sandwiches to unpack and arrange. These pleasant processes were accompanied by the clink of glasses and the pop of beer cans, and a rush and murmur of excited conversation. In the light of the fire the room grew golden. The sound of people enjoying themselves rose to a magnificent roar. The place shook. Four couples were dancing in the middle of the room. Half a dozen were busy in the kitchen, from which the odor of cooking steak began to percolate. Two men in the opposite corner had begun a friendly bout of Indian wrestling, cheered on by a ring of spectators. It appeared to be Bobby Rich and the owner of the boat trying to see which could make the other give up first.

"Listen, you big baboon from Boston, just because you own that boat, don't think you're goin' to put me down!" (Grunt — Grunt.)

"C'mon, Bob! Get your shoulder into it. He's weakenin'! Hey! Watch yore thumb, there! If Bob's face gets any redder he'll bust right down the middle!"

I found one chap buried in another corner with a history book, quite oblivious to the roar and surge. "Yep: I'm interested in the migration of peoples," he said. "Originally my folks were Spanish, but back at the time of the Inquisition they left the home country and came to Italy to live. Now here in Maine I'm a bricklayer and mason — have a nice job up at Dow Air Force Base."

A woman was talking to Fred: "My husband has just taken a job as captain of a private pleasure boat. I just hope that job lasts all year round. We have five children to support, you know. Of course, the kids, the oldest ones that is, help out during the summer months. Take my eleven-year-old, for instance. Gets up at midnight every night and goes out with a trawler crew. He steers the boat while they get in the nets. He gets a bit of a snooze on the boat. But he really doesn't go to bed till they get in at six P.M. . . ."

Sizzling steaks began to come from the grille in a steady stream. The salad, mixed by strong brown hands, was all ready and was being brought to the table where piles of sandwiches had been stacked. Came the cry: "Come and get it!" in a voice that sounded like a blast from a tugboat. Uninhibited male voices, used to the open sea, can ricochet around a room like steel-jacketed bullets. This was not exactly a gathering of dainty adolescents. The men were like trees walking, like bellowing walrus. There were women, too, but large masculine forms and large masculine voices dominated the day. There was an atmosphere of all-out full-bodied gusto: smacking lips as loud as pistol shots, toasts shouted full throat, even the colors seemed brighter than life. Color, sound, form, seemed to weave and unweave before me in a never-ending series of intoxicating patterns. At one point I looked down to see the three-year-old Rich grandson carrying one of my cats through the mob. The animal's two ends hung down like a hairpin from the child's tummy, to which its middle was firmly plastered. CRASH! Someone had fallen over backward in his chair, and now lay flat out on the floor, legs akimbo over the front of the chair. "Aw, leave him sleep — he's comfy," said one of his mates. And so the prostrate form remained, a fine blob of red and black like a giant lobster buoy on the floor throughout the rest of the party.

"Hey! That's my beer! Hand it over!"

"No t'ain't! I got there first!" Gulp gulp gulp . . .

"Who's fer the bushes?" Suddenly the room half emptied as a dozen bodies hurl themselves through the door. Sounds of hoarse laughter from outside. I glance at my bricklayer friend, still in his corner. He, whoever he is (I never did learn how he got to the party), and the supine form of the

fallen lobsterman, are the only quiet objects in the room.
Now the men come storming back in, bringing with them a
wet fragrant breath of outside air and a couple quarts of
rainwater.

Zumph! Zumph! Two men down. "Now look at that!
Slipped in yer own slime, eh? How the hell are you boys
goin' to stand up in them boats o' yours if you can't come
in out of the rain without fallin' all over Challes's floor: it
ain't rockin' hardly at all!"

Everyone seemed to be in too high spirits to sit down.
New groups were constantly being formed and dissolved.
Men and women ate while dancing, ate while sitting on
the floor, ate wandering round, while coming in and out
of doors — all except the bricklayer who continued to sit
wedged into his corner like an owl in the cleft of a tree.
Brilliant red sweatshirts, the green work trousers character-
istic of the region, the bright dresses of the women, emerald
salad, rosy wine, all swam before my eyes like a school of
curiously colored fish, the more so as the dancing had now
become general. Great Hall shook to the steady swish and
plop of moving feet. The food seemed gradually to leak
away and disappear. Nothing left now but half a loaf of
tired-looking bread, and stacks of empty containers and
paper plates. As I circled round the room, snatches of conversation came to me, surfacing loud and clear when I was
slowed down by a press of friendly bodies: "Don't feel so
pert today. When I got out o' bed this mornin' I had to
put my hand on the wall to kind of steady my keel. Doctor
tells me you got this little wheel in your ear somewhere
turns round and round and helps you keep your balance,
like a gyry-scope. Mine must have busted a spoke, I guess,
but what I say is . . ."

"How's your paw?"

"Not so good, all told. You know Paw's gettin' mighty old. Now he tells me he's got Baptists in the bedroom — rows of 'em!"

"Ho ho, Clarence! Ain't seen you since the launchin'! How'd they let you in here, anyway? When I last laid eyes on you, that boat was jest about to let go, and you was standin' so close to her I swear to God I seen her take a shavin' right off your backsides as she went by! A liar, am I? Now all you have to do is to take off your britches, and I could prove . . ."

In the agreeable American way the kitchen filled with a crowd of helpers who washed glasses and silver, swept the floor, emptied the leftovers, and performed other kindly offices, meanwhile singing and talking at the top of their lungs. It was all becoming a vast blur of smiling faces, weaving colors, susurrus of sound, now and then punctuated by a thump as someone put a new log on the fire.

"See out there? That's my boy. Fourteen years old," said a lobsterman pointing toward the sea-facing windows. I could just make out the silhouette of a small boat and fancied that I could hear the roar of an outboard motor through the hubbub in Great Hall. The little craft was pounding into the wind, and as I turned my head to get a better view I could see a smallish figure in oilskins standing in the stern, balancing himself miraculously as the bow rose and fell.

"Scares the hell out o' me, the way he stands up in that boat. Funny thing is I used to do it myself when I was his age and thought nuthin' of it. Will say the boy's pretty handy though — takes after his paw. Now he runs his own line of traps. That way he makes enough durin' summer to buy clothes for school come fall. Hey, Harry! Time to go?"

"You crazy? I aim to stay till the party's over, so's to get the good out of her!"

I looked around again. The bricklayer had finally come down out of his tree and was wolfing a last cold slab of steak. The fallen lobsterman was being tipped by a friend into a vertical position, still snoring loudly.

"Come on, brother! Wake up! Time to go!"

"Go? Go? Jesh got here. Don wanna go. Leave me be!"

Sock! He strikes out with both fists as two burly figures hustle him through the front door.

"Won't go! Leave me down or I'll stave a hole through yer bottom!" The voices diminish into the night.

"Come on, girls! The dishes are all washed up. Let's get on home and leave these folks in peace. Goodbye! Goodbye! Mighty nice launchin'!"

"Nice home you got here, Challes. Fact is I've often wondered what she looked like when you got aboard of her. Never did lay eyes on the insides till today. Well, hate to go. Great party! But I got to get up at three tomorrow mornin' for the fishin'. Tell your missus goodbye for me . . . can't find her anywhere. Hey, Bob, if you get a bigger boat than this'n to build next time, jest see that you put yer foot down with a firm hand and say 'No thanks!' Then the roof won't come off like it almost did this time. Only thing is, in that case it won't hardly be wuth watchin'!"

17

Full Circle

NOW during the few remaining days of our summer the sun was retreating southward again and on nights of scudding cloud as likely as not one could begin to hear the honking of wild geese. Our swallows and humming-birds had gone and the robins were flocking on the Point by the hundreds, ready to depart. And here were the monarch butterflies foregathering for their long mysterious flight south. Why just the monarchs? They were everywhere, orange and black wings hovering over the banks of purple asters in a last echo of color, or folded by the thousands in long clumps, quivering and fluttering: poignant, somehow.

On the last day of our stay I walked out along the old road, noting with surprise that the tops of many of the new trees had now almost reached the telephone wires. Here and there were reminders of the corduroy — scarred old log ends still protruding along the sides of the road under the overlay of new gravel. Incidentally, a bit more gravel in that low spot would help. The cut was now a tangled woodland reaching its green fingers into the road. Next year this would have to be dealt with.

Scrambling down the slope to Twisty-Turvy Land and sliding down the rocks to the beach which now lay bare at low tide, I listened once more to the purling of the tidal spring. We don't need you now, old friend, I thought — "ye that on the sands with printless foot do chase the ebbing Neptune" — we will not disturb you.

And here was the old spring house — full now, its sloping rock floor faintly visible in the failing light. I suddenly recalled those pine siskins and purple finches darting in for a drink heedless of our shovels and of fat baby Rachel with her tin dipper. And the old butter crock that sank: whatever became of it?

As I wandered back toward the cabins, I could see the place where for so many years the tents had been. There was that spot where a rusty nail had stuck out of the bole of a tree. Someone — perhaps Callie — had hung a lantern there. Down on the beach there was no trace of the spot where the great green stone had lain. The remnants of a blackened fireplace were still there, but it would soon be washed away by winter storms. Looking up, I could see long tongues of mist creeping across the bay, licking up the islands one by one. In the other direction, I noticed that the gardens on the hill were still lit by the slanting rays of the sun. The studio, too, in its little orchard, was bathed in a tawny light, the red-lacquer door glowing like a ruby. Farther down the slope a long column of blue smoke was rising from the chimney of Great Hall and at a certain level about forty feet up was spreading into a horizontal layer of mist which began to blend with the fog stealing in over the Point. I could hear, as if it were yesterday, the shouts and laughter of the kids who had helped me work on the roof. Some of them were married now, with children of their own.

Still farther down the hill the windows of Old Cabin were catching the light — a long string of golden squares in the dusk. It was easy to think myself back to the dark forest, to the sound of falling trees, the tonk-a-tonk of a sledge hammer as it drove home the spikes in the newly peeled logs. Just here was a place where a large tree had stood. I remembered it well, because it was the one that had a horizontal branch from which we hung a swing for the children. The tree had been blown over in the hurricane and the stump had turned to mush. Now nothing was left of it except a thick mound of wild blackberry vines, but I could still see those little feet cleaving the air, see Rachel with her pink teddy bear and hear her cry, "Harder! Push harder!" And here was the place where little Erica had put her collection of white stones which nobody was allowed to touch.

The day was dying now, but for a moment just before the evening fog closed in everything stood out in crystal clarity — the gardens, the tower, the studio, the young trees on the hill, the cabins, the green rock at the door. What was it that the angel in Revelations had said? "Hurt not the earth, neither the sea, nor the trees." Well, we had tried to be faithful to this adjuration in our fashion. The whole scene hung there in the gathering dusk, still magically clothed in a soft garment of light from the setting sun. I stood for a moment at the door before going in. The faint strains of music came through the wood. What were they playing? Villa-Lobos? The gulls were now winging in a long line to their nighttime sanctuary. Out in the bay a loon let go a wild summons to mystery. Somewhere between the sophisticated utterance of a Villa-Lobos and the wholly impulsive but ineffable cry of the loon, I thought — that is to say somewhere between articulated man and free-form nature — lay the possibility of the kind of balance or collaboration which we thought of as civilization. Certainly it was not part of the given. It had to be created, and its balance maintained. With all its form and brilliance, it could disappear. And our life at the Point, a similar balance, precariously and lovingly maintained, could be upset and forever undone.

But for now, what was here was tangible, solid. The gift of good things to eat from our gardens was real enough. The gifts of logs, stones, fish from the sea, loam and gravel, were real. And their present arrangement in a new coherence was real. And the intangibles too, they were no less solid, it seemed to me: beauty, fragrance, health, pride of workmanship, family solidarity. Who could take these away? Were they not perhaps the most lasting fruit of our twenty years, yielding us as their final truth that ultimate precipitate — intangible, yet most tangible — a new scale of values? When all was said and done, were these not the essential gift, the real reality?

I could see now that this twenty acres and this twenty years, with all their lights and darks, and all their cabins, gardens, roads, music, and other amenities were only shells. What one passes to one's children, I thought, is not so much an outer form: houses, corporations, machines, money, or even experience. It is, essentially, attitudes. They are the real inheritance. For the moment this inheritance in both its aspects — as value and as form — was here, alive and solid, and so were we. For a space of time, now a generation long, both value and form together had grown from the forest floor like a redwood tree, rooting us to this soil with a thousand strands of remembrance. Time or indifference might bring our domain down. But to all of us, and hopefully to our children's children, it would live on, forever green.